Knowledge and social structure

International Library of Sociology

Founded by Karl Mannheim

Editor: John Rex, University of Warwick

Arbor Scientiae
Arbor Vitae

A catalogue of the books available in the **International Library of Sociology** and other series of Social Science books published by Routledge & Kegan Paul will be found at the end of this volume

Knowledge and social structure

An introduction to the classical argument in the sociology of knowledge

Peter Hamilton
Faculty of Social Science, Open University

Routledge & Kegan Paul
London and Boston

First published in 1974
by Routledge & Kegan Paul Ltd
Broadway House, 68–74 Carter Lane,
London EC4V 5EL and
9 Park Street,
Boston, Mass. 02108, U.S.A.
Printed in Great Britain by
Ebenezer Baylis & Son Ltd
The Trinity Press, Worcester, and London
© Peter Hamilton 1974

ISBN 0 7100 7746 7 (c)

ISBN 0 7100 7786 6 (p)

Library of Congress Catalog Card No. 73-86574

Contents

For Susan

Introduction

As its title somewhat grandiosely suggests, the primary aim of this study is the presentation, elucidation and analysis of the developments which have characterized the sociology of knowledge, and which have set for it the outlines of its major problematics. However, the study is neither exhaustive nor analytically complete. It represents a more or less idiosyncratic journey through the subject-field in which the author picked out those contributions or *œuvres* which seemed to him to have had the most obvious influence upon the progression of a distinctive sociology of knowledge. Thus the analysis excludes—but does not intend to derogate by doing so—such notables as Lévy-Bruhl, Grünewald, De Gré, Znaniecki, Merton and Parsons, all of whom deserve mention in one respect or another. It is merely time and energy which have prevented their inclusion. However, what remains is a particular interpretation of what constitutes the primary elements of a distinctive field of study concerned with a determinate relationship between knowledge and social structure. What I have done is to take each of the most distinctive approaches to the explication of such a postulated relationship, and reconstruct them analytically so as to present a coherent way into looking at how they affect that explication. Consequently I have discussed and analysed the three main 'pre-paradigms'[1] of the sociology of knowledge based in the work of, respectively, Marx, Durkheim and Weber. Each of these 'pre-paradigms'—by which I mean a structured framework of concepts and subject matter which claims to hold scientific adequacy—treats in a distinctive way the determinate relationship between knowledge and social structure. Each pre-paradigm also has distinctive philosophical roots and characteristic expressions. I have tried also to describe the intellectual context in which the problems involved in producing a sociology of knowledge first came to light. That context produced the notion of ideology, in the sense that the political, social or economic interests of a group of know-ledge-producers were seen to be responsible for the distortion of that knowledge in directions suitable to those interests. The whole idea of ideological thought, that existential conditions may affect the validity of thought, is a property of Enlightenment philosophy, which first began to inquire systematically into human social organization. What the Enlightenment produced was a way of looking at the world which had some components, empiricist, individualistic and positivist though they may be, which were at least *sociological*. From these beginnings, and particularly from the critical rationalism which underlay Enlightenment thought, came the rational analysis of social phenomena, the creation of social theory, and the eventual production of a sociology of knowledge.

Traditionally, our knowledge of the world, of ourselves and of other people has been consigned to philosophy, as a problem re-solvable in terms of epistemological theories. The creation of em-piricist epistemologies by Enlightenment thinkers, and notably David Hume, meant that knowledge had to be seen in terms of the existential conditions in which it was produced; in this case the ex-perience of the thinkers.[2] Once it was possible to define that experi-ence in social terms, it became clear that a 'sociology of knowledge'—which could investigate knowledge in terms of the *social* experience of the thinker—was available. The history of the discipline—if we may call it that—has thus centred around its emancipation from epistemology. But it can only be a partial emancipation, since a complete theory of knowledge must include more than purely socio-logical elements: indeed its formulation as a complete theory, in-volving assessment of the ground, truth, meaning, etc. of knowledge starts at an irreducibly philosophical level. But once the theoretical problematics have been set, knowledge becomes open to study by specialist sciences from biology to sociology and economics, via physiology, psychology, or whatever. One important—in fact, prob-ably the most important—strand of the development of a sociology of knowledge has been Marxism, which has argued for a theory of knowledge based on a conflation of the special sciences with a 'his-torical materialist' method which gives primary explanatory power to sociology and economics. In fact most of the positions examined here allot a significance to social factors in the understanding of how knowledge comes to be produced, structured, validated and 'dis-torted'. Accordingly, since it has had to involve itself in questions of truth-falsity and their determination, sociology of knowledge has been concerned to either separate or conflate 'knowledge' and 'belief'. Positivism has played an important role in this for it assumes, on the empiricist model, that a complete distinction can be made between that which is to count as valid knowledge, on the one hand, and that which is to be counted as value judgements, normative statements, or simply beliefs, on the other.[3] Since sociologies of knowledge have been elaborated both on positivist and anti-positivist models of knowledge, it follows that the whole conception of what is to be considered as knowledge, is itself something to be taken into account when analysing the several approaches to the construction of a sociology of knowledge. This issue itself can in fact be taken as one way into looking at the various problematics of the discipline: indeed all sociologies of knowledge have been concerned with the extent to which social factors intervene in, or even produce, the relationship between knowledge and belief. I have accordingly considered analytically how this problem—usually expressed in terms of the concept of 'ideology'—is resolved by each of the pre-paradigmatic positions and their developments.[4]

I have tried to present an account of each of the sociologies of knowledge considered which deals with them in terms of five main areas:

1 as sociologically orientated theories of knowledge, which involves a consideration of their definitions of knowledge, and of its relationship to society or social system;

2 in respect of the intellectual bases, philosophical, sociological, etc., of the theories put forward;

3 as distinctive methods of analysing the relationships imputed between knowledge and social structure;

4 in terms of the extent to which their concepts are:

(a) scientific (rather than philosophical–metaphysical) and (b) at least minimally *sociological* in the sense of referring either to basic units of social action, or to supra-individual collectivities of social actors;

5. the extent to which each of the theories examined is internally consistent.

The conclusion is written in the belief that in some sense these aims have been achieved, and attempts additionally to suggest an inclusive perspective for approaching the problems posed in any attempt to describe and explain determinate relations between knowledge and social structure.

1 Philosophy and the roots of social science: the Enlightenment

To introduce a primarily analytical essay by reference to a group of thinkers whose significance is to many purely historical—bearing no concrete relationship to modern trends in, or theoretical developments of, the sociology of knowledge—requires some justification. Let me very briefly provide that justification by outlining the aims of this preliminary chapter. First, I want to demonstrate that we should consider the Enlightenment philosophes (I propose to use throughout this essay the term philosophes, without quotation marks, as the most acceptable synonym for the men of the Enlightenment: my reasons are based on Gay's reason for the same usage) as those who produced the first steps towards a modern social science in general, and to a modern sociology in particular. And second, I would like to show that in producing an elementary sociology they also produced, largely as a result of the critical rationalism which informed and underlay their whole 'program' (as Peter Gay has called it,[1]) a theory of ideology which can be regarded quite properly as inaugurating the sociology of knowledge as an integral part of Western social theory.

I

The importance of the Enlightenment, both as social movement and period of intense intellectual development, cannot easily be overstressed, particularly as it effects discussion of sociology and the sociology of knowledge. What the philosophes produced, when their gaze was directed towards scientific analysis of society, was characteristically a sociology of ideas and values. In modern terms they were more interested in the cultural components, than in the structure, of the social system, and such an interest arose out of their

1

efforts to break down moral and political philosophy into secular, non-metaphysical and primarily rational elements. Without doubt what resulted was not always objective: the very spirit of critical rationalism which underlay their world implied a degree of commitment to certain values. But those values, which might be summarized as anthropocentric, were not antithetical to a scientific approach to society and to man's role as a social being but rather encouraged such an approach. They were, in the main, scientific values. The philosophes were *engaged* sociologists and anthropologists, but the direction of their engagement led them to unify reason and science into a world view, which when it became systematized, laid the foundations of a science of society. Enlightenment man was committed to progress, change, secularism, humanity and cosmopolitanism, but above all, to *freedom* and to the rights of the individual to determine his own beliefs and values.[2] This 'recovery of nerve' which manifested itself in a 'science of freedom'[3]—a practical science with man at its centre, pursued for his good alone and not for the glory of God or gods—is thus the real source of social science, or as they were termed at the time, the 'moral' sciences. And this term is in itself significant in that it gives conclusive proof of the destruction of moral philosophy (which had operated since the Middle Ages as a branch of theology): the old concerns of moral philosophy with the ethics of worldly princes, the duties of men to their fellow men and their relationships to their rulers, and the sources of law, justice and the social order could now be considered within a non-religious framework: the advent of a science of man meant that they could be examined rationally and with regard to how things actually existed, rather than to how they should exist. The new science looked not for revealed truth, or *a priori* knowledge, but for evidence of man's practices and his social variety and regularities. As a consequence cross-cultural comparison became the accepted method of social inquiry, and a much-needed dose of cultural relativism was injected into the main stream of western social thought, and to a large extent dominated the development of the new science of man.

The new sciences were created in the forcing house of the philosophes' programme, who sought to turn ideas into actions, to unite theory and practice and science with technology in order to produce a change in the social structure of their world. At their most radical these sciences looked forward to a new individual, a new state and a new society and in that very utopian sense prefigured the French Revolution, but did not in any sense determine either *its* programme or the course it ran. However, the conservative response to critical rationalism—positivism—saw in the French Revolution the working out of Enlightenment ideas in practice and made Voltaire, Rousseau, Diderot and the rest, authors of the Terror. They neglected to recall that Condorcet, as typical a philosophe as one could have, was unfortunate enough to be a victim of that same Terror. In truth the linkage between the philosophes and the Jacobins is indirect, though it does exist. But where the Enlightenment relied upon reason and the written word to effect its desired ends, the Jacobins employed revolution. The two are linked, as Marcuse has so carefully shown,[4] but the philosophes were most interested in the social influence of ideas and the consequential effects of social position and privilege in turn upon ideas, values and knowledge in general. They were concerned thereby with the notion of ideology, of the distortion of knowledge to conform with an inequitable social structure, the misuse of social power, and the denial of human rights. In allocating the principal role in the propagation of traditional, absolutist and hierocratic ideas to the church in general and the priesthood in particular, the philosophes developed a notion of ideology which stressed the alienation of men from their true nature, by subordinating man to God. In that sense their theory of ideology, and as a result their first steps towards a sociology of knowledge, are above all else critiques of Christian religion and its social organization. But it is possible to discern a more general view of ideology in the work of some of the philosophes, and even an approach towards a dialectical view of society. We may single out two writers who were interested in, and developed an understanding of, the relationship between social structure and ideas, and whose work significantly affected either their contemporaries or later writers, and consequently had a general effect on the scientific development of the sociology of knowledge. It must be stressed that their effect cannot easily be particularized. As important writers, Vico and Montesquieu were absorbed into the intellectual world views of certain specific periods, and set by their example a certain tone to the discussion of a discrete set of issues. I am not claiming that either Vico or Montesquieu produced a systematic sociology of knowledge which inaugurated that discipline as a branch of sociology. However, they did approach the study of society from a particular viewpoint, and the questions they asked and the sort of answers they found channelled later discussion of the relationship between knowledge and society in a certain direction. What I am claiming for Vico and Montesquieu is that by asking questions about culture, society, political constitution and history in a certain way, they were instrumental in defining some of the subject matter that the prototype social sciences would study, both in the Enlightenment period itself and in the period of conservative Romanticism (which followed Napoleon's defeat at Waterloo) that saw the rise of 'positive' social science as an antidote to 'negative' rationalism, and its social science.[5]

The reader must bear in mind that in the sections that follow, on

Vico and Montesquieu, I am only drawing the *broad* connections between philosophic concerns and what might be termed a modern approach to the sociology of knowledge: to show the connections properly would of course take a good-length book.

II

Giambattista Vico (1668–1744) proved to be what might be called the 'sleeping partner' of the Enlightenment. Unrecognized and largely unread outside of his native Naples, and in his own time, Vico's influence on the philosophes is understandably slight, yet his thought is remarkably parallel to theirs. Although there is evidence that Montesquieu was aware of his *Scienza Nuova*, the remarkably modern conceptions of history and society which Vico adumbrated there remained largely ignored until the 1820s in Europe, when they were taken over and given an historicist and conservative interpretation by French Romantic historians.

In his *Scienza Nuova*[6] Vico aims to produce a new method for studying human history. Whereas, he points out, natural history is not directly open to man's control, existing quite separately from him, human history is in fact man's creation. As such, it follows that an important epistemological distinction can be made, which Vico uses as the basis of his historical and sociological methodology: natural objects may be known only in so far as we may study their external characteristics, whereas human facts may be studied both externally and internally and thus may be known in their totality. From this Vico deduces that all of human society, both past and present, is open to our study. His method of internal analysis of human facts is in many respects similar to the method of *verstehen* developed by Wilhelm Dilthey (who was probably indirectly affected in this by Vico,[7]) and of course it implies a certain degree of relativism and historicism. What Vico was proposing was that to study Roman history say, it was not enough merely to record a chronicle of events, and draw conclusions solely from that about Roman society. What the real, Vichian historian must do is to examine and empathize with the culture of the period—what he called the 'civil world'—which exists in terms of actions, thoughts, ideas, religious beliefs, myths, norms and institutions and is in its totality a product of the human mind. Since it is such a product, we can understand it better than we can the abstractions which we are forced to employ to apprehend physical nature. This is by no means a simple process, for we cannot regard human nature as fixed, or the institutions, customs, myths, which we study as timeless entities: Vico applied to the study of human nature and 'culture' (which in modern terms we would refer to as both 'culture' *and* 'society') a historical perspective which emphasized the changes and developments implicit in both individuals and societies and showed their dialectical relationship. But though he was both methodologically and morally an anti-Cartesian as far as the human sciences were concerned, Vico did believe in the possibility of a universal history which he claimed that his new science could produce. There are, he wrote, common human needs which produce universal institutions and consequently we may derive universal principles from them, though we must always make due allowance for Providence.[8]

Though he based his idea of a universal history primarily on his epistemological distinction between human and natural science—complete knowledge of all human history being in theory possible—Vico supported it with a cyclical philosophy of history, in which human nature is, in its manifestations throughout man's cultural history, a social creation. The cyclical view of history as '*corsi e ricorsi*' is in effect a view of the parallel process of development of human nature and human society. Both man and societies come to develop their self-knowledge over time in the movement from barbarism to civilization, evolving ever more complex forms and cultural expressions. As societies become more developed socially, human nature also develops, and both manifest their development in changes in language, myth, folklore, economy, etc.; in short, social change produces cultural change. Vico was the first to use this organic (and very modern) idea of culture as a system of socially produced and structured elements. In his view of social organization, all the elements of the 'civil world' are inter-related: it follows from such an organic conception of societal '*Weltanschauungen*' that the knowledge, ideas, values, and other cultural elements of any given historical society are explicable only in its own terms, which are linked of course to the structure and content of its language. A language embodies for Vico not merely the 'spirit' or *Geist* of a period: it is also an agent of social change. In a famous phrase Vico claims that 'Minds are formed by the character of language, not language by the minds of those who speak it.' Hence we may discern a dialectical relationship between language, knowledge and society in Vico's work. In producing a cyclical philosophy of (universal) history Vico asserts a relationship between cultural and social development. The one leads necessarily on to the other, and creates the structure and limits within which it can operate. But the process is not infinite: the '*corsi e ricorsi*', the recurring cycle of history, means that the same process will operate over and over again. Whilst primitivism leads eventually to rational civilization, the achievement of such civilization contains the seeds of its own decay, which is quite inevitable and attributable to 'civil providence' as much as to man's own failures. It is simply true, says Vico, that all history is the history of the rise and fall of civilizations and he presents evidence both cultural and historical to prove it. But in this he had not progressed any further than the Graeco-Roman historians from whom he took the idea of human history as a cyclical process.

It is, then, possible to discern an approach to the sociology of knowledge in Vico's principal work, the *Scienza Nuova*. What Vico suggested there was that our understanding of social organization is dependent upon the concepts and ideas which we employ, the language that we use. These 'ideal' elements are closely related to the social structure of the time and place in which they are located: we cannot compare the poetic or mythological wisdom of primitive men with the rational and precise wisdom of an advanced civilization without considering the contexts in which they exist, and in fact no logical comparison is really possible or indeed meaningful. We may only understand the two forms of wisdom by employing imaginative insight into their specific meanings in their own cultures, of which they are crucial elements.

Vico became influential and relatively well read at a curiously important time for social thought in general and for sociology in particular, the period roughly between 1820 and 1850. His principal influence was in France, whose social thinkers were at the time concerning themselves with the 'scientific' and 'positive' explanation of society.

In response to the radical individualism and critical rationalism of the Enlightenment, French (and European) thought in general turned away from Cartesian scepticism, and moved towards Romanticism, ultramontanism and to an organic conception of society and the rights and duties of individual men. This movement, profoundly conservative in tone, was motivated by the French Revolution and its Republican consequences: writers like de Maistre, Bonald, Mme de Staël and Chateaubriand saw in the Enlightenment's criticism of religion and monarchic absolutism the seeds of revolutionary terror, and responded by denouncing reason. Hence in the years following the end of the Republic such writers inaugurated the Romantic concern with the past, and with feelings and emotions, placing sentiments above ideas. In so doing they generated a new intellectual interest in religion, and produced metaphysical world-views which stressed the integrative power of religious belief in society. Ultimately the Romantic idea of the global meaning which history possessed in its movements—in which principal interest was of course directed to the 'catastrophe' of 1789—produced problems and questions only answerable by philosophical meditation on history. History became the means whereby the present state of affairs could be justified: since the present had its roots in the past how could that be otherwise? Romantic conservatism was backward looking, always searching for the origins of present customs in the previous idyll of medieval corporatism, when all the classes in society knew their places and roles in relation to each other, and hierocratic authority was unquestioned. The Enlightenment was seen as disturbing the stability of society, by criticizing religion which had hitherto answered everyone's spiritual needs and provided a source of stability in the old order: by destroying public confidence in religion, the philosophes had allowed the propagation of an atheistic republicanism and thus virtually started the Revolution themselves! It was in this context of an anti-Enlightenment feeling that Vico became influential. With his view of the movement of history as '*corsi e ricorsi*', a repetitive cycle, and his anti-Cartesian methodology coupled with an organic theory of society, Vico became 'sponsor' of the French Romantic view of history, a function which Hegel performed for Germany. By 1830 Vico was part of intellectual orthodoxy. In a course run by Victor Cousin at the Sorbonne, Vico was given equal status to Bossuet and Herder. But although there was diffusion of Vico's main ideas, especially those of the unity of thought and of the 'organic system of the world of societies' which Jules Michelet took over for his philosophy of history, the really significant element of his *Scienza Nuova*—the dialectical progression of social change—was largely ignored. This is understandable in one sense, in that the dialectic implies conflict between the cultural forms of one age and the social forms of the next, and indeed between social groups in each age. Such conflict was unacceptable to the Romantic view of the harmony of (most) historical development, and neither Comte nor Saint-Simon, who are both essentially Romantics, took any notice of Vico in this respect.[9]

Vico then, appeared favourable to the 'positivism' of the early, post-Revolutionary, social sciences, and exerted considerable, though diffused, influence on their early development through the agency of men like Michelet and Cousin. But his influence on socialist thinkers, and particularly on Marx, is surprisingly slight. Marx was living in France at a time (1843–8) when Vico's intellectual standing was higher than either before or since, yet his only published reference to Vico[10] comes in a footnote to *Capital*:[11]

since, as Vico says, the essence of the distinction between human history and natural history is that the former is made by man and the latter is not, would not the history of human technology be easier to write than the history of natural technology? By disclosing man's dealings with nature, the productive activities by which his life is sustained, technology lays bare his social relations and the mental conceptions that flow from them.

B 7

Although a meagre reference in itself, this note suggests that Marx was aware of the connection between Vico's methodological writings and his own elaboration of a sociology of knowledge based on the economic element in social life. Marx had read the authoritative French translation of the *Scienza Nuova* (by Princess Belgioioso) soon after its publication in 1844, and it may be surmised that he was aware of the parallels between his treatment of the 'production of consciousness' in his *German Ideology* and Vico's similar treatment of the same subject in the *Scienza Nuova*, where ideas are considered as social productions in the sense that they are formed by language in the dialectical progression of human nature and culture. However, we will consider Marx's notion of the 'production of consciousness' as a paradigmatic concept at a later point.

One of the few Enlightenment writers to be aware of Vico and the content of his most important work was the Baron de la Brède (Montesquieu). Vico was known in his own period primarily as a juriconsult, rather than as a political philosopher, and Montesquieu undoubtedly came upon the *Scienza Nuova* through his interest in legal theory. There are some superficial similarities between Montesquieu's *magnum opus*, *De l'Esprit des lois* of 1748, and Vico's *Scienza Nuova*, though these are limited mainly to the overall conceptions of the works, and the cultural relativism and historicism which characterize both.

III

Montesquieu's approach to the sociology of knowledge in some ways reflects his role as 'the French Vico'. He was Vichian in the sense of being to a certain extent out of sympathy with aspects of the rationalism of the Enlightenment, but decidedly un-Vichian in his influence on his contemporaries. None of the philosophes, with the possible exceptions of Voltaire and Rousseau, could lay claim to as wide a circle of influence as Montesquieu possessed, principally as a result of *De l'Esprit des lois*, and by the close of the eighteenth century his methods of studying political and social institutions and relating them to their social context were almost orthodoxy in the new, 'moral', sciences.

Montesquieu's sociology of knowledge really amounts to a theory of how the social structure of a society reflects, and in its turn is reflected by, the social values of its inhabitants. The title of Montesquieu's most famous work—*The Spirit of the Laws*—expresses the theoretical content of his sociology of knowledge admirably. For what the book constantly refers to is the underlying basis of civil (i.e. constitutional) law, and what Montesquieu means by this is the type of normative system suitable to a political constitution, and by extension this comes to mean that it is possible to specify a given structure of laws, norms, religious beliefs and ideas as characteristic of a given social structure. Montesquieu did not start his intellectual career with such a sophisticated approach to the study of political and social institutions, however, for he was originally (in the famous, satirical, *Lettres persanes*, 1721) quite a blatant and sceptical rationalist, attacking the conventions, morals and in particular the religious institutions of his time. Travel and experience ameliorated his extreme anti-clericalism, though he never quite gave up the rationalism which underlay it, despite what W. Stark asserts to the contrary.[12] By the time *De l'Esprit des lois* was written Montesquieu took a wider view of society and though he did retain a rationalist concern with freedom and political liberty, these values were tempered by an intellectual move towards historicism and cultural relativism.

The suggestion of what we now term 'sociology of knowledge' as an important theoretical component of *De l'Esprit des lois* is primarily confined to the first half of the book, which as Raymond Aron has suggested, is virtually a treatise of political sociology.[13] In the second section of the book (there is a third discrete section of the book which is in effect a collection of odds and ends relating to a number of minor subjects, references to French politics and legal theory), Montesquieu develops a secondary, ecological theory of social organization, which in a sense defines the limits material environment places on social structure. This seems to suggest, almost antithetically to the first section of the book, that the material basis of social organization determines what ideas, values, modes of thought and other cultural components will come into existence, moulded by the ecological environment in which a society is situated. Even the development of religious and theological ideas, as well as the institutions which support them are traced back to environmental causes in this second section: Protestantism's influence in Northern European Catholicism is explained by reference to the influence of climate and geography upon human nature. This would seem to present a problem in the interpretation of *De l'Esprit des lois*, and indeed the paradoxical nature of the book has not gone unnoticed. However, it will be treated here as if the two theories of social organization, normative and ecological, refer to mediatory factors whose relative importance is determined by the context in which they operate, which I am sure is what Montesquieu himself was getting at.

As outlined above, the first part of *De l'Esprit des lois* forms what might be called a sociology of politics, for what Montesquieu discusses there is the 'principle' and 'nature' of government, elucidating as he does so what might be termed a 'prototypical' theory of the social basis of political ideology and its influence, in turn, upon social structure.

Each society, if it has any form of regularized order—and in Montesquieu's pessimistic view of human nature, somewhat similar to Hobbes's, this is the prerequisite if any continuity is to exist in men's lives—will only flourish and cohere if all the men in it act unselfishly, or at least in concert towards the end of maintaining social stability. There is, asserts Montesquieu, only one type of society in which men rationally choose to live unselfishly for the good of all rather than for themselves alone, and that is what he calls a 'republic'. Republics may be of two forms, either democratic or aristocratic: the democratic being the purest form which most nearly approaches the ideal of political equality for all (male) members of a society. Against the ideal-type of the republic, Montesquieu contrasts two other types of society, characterized in terms of their political constitution, 'monarchies' and 'despotisms', each of which represents a corrupt form of social order in which the rights of the many are subordinated to those of the few or the one, and in which there is no real human freedom. Each type of state has a 'principle', a set of sentiments which in their totality form the underlying normative system for the type of government which it possesses, and which are necessary for the state to have a continuous social order. The totality of sentiments form an integrated whole, appropriate to whichever type of constitution exists, and their function is essentially that of an ideology. These 'principles' thus contain both values and what is defined in the society as 'knowledge': they constrain men to act in certain ways and to recognize a certain power or authority structure as legitimate. As well as providing an ideology for men to believe in, they may also be seen as '*Weltanschauungen*', as recognizable systems of ideas which characterize the societies they are produced by and thereby allow their classification into one of the three types of state which Montesquieu devised. The typology is intended to be exhaustive: all societies past and present (and presumably future societies as well) may be classified according to it. To go with the three types of government, there are three 'principles' or normative systems: for republics, what Montesquieu calls 'civic virtue', involving recognition of the free and equal status of every inhabitant of the society; for monarchies, the 'principle' of government is 'honour', a normative system which implies deference to a personage whose right to rule is pre-ordained and traditional and who justifies his power on that basis in a hierocratic society (conceived by Montesquieu as structured into estates). The final 'principle', underlying a despotic state, is fear. The corrupt nature of a despotism can only be maintained, argues Montesquieu, if people are coerced into acceding to the power of the despot and his minions.

One cannot in any real sense talk of a moral order underlying a despotic society, and in Montesquieu's usage of the type there is little of empirical or analytic value.

Each 'principle' of government is linked to what Montesquieu calls the 'nature' of government, the social distribution of political power, in effect the concrete social structure which the political constitution represents. From this we may legitimately discern a sociology of knowledge in embryo form: by specifying a causal relationship between the social order of a country and its political constitution, Montesquieu introduces the concept of characteristic 'principles', either ideologies or *Weltanschauungen*, which are themselves produced by, or are reflections of, the social relationships of the society. Montesquieu himself confirms this point: 'such as the pattern of public order is in a country, such will be its total life, and hence also its mental life.'[14]

Montesquieu develops his political theory in a way that leads the reader to suspect that his primary concern is in fact political ideology. For his discussion of the content of 'principles' of government turns on the part played by law, mores and religion in providing a system of co-ordinated political values and beliefs. In assigning the most important role in the formation of such a system to law, Montesquieu indicates that he views ideology as fundamentally a constraining entity, as the more important and influential means of social control available to man to curb his own selfish and domineering nature. For it is where the system of social order breaks down, where a unified ideology has not been systematically developed, that despotism and slavery (both of which Montesquieu abhorred) exist. Similarly monarchy, where it exists, depends upon the development of a false ideology—'honour'—which subordinates equal men to an authority system in which they owe allegiance to an individual, and their political liberty is repressed by his absolute and 'divine' power. Only in a republic can man's natural equality be recognized, for it is there alone that the system of social control reflects the reality of human nature. In a republic the laws thus assume the status of a system of knowledge: they tell a man how he should act if he is to act in accordance with the basic uniformity of human nature.

It is legitimate to conclude that Montesquieu's theory of ideology plays a highly significant role in his attempts to produce a science of politics based on some simple sociological laws. In attempting such a project, Montesquieu was indicating the interest of the Enlightenment thinkers in the empirical, rather than metaphysical, study of human institutions, an interest not purely scientific since they believed that knowledge itself could bring about social change. This critical rationalism led naturally to an implicit notion of ideology as irrational or distorted ideas, as knowledge which had

11

become divorced or alienated from its proper object, which was, primarily, *man*. Hence the theory of ideology which developed during the Age of Enlightenment was one which criticized the alienation of man's natural reason, and saw the prime source of that alienation in the propagation of superstitions about religion by a priestly class who used irrational beliefs to justify their own privileges and power. Montesquieu developed this implicit notion of ideology, generalized it and applied to it empirical evidence, so that ultimately he broadened the theory of ideology to produce a virtual 'sociology of knowledge' in his *De l'Esprit des lois*. By transforming the idea of the ideological role of the priesthood into a more general concept of the ideological needs of political and social systems, Montesquieu provided a real step forward in social knowledge.

The conflicting and paradoxical theory of the material basis of political and social structure which Montesquieu elaborates in the second half of *De l'Esprit des lois* can be largely ignored as far as the sociology of knowledge is concerned, for what it does is to suggest an alternative, a 'morphology' of knowledge tracing ideas and beliefs to physiological sources. Montesquieu suggests that climate and geography are responsible for changes in human nature such that specific types of political and social structure are appropriate to specific regions: despotisms flourish in large land masses like Asia, whereas republics exist more happily in cold, small countries like Sweden or England. However, there is no complete determinism intended here: Montesquieu is very careful to point out that human reason can overcome such conditions, and produce republics where, ecologically, they are inappropriate.

Both Vico and Montesquieu were to a certain extent fascinated by the processes of social change and its influence on the political and social structure of states. In their attempts to study this phenomenon they took a wider view of history than had hitherto seemed possible, and what followed from this was a degree of cultural relativism. The critical rationalism of the philosophes really encouraged such a relativism, though it was kept within certain limits, in that their criticisms of contemporary institutions employed cross-cultural comparisons. Very often these were antiquarian, referring to the liberty and reason of classical Greece and Rome, but they also used modern examples and paradigms in their social criticisms (Rousseau's idea of the 'noble savage' is a paradigmatic example of some fame). The conviction that Western society had no inbuilt advantages as far as culture or civilization was concerned was a powerful factor in the development of social science as it encouraged men to take a global view of human institutions and practices. In that sense it encouraged objectivity and whilst there were excesses of rationalist fervour for the virtues of alien civilizations, on the whole the philosophes

12

used the large amount of data available to them intelligently. (One must remember that even in the eighteenth century new lands were being discovered all the time. Travel on an international scale was not uncommon, and there was a ready market for atlases, chronicles and accounts of alien cultures.) None used the data more intelligently than Montesquieu. His work really enlarged philosophic conceptions of the human world, stressing the disparate and varied practices and mores of societies, and setting them (through the use of typologies) in a more systematic and objective framework than before. His work became the model for comparative historical studies, political theory and 'sociology' and was very influential for the Scottish Enlightenment which was itself, in the persons of Adam Ferguson,[15] David Hume[16] and Adam Smith responsible for much of the later development of sociological thought, especially in France during the 1820s when there was an intellectual vogue for 'Scottish' social theory.

IV

The Enlightenment, spreading reason like light, produced social sciences by unifying science with rationality in the best Newtonian tradition. As a result moral and political philosophy were liberated from the chains of theology (and theodicy) and transformed into empirical sciences. But in many respects the Enlightenment failed in its aim of making rational man the centre of scientific study, for its 'program' could be interpreted as a call to revolution, and its contiguity to the events of 1789–94 led to it being vilified in the name of social order. The French Revolution produced a change in ways of viewing the social world, which, when they were linked with the social changes of emergent industrialism, profoundly altered the nature of the problems with which the philosophes had dealt. Political reaction was fused with a social reaction against the new bourgeois society, and a concern with organic, semi-feudal conceptions of society became established. This was an antithesis to Enlightenment individualism and rationality, and social science suffered as a result. The profoundly conservative cast into which sociology was put after 1815 is demonstrated by Comte's 'positivism', which represents most adequately the prevailing reaction to the 'negative' social criticism of the philosophes. Sociological concerns were everywhere returned to moral and political philosophy in the wave of Romanticism which swept Europe after the revolutionary wars, and the organic notion of society was dominant, emphasizing the need for social order and stability. In such a climate, religion became a positive and good thing again, as the basis of society and of man's civilized nature: consequently social philosophy, and the philosophy

13

of history in general, became closely connected with theology. The idealism of Fichte, Hegel and Schelling demonstrates this. In rejecting the utilitarian ethic which had so characterized Enlightenment thought they produced new, metaphysical ethics which though they resulted in theological innovations intended to safeguard both knowledge and virtue from the subversive doctrines of the eighteenth century, ultimately served only religious interests.

In such intellectual conditions the prototype sociologies, including sociology of knowledge, all but disappeared. Of the social sciences only political economy could claim continuous development from the eighteenth century and that only because of its British location and quantifiable (and thus 'positive') nature. In condemning and attempting to erase critical rationalism, positivism and Romanticism together contrived to stifle the development of the empirical sciences of man, and produced in their stead distorted and partial sociologies, psychologies and anthropologies. A sociology which could not be critical of its social environment could not give rise to a sociology of knowledge whose principal element was a theory of ideology. However, the conservative and Romantic attack on reason did paradoxically produce (as a response to it) new, radicalized social sciences. By subordinating social and political discussion to theological and state interests, by repressing criticism of religion, conservatism motivated a new concern with ideology and the development of a whole sociology based upon criticism of the fusion of religious and social privilege with the interests of the state. Starting with the Young Hegelian movement in Germany, criticism progressed from constituting one element of a radical idealist philosophy to a scientific analysis of social structure, via the medium of a dialectical and materialist theory of historical and social change. Hence, to conclude with a sweeping generalization which contains an important grain of truth: there is no real progress in sociological thought, and consequently no development of a sociology of knowledge, until the catalyst of Marx appears upon the scene to reintroduce critical rationalism to European social thought.

The Enlightenment was, with one important exception,[17] barren of consequences for the sociology of knowledge. Yet its influence extended over the period of repression which followed it, since it provided the notion of an explicable and scientifically comprehensible social order which was itself imperishable, though either a conservative or revolutionary superimposition could be placed upon it. Legitimately we may claim that what we now call sociological thought was inaugurated by the 'little flock' of philosophes, and received its first definitive structuring in their hands.

2 Marxism I: Hegel and Marx

I

Hegelian philosophy had achieved the status almost of orthodoxy throughout Germany when its propagator died in 1831, the only pocket of resistance being East Prussia, dominated by the continuing influence of Kantianism in the University of Königsberg (where Kant had had his Chair). In carrying reason and idealism to the pinnacle of universality by his dialectical system, Hegel had created the persuasive view that philosophy and religion, always hitherto opposed (as 'thesis' and 'antithesis'), were reconcilable in reality, in the mediation of the Prussian State, their practical synthesis. But the philosophical system, whatever its value as a legitimation of the Prussian State, was not without contradictions and problematic elements which only came to critical light after the master's death. It then became clear that Hegel had not been precise about either the immortality of the soul or God's personality, or indeed and more seriously, about religion in general. Accusations of pantheism were directed at Hegelianism and were only reinforced by the realization that Hegel had seemed to suggest that God's knowledge of himself was simply man's self-consciousness. The publication in 1835 of Strauss's book, *Das Leben Jesu* (*The Life of Jesus*) immediately raised a storm of controversy by treating the Gospels as mythologizations of the wishes and desires of the early Christians. Although Hegel himself had not considered the historicity of the Gospels to be of much importance, interested as he was solely in their symbolic content, Strauss's book put the issue of the Hegelian treatment of religion in a harsh and critical light and effectively split the Hegelian movement by implying that the revelation and incarnation of divine essence could only be collective, its 'sole adequate field . . . the whole of humanity'.[1]

The split in the Hegelian movement took three initial directions, which Strauss himself characterized using the French *political* terms: left, right and centre. The right, or 'Old' Hegelians, believed that the whole Gospel narrative could be deduced as history from the idea of the unity of divine and human nature, as Hegel had seemed at some times to think. The centre group—which came to include Strauss when the political distinctions became clearer—believed that only a part of the Gospel could be so deduced. The left, or 'Young' Hegelians rejected the notion entirely. In fact, these originally theological and philosophical distinctions were substantially reproduced in the later political divisions among Hegelians and German intellectuals generally. In a theocratic state, as Prussia was at that time, religious divisions automatically became political divisions, or were generalized into them. In the intellectual climate of those times virtually the only 'free' discussion possible *in public* was about religion; censorship prevented until 1840 any discussion of substantive political issues. As a primarily philosophical movement, and one firmly ensconced within German idealism, it is not surprising that the Young Hegelians should have seen everything in terms of theory and ideas, including politics. Indeed their treatment of theology though not originally atheist very soon became a radical criticism of religion logically developing from the speculative rationalism which had characterized the teaching of Hegelian philosophy at Berlin University under Gans, Hegel's successor, where Edgar and Bruno Bauer, Feuerbach, Stirner, Engels and Marx himself had all studied. The Young Hegelians, in developing this speculative rationalism[2] along dialectical lines, were indeed carrying on from an earlier German intellectual tradition, that of the *Aufklärer*: implicit in this was an admiration for the principles of the French Revolution in which they saw, as had Hegel, the practical development of reason. Reason appeared to them as a 'continually unfolding process and [they] conceived it their task to be its heralds'.[3]

The Young Hegelians' development of radicalized Hegelianism was an approach distinctively idealist in its reliance upon 'criticism' as the primary agent of 'world-historical' social change, which they conceived of in terms of a bourgeois social transformation, a sort of humanistic democracy. This approach contained a messianic note; believing (with Hegel) that they were part of an age of transition, they developed the view that 'the revolutionary tendencies of Hegel's thought were hidden and it was his disciples' (the Young Hegelians') task to bring them out into the open'.[4] Producing a revolutionary dialectic somewhat transformed the contents of Hegel's philosophy, however, since the idea of mediation, so central to Hegel's dialectic, became completely changed in meaning. It was replaced by a notion in which the polarities of the historical dialectic were to be, henceforth, 'absolutely negated' by a final rupture which the 'criticism' of the

Young Hegelians themselves would aid in producing. This was all far beyond Hegel's original intentions: as McLellan puts it:[5]

Hegel's close attention to empirical reality, his distaste for prediction, his dislike for ideas that were too dogmatic, the moderation and precision that the concept of mediation gave to the whole of his philosophy—all this was lacking in the Young Hegelians.

The Young Hegelians themselves, however, still thought they were being faithful to Hegel, and they were seen as such by the ruling class in Prussia. When, in 1840, the accession of Frederick William IV to the Prussian throne was followed by a relaxation of the censorship laws, the only opportunity for Young Hegelian political action appeared. But they were not a political party, and had no real following amongst the German middle class. Action was limited to political criticism, roughly along the lines of opposition to the Christian base of the Prussian State and couched (under the influence of the Bauers and Feuerbach, its leading lights) in a highly atheistic vein. A journal, the *Rheinische Zeitung*, became its chief mouthpiece, directed mostly against the *Kölnische Zeitung*, a journal of reactionary, pro-religion and state views: in the *Rheinische Zeitung* most of the characteristic views of the Young Hegelians were aired—their doctrine of the rational organization of the state, disestablishment of the Church and Jacobin notions of social justice. The new regime (in which Hegelianism now had no support) did not take the criticism at all favourably—the king was a Christian romantic, a pietist opposed to liberalism who saw social change and political development in terms of the evolution of traditional forms—and by the end of 1842 various measures were taken to stop Young Hegelian criticism, identified simply as Hegelianism. Schelling replaced Gans at Berlin with orders to root out 'the dragon-seed of Hegelianism', Bauer was deprived of his teaching permit (thus barring Marx from a teaching job via his influence) and the *Hallische Jahrbücher* which had been sympathetic to Young Hegelian policies was forced to publish in Saxony because of its criticism of the Prussian government. Marx himself, who had been working on the *Rheinische Zeitung* after writing for Ruge's *Deutsche Jahrbücher*, came into contact with Moses Hess, the first German communist, and began to develop his Young Hegelian ideas on the role of religion in the state. By October 1842 he took over editorship of the journal and began to be more concerned with questions of a wider political nature, though he was unimpressed with communism and socialism. However he did attack laws against the collection of scrap by the poor and the miserable conditions of the Moselle winegrowers. In March 1843 the Prussian government could not tolerate criticism any longer, and Marx was out of a job when the *Rheinische*

Zeitung was suppressed. He moved to Paris to work with Arnold Ruge on his *Deutsche-französische Jahrbücher*: by this time he had almost broken with the Young Hegelians and was working on a critique of Hegel's political philosophy (the 'philosophy of Right'), in which he conflated humanism, communism and democracy. In France, Marx moved further towards communism, attending workers' meetings and eventually breaking with Ruge over his attitude towards socialism. He also began to get interested in economics, especially the development of political economy by Smith and Ricardo. He came into contact with Frederick Engels, another Young Hegelian, and they decided to collaborate on a book, so similar did they find their views on revolution, communism and economics. The first real product of that collaboration, and the book which really indicated Marx's break with Young Hegelian philosophy (as he wrote later, it was 'to settle our erstwhile philosophical consciousness'), was *The German Ideology* which is at the centre of any understanding of the development of a Marxian sociology of knowledge.

II

Engels said that Marxism had three essential components: 'German idealist philosophy, French socialism and English economic theory'.[6] The first work in which all three appear as connected components is the 'Economic and Philosophical Manuscripts', the Paris manuscripts of 1844. It is in this work that the central ideas with which Marx comes later to see knowledge as an element of social reality, rather than as something separate and autonomous, make their first appearance. The work is a testing out of Feuerbachian materialism—there is much talk of its 'empirical' basis—and an attempt by Marx to conceptualize the primary characteristics of bourgeois social relations in a world coming to be dominated by capitalism. In that sense it is a complete rejection of the idealism of Bauer, Stirner and the other 'critical theologians', who used the Hegelian dialectic in an abstract way; Marx claimed to be using it 'practically', at least in the first part of the Paris manuscripts which form a critique of political economy and the way in which it treats 'the state, law, morals, civil life, etc'.[7] The second part of the manuscripts forms an analysis of Hegel's *Phenomenology of Spirit*, and a criticism of Hegel's idealism, which Marx contrasts with his own consistent naturalism—a form of humanism which avoids both idealism and (Feuerbachian) materialism.

As is well known, what the Economic and Philosophical manuscripts deal with above all else is *alienation*. The concept of alienation is as central to what constitutes Marx's sociology of knowledge as it is to his work *as a whole*. I do not intend to be contentious about this point; although it has been alleged that the concept of alienation is a part of the *œuvre* of the 'Young Marx' only, the concept continues, in one form or another, throughout Marx's whole work. Indeed its centrality is indicated most unequivocally in the *Grundrisse* which (though only in draft form) gives us Marx's view of the development of the materialist method in its application to history and to capitalist society. *Capital* was only a part of Marx's great aim of producing a *magnum opus*, which he termed his *Economics*, which would deal with the whole issue of the alienation of man through capital and the state (bourgeois 'civil society'), and which is sketched out in the *Grundrisse*.[8] This work, which Marx himself felt to be the work of the 'best period of my life' is as Hegelian in tone as the Paris manuscripts and deals with alienation as much as that earlier production does.[9]

The development of Marx's important work, then, starts in 1844. The Paris manuscripts, in explicating the conceptualization of human alienation, show Marx in his first attempt to apply his version of the Hegelian dialectic to an empirical problematic, the failure of the classical economics of Smith, Ricardo and Jean-Baptiste Say to explain the relationship between capital, labour and private property. The manuscripts are 'materialist' in the sense that they deal with society as a historically determined, as a specific *structure* of social relationships between *real* men, rather than the interrelationships of abstract 'ideas' as in Hegel, or human consciousnesses, as in the Young Hegelians. But it is not 'materialist' in Feuerbach's sense of a perceptual materialism positing a static conception of the relationship between consciousness and society, but in a dialectical sense. The relation between thought and being is not as two separate, ontologically different, things but as two elements of reality which mutually affect each other to produce a reality not subsumable either to the material substratum or human consciousness alone. 'Alienation' expresses how the relationship between the material basis of life—work —and man's conceptions of himself as a social being is distorted, to produce in capitalist societies a *reification* of social relations, a reduction of their human nature to the status of things, as mere 'objects'.

We shall discuss the development of Marx's concept of alienation, and its crucial connection with the development of a Marxist theory of knowledge predicated in sociological terms, by reference primarily to the 1844 manuscripts, *The German Ideology*, the *Contribution to the Critique of Political Economy*, *Capital*, (the last two by reference also to the *Grundrisse*) and *Theories of Surplus Value*.

What Marx does in the 1844 manuscripts is to take the 'classical' political economy of Smith, Say and Ricardo and indicate its relationship to the socio-historical context of capitalism, to show how this contextual situation provides it with a particular view of social relations. Though it has some scientific value, the inadequacies of classical economics especially in its treatment of labour and private property derive from its refusal to see how the categories it uses are a part of the social reality they express and not abstract laws of all human societies. Classical economics presupposes, initially, the demotion of the worker to the status of a commodity, a thing whose misery is 'inversely proportional to the power and volume of his production'.[10] It presupposes also that capital will be concentrated into a few hands and the whole of society divided into two classes, property owners and property-less workers (Engels had pointed this out in his 'Umrisse zu einer Kritik der national Oekonomie', an essay which had greatly impressed Marx when it was submitted for publication in the one and only edition of the *Deutsche-französische Jahrbücher*). In short, political economy proceeds from the assumption of private property as a *given*. It does not explain the concept, but uses it in a general abstract way as a 'law' of society assuming the interests of the capitalist alone to be adequate. In particular and as a result of this subordination of science to the social interests of a particular class, the relationship between division of labour and exchange does not appear as an object of analysis anywhere in classical economics—it is systematically excluded from study. Marx saw in this ignorance of the connectedness of division of labour and exchange that certain facts disappeared from view, most importantly that 'the worker becomes poorer the more wealth he produces, the more his production increases in power and extent'.[11] The value of the worker is depressed, it declines to the level of the value of things: in capitalist society, labour thus produces both the commodity and also the worker himself as a commodity. What labour produces becomes alien to its producer, since it is 'objectified' into a commodity which only embodies abstract human labour. Consequently appropriation of the object of labour is experienced as 'externalization', as alienation. What belongs to the worker, his labour, embodied in its object, is separated from and set against him; as in religion, 'the more man attributes to God, the less he retains in himself', so in capitalist society: 'the life [he] has given to the object confronts him as hostile and alien' and the worker falls under the domination of his product—capital.[12]

But it is not the economic relations of capitalism alone which produce alienation, but the whole structure of capitalist society which affects the most profound of man's relationships, that which he has with nature. The progression of capitalist social relations to a more and more developed state thus results in a greater and greater appropriation of nature; the more it becomes a factor of production the less it is a means of life for the worker in two important respects. The 'sensuous external world' ceases to be an object belonging to labour because of its appropriation in the commodity, and it ceases to be a means of physical subsistence for the worker. The changes in the man–nature interaction brought about by the mode of capitalist social relations thus reduce the worker to the status of slave of what he produces—he *receives* labour and the means of subsistence: 'the terminus of this slavery is that [the worker] can only maintain himself as a *physical subject* so far as he is a *worker*, and only as a *physical subject* is he a worker.'[13] Alienation is not however a phenomenon which affects the worker alone, but characterizes the process of production as well; the 'active externalization' of labour which makes of it something coerced from the worker on the basis of his need to exist, since he has been deprived of the means of subsistence. Man as worker loses his individuality in this process; he can feel conscious of himself as an individual human being *only* in the 'animal functions' which ensure his continuing existence. This is man's self-alienation, the objectification and externalization of his qualitative individuality, that which makes him conscious of himself as a human being. Man's alienation in capitalist society does not stop there, however. There is a more fundamental form of alienation resulting from the operation of capitalist society: man's alienation from his 'species-being' (an essentially Feuerbachian concept) devolving upon his consciousness of himself as a universal and consequently free being. Man's species-being comes to exist as he makes his life activity conscious, a part of his will. Where animals produce specifically for their physical needs, man produces 'universally' and in that sense his production is only genuine when it is free of the constraints of physical need. As Marx puts it, man reproduces the whole of nature, whilst 'the animal only produces itself'.[14] In fact, this universal nature of (ideal) human production allows man to produce to standards which do not relate solely to the physical needs of the species, but to extrinsic standards, (virtually to universal values) such as 'beauty'. The object of labour is thus 'the . . . objectification of man's species-life', life in the sense not simply of human activity, but of human consciousness as well. In alienating man from nature, and man from his own self-consciousness, alienated labour thus externalizes and estranges the species from him and makes of it an *abstraction*. Species-life is thought of solely as the *process* of subsistence; human nature recedes from reality to become a wholly abstract conception. Any knowledge of man and his social relationships thus becomes as unreal, as atomized, as his social relationships are unreal and expressive of a social atomism.

What are the causes of these consequences of capitalist modes of production? Primarily, a particular type of social structure, in the sense of systematically reproduced social interactions. For as much as the product of labour, alienated from the worker, can only belong to a man not subject to this externalization of the product of labour, a non-worker (e.g. a capitalist), then alienated labour implies a set of social relationships which structure the relation of worker to capitalist, predicated on the basis of private property. Private property is thus 'product result, and the necessary consequence of externalized man'; it is the product of alienated men.[15] Political economy, bourgeois 'social science', confuses this relationship. By treating externalized labour as the result of the movement of private property, it reverses the true relationship (and thus functions as an *ideological distortion*, we may add). Though private property appears as the cause of externalized labour it is in fact its consequence. Thus the equalization of wages (as had been argued by Proudhon and some other of the French socialists) could not in any sense abolish capitalism, since all that would occur would be that society itself would become an 'abstract capitalist', and a completed and universal alienation would operate. Only by the emancipation of the worker can society be emancipated from private property and thus from the alienation separating the worker from his product.[16] Marx uses his explanation of the social functions of private property to show how it is possible to develop *all* the categories employed by political economy 'through analysis from the concept of alienated externalized labour' and thus to show that classical economic theory, far from being a formal, universal science, is rooted in a particular structure of interests, values and social relations itself, and operates to place a particular, *class based*, interpretation on reality.[17] And by indicating in this way the partial nature of the categories of political economy Marx really inaugurates his theory of ideology as the connection of what purports to be a 'general theory' of society with a ruling class, the theory being ideological in the sense of having its explanatory power *limited* because it functions as an expression and legitimation of the interests of that class against the interests of the classes subservient to it. The organizing concept of this theory of ideology is thus 'alienation' as a category central to the operation of class societies. In particular, the social structure of capitalist society gives rise to a situation in which men are forced to work in such a way that their individual qualities are suppressed, and they cannot relate effectively—or humanly—to their fellow men. As a class, workers are socially atomized and have only a limited and impoverished conception of themselves and the society they live in as a result of the alienation of their labour (of course, definition of 'class' is central to the whole Marxian theory of society, as well as those elements constituting its sociology of knowledge). Programmatically, in the future communist society there would be no disparity—as there now is—between what men think about society and how society actually functions, such that the overcoming (or transcendence as Marx puts it in a very Hegelian fashion) of private property means the emancipation of all human senses and aptitudes, henceforth developed in the social context of man's realized species-being. Although Marx is relatively non-specific about the mechanisms of social change, importantly for our analysis of his sociology of knowledge, he does allot an important role to natural scientific knowledge, which is an agent of change in so far as its advances facilitate the development of the means of production—industry—which although a momentarily alienative agency is also the ultimate agency of human emancipation. In that sense, with social change, natural science changes its nature: communism allows it to lose its 'idealistic' tendencies and become 'the basis of human science'.[18] A distinctly positivist tendency is thus obvious in the development of Marxian thought: man is the immediate (e.g. given) object of natural science, nature the immediate object of the human sciences, hence there is the real possibility of the unity of sciences, a unified science of man and nature in which no distinction is made between the basis of human and natural existence —a properly naturalistic unified science (such a goal—unified science —is even now still in existence, so tied up is it with the dominance of positivist ontology in science). This positivism illustrates better than anything else Marx's connections with critical rationalism. The aim of a totally *liberating* knowledge was in the forefront of Enlightenment positivism and was a component of a programme essentially similar to that of Marx; the production of a qualitatively new social structure in which each individual would be able to fulfil his individual needs and achieve a total happiness.

But we are not concerned with such ideological similarities as such, though they illustrate the continuity of certain types of social idea, but with the paradigmatic development of Marx's sociology of knowledge.[19] This development is tied up with Marx's break with Young Hegelian critical criticism as much as it is with his brief espousal of Feuerbachian materialism. By taking from Feuerbach the materialist conception of reality, that what man had previously sought in religion and pure thought could now be realized in fact, Marx accepted the viewpoint that nature is the 'primary' and thought the 'secondary' reality. Feuerbach himself expressed this point in his *Theses on the Reform of Philosophy*: 'The true relation of thought to Being is this; Being is subject, thought is predicate. Thought springs from being, but Being does not spring from thought.'[20]

And this is essentially the presupposition of the Marxian sociology of knowledge. I do not want to be confusing here: Marx rejected, in the *Theses on Feuerbach*, the perceptual materialism which was a static conception in Feuerbach's understanding of the relationship between consciousness and society, but he does retain the crucial epistemological assumption that concrete reality, material facts are *prior* to thought, departing from Feuerbach in conceiving of thought as a produced part of reality and ontologically the same as matter. The crucial difference comes from Marx's use of the Hegelian dialectic, in which he resolved the epistemological problems raised by Feuerbach's naturalism which reduces truth to the level of simple sense-perception, and leaves nature as something immutable, unchanging. Marx criticized Feuerbach, in terms derived from Hegel, for ignoring labour and its transformation of the natural conditions of human existence into social conditions, with the result that he mistook sense perception for nature and thus could not understand nature as practical human activity (praxis) (thesis 9).[21]

III

Having raised himself above both Young Hegelian critical criticism and Feuerbachian naturalistic materialism, Marx felt himself able to criticize both positions—'our erstwhile philosophical conscience' as he put it—as 'ideological'.

Written in 1845 in collaboration with Engels (and with a little assistance from Moses Hess), *The German Ideology* takes up the critique of capitalist society developed in the Paris manuscripts, but its larger part is devoted to a lengthy critique of Bauer, Strauss and Stirner, polemical in tone and now of little more than historical interest. It will not concern us here in any detail.

In the earlier work, Marx had shown that the economic categories and processes of capitalism were merely reified expressions of the social interactions between the (economically defined) classes of society. A suggestion of the connection between knowledge—consciousness—and society had been plotted, and *The German Ideology* takes this up in the context of a general critique of German philosophy. Marx took issue with the Young Hegelians primarily over their interpretations of German history. They had, as was pointed out earlier, continued the trend of Hegel's early political philosophy by allotting the principal role in socio-historical change to human reason rather than to 'real' factors, as for example, social revolution. This had led them to proclaim that their revolution in thought—'critical criticism'—was as important for German history as the French Revolution in the historical movement towards human freedom posited by Reason. Marx recognized the fallacy in this position. Although German thought, idealism, was most concerned with the idea of freedom (the reality of which the French Revolution had approached), it could only accomplish freedom in the realm of pure thought. Real freedom required real action, and, since the Young Hegelians deprecated such 'materialism', they could not achieve the *social* changes they apparently wished for. Marx's introduction to French socialism (especially through the 'League of the Just' in Paris) and his faith in the labour movement led him to see the industrial proletariat as the primary agent of social change. The Young Hegelians themselves tended to derogate the masses and deride communism, clinging to essentially middle-class notions of change. Even the Young Hegelian criticism of religion, the central element of its political position, was, as Marx pointed out, to take religion for granted, reducing everything to essentially religious conceptions (the heritage of Hegel's Absolute Spirit). In considering all products of consciousness as 'chains' the Young Hegelians limited themselves to changing conceptions of reality—'to interpret [it] another way—'effectively, they ignored the real world: 'It has not occurred to [them] to enquire into the connection of German philosophy with German reality, the relation of their criticism to their own material surroundings'.[22] Marx sets against this idealism his own concern with the 'real premises' of history whose basis is 'empirical' and can be 'verified' as such.[23]

In the view of Marx and Engels, the first real premise of history is the human individual: all understanding of history and society must start from that point. The distinguishing activity which separates man from animals is his production of his means of subsistence. This starting point becomes the basis, the developed and dialectical, materialism of what constitutes the definitively Marxian sociology of knowledge. In the first sixty pages or so of *The German Ideology* is sketched out the development of Marxian theory; there is certainly no greater development of the basic epistemological position formulated by Marx and Engels.

A basic equation is implicit in the Marxian social theory; the mode of the production of man's subsistence is the mode of life of individuals and *determines their social relationships*. As the mode of production develops through history, its development is indicated by the division of labour in which the productive process is split up into a set of specialisms. Another equation is denoted here: the consequence of the division of labour is the separation of town and country, of commercial and industrial labour, and the opposition of their respective interests. The *stages* in the development of this sociological equation may be characterized as, typically, stages in the nature of property ownership.[24] Hence, the division of labour provides the primary determination of human social relations. There are three pre-capitalist systems of property ownership and thus three main types of non-capitalist social structure dependent on them in the sense that they are predicated by specific forms of the division of labour. The three are: one, 'tribal' ownership, based solely on the family division of labour being accomplished on the basis of kinship criteria; two, 'ancient communal and state ownership' in the early city states based on the division of labour between owners of property and their slaves, the most important element of that property; three, 'feudal or estate property', a primarily rural social formation composed of land-owners with a serf class set against them.[25]

Having established the bases of his historical materialism Marx turns to discussion of the 'production of consciousness'. In the early stages of man's social existence, the production of ideas and consciousness was 'directly interwoven with the material activity and material intercourse of men, the language of real life'.[26] Men are thus the sole producers of their conceptions since their consciousness can never be anything other than their conscious existence. The corollary of this is that ideology, which Marx defines as men's false conceptions about themselves as social beings, in its inversion of men and their social conditions, is a consequence solely of the historical situation in which they live, the social structure pertaining at that time. This simply stated thesis thus provides the basic outline of the Marxian paradigm of the sociology of knowledge from which all development of the social conception of ideology and the relationship between knowledge (consciousness) and society proceed in Marxist thought.

Starting from men's 'real life processes', Marx demonstrates the superiority of his historical, materialist method over that of German idealism ('German philosophy'). In contradistinction to the idealist position, Marx maintains that the 'real life processes' are related *reflexively* to ideologies, that ideologies do not arise independently of men's existence and that this can be 'empirically verified' in that this approach starts from the premises of 'real men' and not their idealized self-consciousness.[27] Consequently, the second main assumption of the Marxian sociology of knowledge advances logically from this point; *consciousness is altered when men change their real existence*, i.e. the structure of their social relations. Study of these 'real' bases of ideology, and of ideology itself must, it follows, be detached from philosophy—which idealizes them—and become a part of science. But this 'science', as we have argued elsewhere, requires some conceptualization or definition of social structure and what it is that makes it distinctively 'social'. Marx provides this in his outline definition of social structure as 'the co-operation of several individuals'; structures are historically differentiated to produce an equation in which the stage of development of the mode of production as a productive force on the one hand, combines with an appropriate social structure as another productive force (in the sense of division of labour) on the other, the totality thus produced determining the nature of society, the total social system.[28] Human history is thus quite simply the history of material forces, and their incorporation in various distinctive social forms. It follows that since all existence is material, social, there can be no such thing as pure consciousness. At its simplest level, thought is connected with language, itself a material interaction, only 'agitated layers of air' in Marx's famous phrase. Both language and thought can only arise through social intercourse; 'consciousness is a ... social product, and remains so as long as men exist at all'.[29] The historical development of consciousness is then linked closely to the evolution of social relationships, locked in a causal chain with this process. The appearance of forms of abstract knowledge is consequently explained by Marx as the result of a *social* transformation, the division of mental and material labour, which separates consciousness and existence to produce 'pure' thought—philosophy, theology, ethics, and theory[30] a form of thought apparently contradictory of existing social relations. Contradictory, because of the practical antagonism between production forces and social structure, itself a function of the division of labour. In this formulation, the division of labour, by fixing men into specific social relationships produces a social structure in which the individual and the community necessarily conflict because of their opposing interests; this conflict is formalized and perpetuated by the transformations of the community into an abstract state, which whilst it is divorced formally from both individual and community is still based on the *real* relationships between them. The *development* of the state is linked with class-struggles within the society where groups of individuals with similar, primarily economic, interests strive for power, to represent their interests as the common interests of state and society. The state is as much a production of the prevailing social formations of society as is thought in general; law and the statutory regulation of human relationships are an ideal superstructure based on the development of the social base of society.

The dissolution of the conditions under which the proletariat is enslaved in capitalist society (outlined in the Paris manuscripts), by means of the communist revolution abolishing private property would allow the real intellectual wealth of the individual to develop. Estranged under capitalism, the intellectual capabilities of men— dependent upon the 'wealth' of their social relationships—would be reunited with their social existence in the communist revolution so that both could be seen as parts of man's production, material and intellectual.

The view of history which Marx develops in *The German Ideology* involves two important elements constituting the central core of his critique of idealism. First, the production process derives from that of life itself; second, that process is intimately related to social structure such that a clear connection can be made between theoretical productions and their specifically social foundation. Marx extrapolates from these elements his fundamentally *political* thesis: the forms and productions of knowledge and thought cannot be dissolved by any purely mental methods but only by a removal of the social conditions which give rise to them. Not criticism but revolution is the driving force of history. But such a revolution is impossible without both material and mental bases: there must be a revolutionary class *and* the idea of revolution. The revolutionary class—in capitalism the proletariat—must be prepared to revolt against the *whole* of the existing order and possess the consciousness of the idea of revolution. As an illustration of the foregoing theses about consciousness and social change, Marx describes the conditions of production of German historiography, which had operated (prior to Marx) in terms of 'theoretical' forces, rather than social or material forces. Idealism thus understood history *only* in its ideal terms and with the aid of fundamentally religious concepts (e.g. *Geisteswissenschaften*). These concepts are themselves related to the social structure of German society and will only be 'dissolved' by changing it. The 'struggles' of German thought thus exist as a purely ideological contest, fought against a real enough foe (e.g. Prussian censorship) but whose content had no relevance to the social reality of Germany at that time apart from the fact that its abstraction indicated the alienation of thought from concrete social existence.[31] All of the issues dealt with by philosophers, commonly presented in an abstract, unreal fashion, have an important substance in reality, which is obscured, and inverted in the ideological constructions of philosophical thought. Philosophy is then merely an ideological presentation of scientific, empirical problems: the relation of man to nature dealt with by Bauer in idealistic terms of 'absolute self-consciousness' is nothing more than production. Similarly the natural science which Feuerbach understands as 'pure thought' is itself provided with goals and a subject matter only by trade and activity, by 'sensuous' activity. Feuerbach cannot see this and separates his materialism from history, from the realm of the social.

Having established his critique of idealism and materialism Marx turns to an exploration of the precise connections between knowledge and social structure. The basic assumption behind this connection is that the way knowledge is produced, and its content, are in direct relationship to the power structure of society (power having in this context a relatively precise meaning of control, ownership, of the material means of production). Hence, 'the class, which is the ruling *material* force of society, is at the same time its *ruling* intellectual force'.[32] Quite explicitly, then, ideas are an *expression* of social relationships; an ideal, theoretical formulation of the facts of material dominance. As a class rules materially, its rule extends into the field of knowledge and culture as well, 'regulating the production and distribution of the ideas of [its] age'.[33] Whether this means that the *content* of knowledge is directly related to the structure of society, mediated through the *interests* of the dominant class, is unclear. Also Marx does not talk in any specific sense about the forms of knowledge, merely the relation of 'knowledge', as a whole, to society. But in this conceptualization, ideas have about the same social facticity as economic categories: they are expressive of something *distorted* in human relationships. Thus they are subject to the same sorts of 'laws' as the more mundane and prosaic units of the economy, liable to the same alienation from their producers as are commodities. Indeed, with capitalist society they become reified into commodities (which is the central issue of Lukács's development of Marxist sociology of knowledge), precisely because of the social division of labour which only allows the production of knowledge to take place in one strata of one class in society, the bourgeoisie. There are thus 'ideologists' who make a living as such, constructing illusory and distorted ideas and theories about their class for the consumption both of *other* classes and for the more passive and receptive elements of their own class. What follows from this is that although there may be internal dissensions about ideas, philosophies within the bourgeoisie, they disappear when the class as a whole is threatened, for the ideas only have power in that they represent the social position and interests of the ruling class, only as they are articulated *in accordance with* the facts of that class's material dominance. They may continue to exist thereafter, but they cannot have any real influence if the social conditions which they expressed have disappeared. Theories of vassal homage, for example, are *only* interesting antiquities in modern capitalist or socialist societies: they have no possible influence or relevance for modern authority relations, which are based upon quite different social relations.

It is important to be aware that Marx's development of the notion of ideology here is quite clearly different from that developed by the 'bourgeois rationalists'—or philosophes—of the eighteenth century. For them, ecclesiastic or aristocratic élites propagated 'superstitions' about God, law, social relationships so as to *intentionally* conceal the real situation from the dominated social groups, to conceal the fact of their immoral exercise of power. But for Marx, both proletariat and bourgeois alike, ruled and ruler, are subject to ideological conceptions and accept them as true because of their mutual existence in a system of social relations. Ideology is not then produced to 'cover up' reality in a conspiratorial fashion, but is systematically generated by the structure of social relationships, by the social division of both mental and material labour. Each new ruling class, in presenting its interests as the common interests of all and as the only rational and valid ideas, does not do this in order merely to confuse the rest of society (although of course the attempt to gain power for one group alone involves the intentional production of ideology *as well*); it actually believes in the rightness of its claim to hegemony and authority. For, inasmuch as capitalist

29

society relies upon the abstractions of reified economic categories and social relations (as, for example, the 'fetishistic' commodity, which we will discuss later) to maintain its dominance over the industrial proletariat, a conception of history which views presently existing social relations as the consequence of changes merely in concepts, rather than in configurations of social power, misrepresents the true social situation now as well as the history it purports to explain. And this provides an ideology which creates a 'false-consciousness' of reality afflicting *both* bourgeoisie and proletariat; the bourgeois *believing* that his society is the apotheosis of human freedom and reason, and his ideological productions exhorting the proletarian to believe this too and acquiesce in his subordinate and exploited position as his 'natural' role in society.

The 'cause' of the ideological nature of bourgeois knowledge is not in principle separable from the causes of capitalist socio-historical development. In particular the evolution of class relationships as the fundamental characteristics of social structure, which only becomes possible with the desuetude of feudal society, and the emergence of an economically powerful middle class, is the primary source of capitalist forms of ideology. Although of course Marx is not specific about pre-capitalist social formations here, *all* social structures in which there is a hierarchy of power and economic interest, based on differential ownership of the means of production, imply the production of ideological knowledge, of 'false-consciousness'. In the development of capitalist society, class becomes the sole structural determinant of life style, personal development and ideas and its control over these aspects of existence is terminable only by the abolition of the 'means' of producing class society—private property. The logic of capitalist economic development reduces all social relationships to the level of the money relationship between capitalist and worker. The influence of economic motivations extends even to science, Marx argues, citing the popularity of Newtonian theoretical mechanics in eighteenth-century France and England—both developing industrial middle classes requiring technological advances—in support of this (interestingly enough, Everett Hagen provides more systematic support for this assertion—cf. his *On the Theory of Social Change*, Homewood, Ill., 1962). Natural science becomes, as a result, subservient to capital, such that all natural relations are resolved into 'money relations'.[34]

The possibility of possessing true, 'scientific', knowledge of society, systematically excluded by the structure of social relationships in capitalist society, can only be achieved by a complete transformation of society. Carrying his analysis of alienated labour over from the Paris manuscript, Marx shows that within this social theory, the inauguration of 'civilized production'—implying a division between mental and material labour on which rests the power and complexity of the whole economic system—results in productive forces appearing as alienated from the individuals to whom they belong. The means of production dominate the producer instead of being subject to his control. The only way in which the producers can control their production is to appropriate the means of production, by the creation of a class opposed to the existing productive forces, a class having a consciousness of its own situation within society, a knowledge of the means to transcend it, and an antagonism to all other classes. It is thus possible for a revolutionary proletariat to develop real—scientific—knowledge of the whole of society involving a perception of the fundamental and structured irrationality of the bourgeois system; a knowledge which implies a going beyond of the immediately given rationality of capitalism and its economic 'laws'. The communist revolution of the proletariat will also facilitate the future production of non-ideological social knowledge since it does away with *labour* as a socially specific human activity divided by partial and reified conditions. This specification for the liberation of the conditions under which knowledge is produced, is thus integrated with his ideas of the 'abolition of labour' which will occur in communist society, e.g. a completely free human activity:[35]

> In communist society, however, where nobody has an exclusive area of activity and each can train himself in any branch he wishes, society regulates the general production, making it possible for me to do one thing today and another tomorrow, to hunt in the morning, fish in the afternoon, breed cattle in the evening, criticize after dinner, just as I like, without ever becoming a hunter, a fisherman, a herdsman, or a critic.

IV

The development of Marxian social theory from the 1844 manuscripts and *The German Ideology* through to the *Grundrisse*, the *Contribution to the Critique of Political Economy* and *Capital* itself, are fundamentally one of increasing concentration on the economic mechanisms reinforcing the characteristic social organization of capitalist society. Thus the wide range of the earlier works, in which Marx (and Engels) could take more account of the general connections between say, capitalist society, alienation and the production and content of knowledge, for example, are not continued in anything but the *Grundrisse*, that master plan for Marx's *Economics* which would develop *all* of the ramifications of capitalism, only realized in the *Contribution* and *Capital* to a very limited extent.

Consequently we are left with little on which to base any further analysis of Marx's theory of knowledge than the early works, and I will conclude this section with some general observations on those elements of the 'mature' works which seem to bear on the issue.

First, the *Grundrisse* illustrates an important change of Marx's attitude towards economics, in that having achieved a synthesis of his economic and philosophic ideas, he could approach the subject from a more clearcut position. In the earlier writings he tended to concentrate on labour itself and the mechanisms of exchange: beginning with the *Grundrisse*, Marx looks at production and labour power, the two main elements of the theory of surplus value developed in *Capital*, whose basis is (rather tiresomely) explicated in *Theories of Surplus Value*. Surplus value is not, and cannot be, derived from exchange alone; it is related to the historical development of the means of production in that the capitalist can employ the use-value of the proletarian's labour power to produce values much greater than the exchange value of that labour power. With his discovery of this theory, Marx was able to demonstrate the historically relative nature of class-exploitation possible under capitalism, and his primary concern in the later works is with the specifically economic causes of this exploitation.

As far as *development* of the sociology of knowledge paradigm outlined in the manuscripts and *Ideology* goes, *Capital* and the *Contribution* only elaborate specific elements of it, primarily those which deal with the nature of classical political economy as an ideology, and the general influence on proletarian consciousness of commodity relations, both under capitalism. It is as well to remember that, apart from a number of articles written whilst he was engaged in political journalism for the *Rheinische Zeitung*, Marx's definitions and analyses of ideology deal mostly with classical economic theory rather than as generally supposed, with religion, on which Engels wrote a great deal more. Marx's critique of classical economic theory rests upon its treatment of capitalist social relations as the starting point of its studies: it accepts unquestioningly the 'facts' of capitalism rather than analysing the historical nature of their sociological base. What this uncritical acceptance of 'reality' does is to produce a method of study which sees the social relations of capitalism as natural relations. By this method political economy produces an ahistorical economics which sees the bourgeois economic system as 'irrefutable natural laws of society *in abstracto*'. Political economy then cannot provide an adequate or properly scientific analysis of capitalism since it refuses to comprehend its historically relative nature and is in consequence, ideological. The concepts and categories which political economy produces *are* related to the socio-historical context of capitalism, but their relation is distorted, inverted; instead of understanding these categories as simple expressions of a complex concrete totality, they are taken to be expressions of a set of simple 'facts' about the functioning of the economic system. As an ideology, bourgeois economics is not straightforwardly either wrong or untrue, it is rather a systematically distorted cognitive structuring of reality in which the vital historical dimension of that reality is left completely out of account. The aim of a properly scientific understanding of the economic and social system would in Marx's own terms be a 'reproduction of the concrete situation' rather than a reduction of concrete reality to the level of a set of 'abstract definitions'.[36] Abstraction, however vaguely Marx uses the term, does seem to have a definitive meaning in the Marxian analysis of ideology, that of distortion by *reduction*. What is characteristic of the ideological formulations of classical economic theory is their reductionism, the assumption that capitalism can be explained in terms of simple economic concepts, rather than by analysis of its existence as a historically relative social system.

The operation of the various mechanisms of capitalist society illustrates how the abstract concepts of political economy are related to the social relationships of 'civil society', a thesis Marx demonstrates by his treatment of the 'Fetishism of Commodities' in Volume One of *Capital*.[37]

Basically the first section of *Capital*, of which the 'Fetishism of Commodities' forms a part, is devoted to an analysis of commodities and their values, commodities being defined as objects which are external to the individual and which satisfy human needs. The 'mystery' of the fetishism of commodities derives from the reification of the commodity in consciousness into something both palpable and transcendental. But this 'enigma' derives not from the use-values of commodities, nor from the nature of the various factors of value, but from the fact that the commodity 'mirrors for men the social character of their own labour', and becomes a property of their 'social–natural' products.[38] The status of the commodity is thus not physical, it is not merely a natural object, but social; its nature analogous with that of religious thought in which the products of the human mind become 'independent shapes' able to enter into relationships with men and women. (Did Marx think these 'relationships' wholly illusory, or did he allow that they could have a purely mental and mystical reality?) Commodities as material products operate in the same way and possess a fetishistic character generated by 'the peculiar social quality of the labour which produces commodities'.[39] Knowledge of the commodity which men in a capitalist social system can have is then necessarily transformed or, as we have put it earlier, *systematically distorted* in a direction which is related to the structure of social relationships where they reduce human interaction to the level of interactions between *things*. The reality of this fetishism—the social nature of production on which it is based—cannot manifest itself until commodities are actually exchanged, which exchange produces an 'inversion' of the relationships involved: '*Material* relations between persons and social relations between things.'

It is not until labour products, the objectifications of labour-power, enter the process of exchange that they acquire their requisite social value-objectivity since exchange renders all products of labour as equivalent, reducing them to their common element, what Marx terms 'abstract human labour'.[40] Political economy plays an important role in this mystifying process, for it treats of the commodity as a concept which expresses the production relations of one specific mode of production in purely general terms, ignoring its basis in the *social* relations of this form of production. As Marx puts it, the concept of the commodity 'enwraps as with a fog' the real production relationships—exploitation of the workers' labour to expropriate the surplus-value created by that labour—and the real nature of the labour products of this form of production.[41]

Interestingly (for our purposes) Marx ties in this process of reification of social relationships under capitalism—a process by which their social nature is transformed into natural, alienated objects subject to 'natural' and 'immutable' laws of society—to the ideological distortion of religion. Marx argues that specific religious belief-systems may function so as to reinforce normative systems constraining acceptance of the alienation of the worker from his labour product not only within bourgeois society but in pre-capitalist social formations as well. Protestant Christianity operates in a way appropriate to capitalism because of its 'cult of the abstract human being', its whole theological structure acting as a 'veil' on reality, forcing perceptions of society through a systematically distorting cognitive framework whose basic elements emphasize man's spirituality, as opposed to his wholly material being (the similarity of this conceptualization of the relationship of Protestant beliefs to the development of capitalism to that of Weber should not be ignored). Such a framework makes society appear as an opaque and problematic entity. In pre-capitalist societies, the less highly developed nature of social productive systems meant that the folk and natural religions of that period were less systematically alienating: hence, religious ideologies function in direct relationship to the exploitative power of the existing division of labour, and the existing stage of development of the instruments of production. Indeed, in the development of classical economic theory, religious ideology seems to Marx to play a part in its suggestion of the concept of the 'abstract human being' so dear to the hearts of both political economists and Protestant reformers.

Marx seems to have seen in the conceptual structure of political economy that it expressed *both* the reality of capitalist society as a totality of precisely structured social relationships based on a dominant economic relationship, and that it provided the legitimation of the normative basis of bourgeois social and political authority in terms of a 'natural' science. As a result of this dual expression, in which the values of capitalism as a moral system are reinforced by its economic theory and vice versa, political economy can appear to be a universal science with general categories. Marx's critique of political economy shows it to be partially, indeed, scientific or 'correct' in so far as it describes the economic aspects of capitalism in a reified fashion, but ideological, false, in so far as it treats such a group of alienated social relationships as universal, rather than as they are, expressive merely of a particular type of societal configuration and subject to social–historical changes which would sweep them completely away. Ignoring the social transformations which allowed political economy to exist as bourgeois social theory it is ignorant also of the transformations which would make its categories wholly illusory. In treating society as an immobile entity, in which 'history' has in effect come to an end in the continuous present, political economy converts actual social relationships which are dependent on specific historical conditions into universal laws of economics.

V

To the extent that Marx's work, as a whole, represents a developed theory of society, a sociology, and that can only be in a relatively loose sense, then we can, I think, discern that his theory of knowledge —what I have chosen to call his 'sociology of knowledge', contentiously identifying it as the first paradigmatic formulation of that area—is in fact an implicit part of that social theory and central to its basic presuppositions. Two conceptual issues need to be clarified at this point: the meanings of the terms 'ideology' and 'reification'. Without going into any real depth, suffice it to say that ideology is most clearly understood as 'systematically distorted knowledge'. That is, knowledge distorted in a fashion which is not haphazard, but bears a systematic causal relation to the structure of social relationships, in particular as to how they affect the production of knowledge, the distortion being affected (in general) by the structures of interests and values underlying the activities of the groups producing *and* consuming knowledge. Reification seems (to me) to express a specific—no doubt historically specific, e.g. to capitalism— form of ideological distortion in that Marx appears to mean by the term the practice of transforming social relations into relations between things. It is these two concepts which have played such an important role in the evolution of a distinctively Marxian and Marxist approach to the sociology of knowledge.

We shall now consider the further development of Marxian ideas, moving towards an understanding of three main sources of distinctively Marxist sociology of knowledge exemplified by the works of Georg Lukács, Lucien Goldmann and the Frankfurt school—Adorno, Horkheimer, Marcuse and Habermas.

3 Marxism II: Lukács

I

In order to talk about the evolution of a characteristically Marxist sociology of knowledge as something distinct from the general development of Marxist social theory, in which, as pointed out earlier, a sociological theory of knowledge is a central element, we must show how a distinctive set of concepts and a relatively separate—yet of course characteristically Marxist—methodology are developed to take specific account of what we have called the determinate relationship between social structure and knowledge. I think that there are two discernible directions which the sociologies of knowledge *influenced* by Marx took (ignoring, for the moment, the development of *orthodox* Marxism, in its 'scientific' form). The first, which I will not deal with at this point, is exemplified by Mannheim's phenomenological relativism, which employs distinctively Marxist conceptions of the relationship society/knowledge, yet develops them into a non-Marxist (and neo-Weberian) theory of the sociology of knowledge. The second, which will concern the whole of this part of the chapter, has its foundation in a particular book, Georg Lukács's *History and Class-Consciousness* and the influence which that had upon a number of German social philosophers and sociologists in Weimar Germany, as well as the general development of Lukács's ideas in the only realm open to him after 1924—aesthetic theory—which exerted a particular influence upon Lucien Goldmann's sociology of literature, itself predicated on a sociology of knowledge owing a great deal to *History and Class-Consciousness*.

What is common to both the Frankfurt school and Lucien Goldmann's work is a Hegelian interpretation of Marx which runs counter both to Old Left 'scientism' and New Left ultra-radicalism—it is labelled either 'humanist' or 'idealist' by both, the terms being ones not of classification but derision. This Hegelian interpretation of Marx—it concentrates on the issues of alienation, objectification and consciousness in avowedly dialectical terms—has its basis in Lukács's 1923 essay collection, itself an attempt to get away from the too 'scientific' interpretations of Marxism made popular by such as Engels, Kautsky and Bernstein in which a mechanistic materialism takes the place of a properly dialectical method, and reduces consciousness to the level of a simple reflection—a 'superstructure'—of the underlying material basis of society. Much of the content of the essays is a simple reworking of the main issues raised by Marx in the *Contribution to the Critique of Political Economy, Capital* and *Theories of Surplus Value* with some consideration of earlier works like *The German Ideology* but of course no account of the Paris manuscripts which remained undiscovered at the time when Lukács was writing, or of the *Grundrisse*, similarly hidden. However, the essays rework the themes in a distinctively Hegelian way such that they appear as striking precursors of the discovery of a 'Young' Hegelian Marx which was not to occur until the late 1930s in Europe, and even later in the English-speaking world. As such, Lukács's essays, dense as they are and philosophically quite complex, seem remarkably modern in terms of Marx exposition. But what is their value for the sociology of knowledge?

One of the main hindrances to development of Marxian ideas in a sociological direction was their excessively materialist and ultimately crude dissemination by the communist and social-democratic parties in the late nineteenth and early twentieth centuries. As we have shown, it is the infusion of Hegelian ideas—albeit transformed—into Marx's work that allows one to speak of a sociology of knowledge and a sociological method as being contained within his social theories. With a mechanical and overtly materialist interpretation (which owes something to Engels, though he should not take all of the blame), these elements which gave the theory its intellectual interest and flexibility disappeared. Lukács wrote the majority of essays in *History and Class-Consciousness* as a necessary corrective to these reductionist and philosophically unsophisticated tendencies in Marxism. As such, though its content is preponderantly theoretical, the book is a fundamentally political polemic arguing for a different strategy in making Marxism the ideological weapon of the proletariat.

The 'spectacles' through which Lukács approaches Marx and Marxism are composed of several perceptual elements deriving from his intellectual development. The path of this development included some important (for our, as well as Lukács's, purposes) exposure to the sociological influence of Simmel and Weber, as he pointed out in his prefatory remarks to the latest edition of the essay collection:

'At the time (1908—when he was engaged in study for a work on the modern drama) then, it was Marx the "sociologist" that attracted me—and I saw him through spectacles tinged by Simmel and Max Weber.'[1] Although his earliest training in philosophy (at Budapest to 1906) was markedly neo-Kantian (e.g. seeing philosophy as concerned primarily with logic and epistemology), Lukács's exposure to Georg Simmel's brand of neo-Kantianism (itself based in the work of Windelband and Rickert, opponents of the classical Marburg school of neo-Kantianism which made a sharp distinction between theory of cognition [*Erkenntnistheorie*] and speculative metaphysics), was fundamentally anti-positivist in the sense of believing that 'real essences were cognizable through an act of intellectual intuition'.[2] In fact Lukács's exposure to the dissolution of neo-Kantianism into irrational intuitionism during his periods at Berlin (1909–10) and Heidelberg (1913–14) undoubtedly had a great effect upon his later work since it established an early interest in seeing social knowledge in fundamentally anti-positivist—and almost anti-scientific—terms. The corrosive influence of Dilthey's hermeneutic '*Geisteswissenschaften*'—a sort of neo-Hegelianism which led, in its rejection of causal explanation for the understanding of cultural phenomena, to Husserl's phenomenology—altered the development of German sociological thought from its fundamentally Kantian directions towards an anti-natural scientific conception of its explanatory role. Max Weber, himself influenced by Windelband, Rickert, Dilthey and Simmel, produced as a consequence his highly influential sociological method, *verstehende* sociology. These idealist tendencies could not but influence Lukács, and though he rejected their logical extension into irrationalism—primarily, I think, by his attempts to draw systematic connections between the dialectical methods of Hegel and Marx—some important aspects, notably anti-scientism, do appear in the *History and Class-Consciousness* essays.

II

There are, I think, three main strands in the essays. The first, involving the concept of class-consciousness, derives essentially from Lukács's reading of Hegel and his exposure to the neo-Hegelianism of Dilthey's *Geisteswissenschaften*—sciences of 'spirit'—involving the intuitive perception of *totalities*, in this regard based, I would argue, in the Hegelian notion of the 'spirit of the people' suitably historicized so that it could refer to specific structural entities—social classes and the totality of their consciousnesses. The second emanates from his sociological interests, based themselves in the modified neo-Kantianism which characterized the thinking of both Simmel and Weber and which involved the assumption that explanation and knowledge of social phenomena involved intuitive understanding: interpretative, hermeneutic rather than causal, positivist, modes of cognition. As we shall see, Lukács characterizes proletarian knowledge in terms of its *understanding* rather than 'explanation' of the social context in which it exists. The third strand is directly Marxian, and provides the basic conceptual framework by which Lukács constructs his analyses and in a modified sense also provides the methodology by which the construction is effected. By taking these three, fairly disparate, strands and integrating them into a relatively unified argument, Lukács does, I think, provide not merely a set of theses about the political strategies of Marxism but also (and I think because he was primarily a politicized intellectual and not vice versa) an important extension of what I have characterized as the Marxian sociology of knowledge, precisely because he focuses on the same sort of issues as Marx had in his early work. In attempting to sort out the connection between social structure and consciousness—including knowledge—Marx had sketched out a theory of a social epistemology. What Lukács did was to fill in elements which Marx had, for whatever reasons, been unable to consider, and to extend the scope and sophistication of the argument. As such he provided a basis for further, more systematic and properly sociological approaches to the development of the Marxist theoretical orientation in the sociology of knowledge.

Lukács's first essay 'What is orthodox Marxism?' deals with the basic groundings of his approach to the treatment of class-consciousness, his interpretation of what constitutes the distinctively Marxist methodology. This means the sort of conceptual preconditions which allow that *only* Marxism as a theory of society *and* a practice of transforming it can: (a) provide scientific, in the sense of true, undistorted, knowledge of society; and (b) provide the means by which the proletariat can recognize and realize its role as the subject and the object of history. This conjunction of elements indicates that to Lukács the development of proletarian class-consciousness to the point at which it is a philosophical negation of bourgeois rationality and its 'scientific' nature, is not to be understood as a contradiction of philosophy, but rather the expression of a philosophically sophisticated concept of dialectic and totality as a mode of unreified cognition. For although Lukács talks about historical materialism as a 'science', the essay collection as a whole must be seen as a refutation both of positivism and any view of Marxism as a positive science. The proletariat is seen as performing a primarily philosophical role, the *negation* of bourgeois society. Lukács's definition of orthodox Marxism is, then, distinctly unorthodox since it focuses attention not on the content of Marx's later 'scientific' work, and the categorical system which he developed from his empirical analyses, but on

40

method. However, orthodoxy does not mean a unified methodology alone, but also a commitment to Marxism as the only means to true knowledge: 'the scientific conviction that dialectical materialism is the road to truth . . . [and] that all attempts to surpass or "improve" it have led and must lead to over-simplification, triviality and eclecticism.'[3] Involved in this faithlike certainty of the veridicality of Marxist dialectics is the conviction that the method, defined in exclusively 'dialectical'—rather than materialist—terms, is the only *revolutionary* dialectic, the only means by which theory can be effectively related to practice. The unity of theory and practice can only be possible, argues Lukács, when a class in understanding itself also understands society as a whole and realizes itself as subject and object of knowledge.[4] Historically such a situation can only exist when the proletariat emerges as a class in capitalist society. In employing the dialectical method to understand itself and its role in society, the proletariat demonstrates that the method implies—that indeed its very existence is predicated upon—the transformation of social reality. Its aim is thus not primarily scientific knowledge, but socialist revolution.

The 'value' of the dialectical method consists in its reliance on holism and in the fact that it does not take the structure of existing reality as 'given', and that this 'given' reality is shown to be a mere appearance obscuring an underlying reality. To Lukács, this anti-empiricism, the tendency to look at the totality of the social world in the explanation of 'facts' isolated from it constitutes what distinguishes dialectics from bourgeois social science. For 'bourgeois' social science merely takes the laws of capitalist society as given, as the unquestioned basis of its scientific method. Marxism—in its properly dialectical form—shows the necessity of dialectical and historical analysis of the 'facts', and thus can penetrate to the historically specific core of the laws of capitalist society: it can make distinctions between the 'real existence and inner core' of phenomena and understand the relation between the two in terms of their historical context. True knowledge, freed from the ideological obscuration of ahistorical 'bourgeois' conceptual systems, is thus made possible when the 'isolated facts' of social life are integrated into a totality, a knowledge based on a 'conceptual reproduction of [social] reality'.[5] Based on Marx's discussion of 'bourgeois' economic theory in the 1859 *Contribution to the Critique of Political Economy, Capital* and *Theories of Surplus Value*, Lukács employs the critique of bourgeois social science which is the basis of Marx's epistemology, but subverts it in the sense that he extends it to an attack on a scientific explanation of social reality. Proceeding from the assumption that what makes bourgeois social science ideological is its systematic ignorance of a concept of historical totality—which allows the fetishistic reification of human relations into timeless laws—Lukács arrives at a point where he finds the natural science model, i.e. positivism, ideological in its application to society. Such a view, antithetical to that of the mature Marx, who held up the goal of positive science for Marxism, derives primarily from the influence of Dilthey and the reaction against science so characteristic of early twentieth-century German social theory. As Lukács himself recognized, his portrayal of the dialectical method made it seem to construct social reality in an unscientific way, but, he argued, if the natural science paradigm is employed then contradictions in social life appear merely as limitations in the theory employed and not as a part of the social system. Their existential reality is reduced to the level of a theoretical problematic. Only the dialectical method and its utilization to understand the totality will allow such contradictions to be seen as contradictions necessary to the social structure of capitalism which will disappear only when capitalist social relations themselves disappear. Lukács employs Marxism to *attack* scientifically based social knowledge. 'When the ideal of scientific knowledge is applied to nature it simply furthers the progress of science. But when it is applied to society it turns out to be an ideological weapon of the bourgeoisie.'[6] Such an attack on scientism, it should be realized, is not just an attack on bourgeois social science for its own inadequacies, but on 'science' as an oppositional method to dialectics. The inclusion of positivist elements in Marxism—which Lukács sees as the responsibility of the 'vulgar' Marxists, Kautsky, Bernstein, Max Adler and even Engels—are then treated as anti-dialectical, either in trying to remove the dialectics from 'proletarian science' (a term never defined, but presumably meaning systematized proletarian class-consciousness) or to reduce it to mere antagonisms or conflicts: in both cases history becomes unknowable as a unified process.

In championing the totality, the dialectical method, Lukács is putting forward a philosophically self-conscious Hegelianized Marxism; philosophically rather than scientifically based. We shall see that this is also what characterizes both Frankfurt school 'critical theory' and Goldmann's sociology of knowledge: the critique of 'positive science' is primary to their analyses. What Lukács did was to present a Marx seen through the eyes of Hegel, but with other less obvious elements present in the exposition—notably the Weberian conceptualization of capitalism as reificatory rationalization—his aim being to preserve a role for philosophy and sociology in the face of the real Marxist orthodoxy—Leninism. Lukács was not simply trying to shield idealism from the corrosive influence of a vulgar materialism: far from it. He provides a critique of Hegel which concentrates on his epistemological dualism, the distinctions between thought and being and between theory and practice. Marx, in Lukács's view, took the implications of Hegel's philosophy—that the dialectical method implies the realization by man of his social nature, as the simultaneous subject-object of history—and put them on a proper epistemological foundation to locate the crucial role of understanding society in the consciousness of the proletariat. The knowledge of reality produced by the dialectical method is identical to what Lukács means by the proletariat's class-standpoint (a far less simple thing than it seems, as we shall see). The development of such knowledge—in a historical materialist form—is consequently conditioned by political events since its method is 'inseparable from the "practical and critical" activity of the proletariat: both are aspects of the same process of social evolution.'[7] And as it is predicated on social evolution, the emergence of historical materialism depends on the existence of a class-struggle, on the objective conditions in which there can be a relatively advanced proletariat. How Lukács actually unifies theory and practice and situates himself *between* Hegel and the later Marx, (which gives rise to Lichtheim's view of *History and Class-Consciousness* as a premonition of the discovery of a 'young' Marx in the late 1930s) involves an *association* between the knowledge produced by the dialectical method and the knowledge required by the proletariat if it is to emancipate itself from capitalist relations of production. But the dialectical method is thus made something separate from the proletariat, something which it needs—a theory both of society and of social action—but is not produced by it. Hence Lukács's view of Marxist method, and his disavowal of substantive concepts, indicate I think quite clearly his élitist view of the production of revolutionary theory, and its metaphysical rather than scientific (and thus generally available) ethos and lead him into seeing the theorist as a charismatic figure: 'Marxist orthodoxy is no guardian of traditions, it is the eternally vigilant prophet proclaiming the relation between the tasks of the immediate present and the totality of the historical process.'[8] The Marxist theoretician has been given a messianic, prophetic role in the socialist transformation of reality.

Having established an important role for philosophy—its production of a polemical sociology of knowledge traced the connection between capitalist society and the development of proletarian thought—Lukács was faced with a problem. Although Marx was regrettably unspecific about what he meant by class—the manuscript of *Capital* breaks off at the point where he is about to tell all—there are enough indications through his mature works to be able to construct a straightforward sociological definition of class as relationship to the means and mode of production. Lukács was, however, unsatisfied with this, since it was used to mean that proletarian consciousness was merely a reflection of the social structural situation of the proletariat in capitalist society. He saw the 'meaning' of class-consciousness as in fact something problematic and requiring clarification. His solution to this problem—the determinate nature of class-consciousness—essentially revolves around a concept of 'imputed' class-consciousness achieved through an analysis of the concept of 'false-consciousness'. Engels had assumed that the real events of history are independent of human consciousness, such that bourgeois thought could only comprehend an abstraction of the historical reality within which it was situated: it was 'false-consciousness' then to assume that bourgeois economic science was in fact scientific, since that would ignore its location in specific, untheorized social contexts. Consequently men may act consciously in performing historical acts, and yet still have a 'false-consciousness' of what they do. It is necessary then, to treat this false-consciousness as an aspect of historical totalities, as a stage in the historical process. Such a treatment, which aims to elucidate consciousness holistically, thus sees it in terms of the whole of the society in which it is produced. It is in that sense possible to have a 'consciousness of existence'—knowledge—that is subjectively justified in the socio-historical present *and* objectively fails to express the evolution of society adequately, and thus is 'false-consciousness'. False-consciousness is then dialectically determined in its construction; it goes beyond mere description alone and the material of analysis. Consequently an important theoretical point may be developed: it is possible to 'construct' the thought and feeling of any given historical period or class-structure location on the basis of the relation (and mode) of production. 'Now class-consciousness consists in fact of the appropriate and rational reactions "imputed" [*zugerechnet*] to a particular typical position in the process of production.'[9] But the quality of class-consciousness which allows such a constructed typification is its essentially holistic nature, a primarily sociological concept in the sense that Lukács argues it. For it is held to be possible to take the *total* consciousness of a class whose actions can be understood only by reference to it. Class-consciousness cannot then be said to exist at any particular point of time or be expressed in an unequivocal form as an utterance of an individual or group: it is rather an abstraction, methodologically necessary to the understanding of society. Characteristically, Lukács expresses the nature of class-consciousness in terms straight from Weber's *verstehende* sociology: it seems to be 'understood' implicitly by some hermeneutic means and constructed in terms of an ideal-type. Class-consciousness is an 'expression' of the character of the social structure of a class, represented as the logical consequence of its position and function in the relations of production and the context of historical progress.

What Lukács thought he was doing by allotting some autonomy

to consciousness in the explanation of social reality was to change the structure of Marxist theory in its treatment of knowledge, from a simple *representational* perspective to one in which material base—social relations—and mental superstructure—socially available knowledge—are dialectically related. It is highly questionable whether Marx ever employed are presentational theory, or even that Engels (cf. his letter to Bloch of 21–2 September 1890[10]) did: but nevertheless, that is how Marxist theory appeared to Lukács at that time. Thus the 'imputed' nature of class-consciousness (what Goldmann calls 'potential consciousness') is explained by Lukács as a sociological variable, in terms of its rooting in the class-structure, the network of relations between a society's productive forces. Far from being an idealist (as he was criticized at the time) Lukács was merely insisting on the fact that class-consciousness was as necessary as force in the class-struggle between bourgeoisie and proletariat: history had, he thought, shown that those classes best able to present their interests as general were those most likely to gain the power to organize society in terms of those interests. The proletariat, alone in history, was the class whose interests were genuinely general. It followed that it needed to develop its knowledge of itself and its societal context, to recognize itself as the identical subject-object of history in order to make its victory in the class-struggle more certain.

But we must be aware that class-consciousness, as a sociological variable, is historically specific. In pre-capitalist social formations, and strata in capitalist societies, the nature of economic production is such as to prevent any clear expression of a class-consciousness. A caste or estate system of stratification entails the fusion of economic elements with political and religious factors. Pre-capitalist societies have so little cohesion as compared with capitalist societies that they cannot separate such elements out: as a result the strata cannot relate to the whole of society in a way that gives their 'imputed consciousness' an economic form. In antiquity, for example, class conflicts and economic problems assumed either natural, religious forms (i.e. as expressed mythologically) or politico-legal forms as between debtors and creditors. Knowledge of the objective economic conditions and thus of the true nature of the social structure is thus quite incomplete and does not exist in any coherent form. Structurally, then, 'There is no possible position within such a society from which the economic basis of all social relations could be made conscious.'[11]

Sociologically, the differentiation between the economic systems and the social structures of societies is the primary determinant of class-consciousness: in fact, Lukács's presentation of it means that properly speaking we can only find actual *class*-consciousness in capitalist and post-capitalist societies. Only abstractly can we talk of class-consciousness in pre-capitalist societies, as a 'construction'

45

from the disparate strata of less differentiated societies in which the forces of production and their control are less rationally and extensively ordered. Only in capitalist societies does economic class interest emerge clearly as the 'motor' of history and class-consciousness become explicit: the struggle for power then resolves itself as a struggle for consciousness: for the ideological veiling or scientific exposure of the class-basis of society.[12]

Although Marxists do not agree on the non-existence of classes in pre-capitalist societies (cf. Marc Bloch's work on feudal society[13]), Lukács's main point is that in capitalism only two classes can organize society as a whole, their potentialities in this respect being solely connected with consciousness. Both petty-bourgeoisie and peasantry lack a sufficiently independent consciousness to act as coherently revolutionary forces; their aims are inherently unrealizable. Bourgeois consciousness, however, can organize society but it is faced with severe problems, for it is dialectically antagonistic to its class interests: Lukács expresses this in terms of two modes of contradiction involving it.

1 Class-consciousness cannot appear in any general sense due to the position the bourgeoisie holds in the mode of production—both mental and material—and the consequent structure of interests this generates.

2 For the bourgeois class, a consciousness is produced which contains the fatal contradiction that the 'freedom' it achieved by its victory over the feudal regime was in reality the means of its oppression of the proletariat, by the reification of commodity production and its destruction of the individual.

In focusing on production and forced by its position to ignore distribution, bourgeois knowledge is contradictory of social reality because of the structural contradictions of capitalist society-capital being both individual *and* social. Bourgeois thought produces a confrontation between the individual and the impersonal 'laws of nature' which impel social phenomena, making completely impossible the discovery of 'theoretical and practical solutions to the problems created by the capitalist system of production'.[14] The social form of the objective economic limitations of capitalist production provide a consciousness-limiting mechanism: the bourgeoisie cannot recognize these limitations because of its role as dominant class. As far as the class struggle is concerned, this bourgeois false-consciousness is accentuated as conflict is exacerbated, such that it is transformed from an 'objective' presentation of the bourgeoisie's social position into a 'mendacious' consciousness, the theoretical (cognitive) limitations of its thought becoming a mere 'moral posture'.

Lukács was hoping to change the conception of the class-struggle which 'vulgar' Marxism had put forward: that all that was involved was a power-confrontation, a situation in which the strategies of '*Real politik*' would win the day for the proletariat. This ignored the 'great battle of principle' between socialism and capitalism (almost, I think, their antagonism as competing *ethical* systems) rooted in the 'ultimate problems of the objective economic process'. Vulgar Marxism largely ignored consciousness, preferring to believe that it was a secondary factor not able to play a strategic role in class warfare—it was merely given by the existing social relations. To Lukács this gave vulgar Marxism an internal structure similar to bourgeois thought in that it separated consciousness from existence: in fact, he said, the proletariat possesses the only 'viewpoint'—perhaps what might today be termed a system of 'domain assumptions' or a paradigm—from which society could be known *as a whole*. Proletarian class-consciousness then provides the clue to the unification of theory and practice and plays an active role in the social transformation from capitalism to socialism.[15]

But complete knowledge of capitalist society is not straight-forwardly accomplished: there are social limitations on what can be produced, arising from the reification of capitalist social relations which separate the proletariat's economic from its political struggles. For its action to be effective, the proletariat must choose between a multiplicity of immediate goals and be aware of the dialectical contradiction between them and its ultimate aim. Only if the gap can be closed between actual and possible knowledge can immediate action contribute to ultimate goals. The development of sociological knowledge is thus identical with the development of a class's social knowledge, we may argue, and as far as Lukács is concerned sociological knowledge is a politically motivated and structured mode of cognition. Consciousness, knowledge, is not *external* to history, as Marx recognized in contradistinction to both Hegel and Feuerbach, but immanent in it as practical-critical activity with the task of changing the world (cf. the theses on Feuerbach; thesis 9). This gives to the proletariat the responsibility for developing its imputed class-consciousness in a specifically revolutionary direction against the 'devastating and degrading effects of the capitalist system'.

In the essay, 'Reification and the consciousness of the proletariat', Lukács took his analysis of class-consciousness and set it in a context which owes a great deal to Max Weber. Weber had seen the rise of capitalism as an essentially Western phenomenon, linked very closely to a process of disenchantment (*Entzauberung*) of the world in terms of a development of technical rationality. Capitalism and industrialism both depended for their extension on such a rationality, which came to characterize not merely economic and technological processes, but institutional social relations as well. The imposition of systems of technically rational rules in all spheres of life was thus the most characteristic aspect of modern capitalism. Lukács took over this conceptualization of the trends of capitalist development, and allied with it the Marxian idea of 'reification', the reduction to dehumanized abstraction of social relationships, such that he could conceive of capitalist social development as a process of increasing reification through more extensive technical rationality.

Following Marx, Lukács identified the commodity as the most obvious example of reification, and took the process of reification to be most characteristic of the development of bourgeois thought: knowledge in capitalist societies thus exhibits a reified structure and content from which proletarian thought must escape. The commodity is the most highly developed form of reification with both subjective and objective functions. Subjectively, the development of the market economy and capitalist social relations estrange man's activity from him so that he becomes a commodity subject to natural laws—a 'thing'. Objectively a world of relations between things exists, composed of commodities and their movements: a 'mysterious' world not amenable to human control. Human labour is made abstract, both subjectively and objectively, by the mechanism of commodity exchange of bourgeois society, its means of reproduction. The result of this is *rationalization*, a process in which the worker and his labour are segmented into quantifiable units (cf. Taylor and scientific management) which can be more easily assimilated and compared with the 'abstract laws' governing production. Both space and time lose their qualitative characters, and are transformed into calculable quantities which can be manipulated, employing technical rules, as mere things. Time is reified into a sort of space. Reification thus affects all of society, all men being dehumanized by having to present themselves as commodities: but it is not thereby a static force, but one which in the historical development of capitalism is 'potentiated', the structure of reification sinking deeper into men's consciousness.[16] The whole process of rationalization which constitutes the impact of capitalism on society establishes a (basically superficial) structure of formal laws: a generalized 'adjustment of one's way of life, mode of work, and hence of consciousness to the general socio-economic premises of the capitalist economy'. The division of labour assists this process, in so far as it leads to the existence of intellectual specialisms 'ruled by their own laws, seeking an internally coherent expression'. This atomism is exemplified by the progress of science: the more it develops methodologically, the more it becomes a closed system of partial laws moving away from a grasp of the totality of the material world which provides it with its underlying reality. Quite clearly, the extension of this critique to 'bourgeois' social science— which employs a naturalistic methodology of specialism—shows that it is ultimately impossible for bourgeois thought to encompass complete understanding of its own social world. (An example is the problem of explanation posed by economic crises.) Of course such a view of science and its 'limitations' is strictly speaking quite untenable—conceptual specialization not having any logically necessary consequence for the adequacy of scientific knowledge—but Lukács's point is not so clearly wrong as we may too easily assume. For in epistemology—one important realm of so-called bourgeois (i.e. non-Marxist) thought—the point may be taken to have limited relevance: an over-riding concern with method rather than reality as such, obscures the relationship between philosophical thought and the social world in which it is located.

The locus of Lukács's argument about the mystificatory and ideological nature of bourgeois thought, which proceeds from its social role and interests, its development of a technical rationalism which dehumanizes man, he traces to a set of problems in philosophy, in characteristically German idealist fashion. In developing this argument he cut himself loose from the philosophical errors and inconsistencies perpetrated by Engels, whom he criticizes. What Engels had done was to make of Marxism a straightforwardly 'positive' science which relied upon a distinction between the 'real' world expressed as objective 'facts', and the subjective conceptions which individuals held about the nature of the real world, the latter being decidedly unscientific. At the heart of this was the old battle between idealism and materialism: Engels was trying to give historical materialism an acceptable 'scientific' tone. But what this did was reduce the element of thought and consciousness to a secondary level. Lukács believed this was not what Marx had himself intended —which was more in the nature of a resolution of the materialism-idealism debate by transcending it to a point where *practice* may be seen as the union of thought and reality, where our conceptions of the world may be tested in attempts to change it.

Bourgeois thought, and non-dialectical philosophy in particular had operated (like Engels) with an idea of the disjuncture of the subject and object of knowledge which led it to conceive of reason as purely contemplative: and as a result to erect a barrier between philosophy and science and more importantly between a knowledge of society, social theory, and a practice of transforming it. Bourgeois knowledge thus became wholly theoretical, philosophy being consigned to the level of arbiter in methodological disputes. This distinction between subject and object is an important limitation on knowledge, since it reduces it solely to the level of the exact, or 'objective' sciences: thought and reality become quite separable cognitively. Without going into the ramifications of his philosophical argument, we can say that Lukács solved this problem by reference to Hegel, and the way in which Hegelian epistemology was taken over and modified by Marx.

Hegel is important because he provides a conceptual mechanism by means of which the problem of rationalism—its opposition of form and content, and the fact that as Kant showed, our knowledge of the objective world is achieved *through* the categorical structure of thought—may be resolved, through the use of dialectics. For Hegel saw that only if the subject were seen as both product *and* producer of the dialectical process in a world impressing itself as a given objective reality upon the subject, would the subject-object, thought-existence antitheses be resolved in a manner that would also unify freedom and necessity. Whereas the eighteenth-century rationalists conceived of history as a bar to a rational epistemology and treated it as 'an eternal and indestructible limit to human reason in general', the dialectical method involves the analysis of history and is predicated upon the historical evolution of new concepts. When we finally understand that it is we who have made our own history, reality becomes our 'action' in which theory and practice completely coincide. But having achieved this position, a new set of problems present themselves. Who do we take to be the subject of the action? How does the unity of subject/object result in the unity of the genesis of determinants of thought and the history of the evolution of reality? What 'position' can be taken to solve the problems so raised? And: 'What *is* the "we" which is the subject of history . . . whose action is in fact history?' 'Classical' (German idealist) philosophy, as Lukács shows, was unable to answer such questions, and Hegel himself only gave unsatisfactory answers—the 'world spirit' as the 'we', made up of the spiritual totality of the individual nations—in an essentially metaphysical form. Importantly, the reason why 'bourgeois' philosophy was unable to answer such questions lies in its social situation, capitalist social relations, which it reproduces in its social theory. To answer the questions adequately would have meant that it was in the paradoxical situation of searching for a theory 'that would mean the end of bourgeois society and to resurrect in thought a humanity destroyed in that society and by it'.[17] Hence the gist of Lukács's argument is that bourgeois society, in destroying humanity through alienation and reification—reducing everything to rationalized commodity relations—in its thought conceives this social reality as an epistemological problem, the separation of subject and object. Because of its social position, however, the solution to this philosophical problem becomes unavailable, since what it postulates is the sweeping away of all class-relations and material foundations which are reproduced in bourgeois thought. The real solution to the problem lies in the abolition of bourgeois rationalism, the dialectical method alone pointing beyond bourgeois society. It is clear to

Lukács that the one class able to employ the dialectical method is that which has no interest in the reproduction of existing social structures, the one class 'able to discover within itself on the basis of its life experience, the identical subject-object, the subject of action; the "we" of the genesis: namely the proletariat'.[18]

The reasons why the proletariat had not, despite its ideological advantage, achieved a universally revolutionary role were primarily based in the reificatory power of bourgeois social institutions. What these allow are two forms or categories of socially based 'mediations' by which the immediate conditions of social relations are raised to consciousness. Given that these categories are—as Lukács asserts—fundamentally different for the two classes, those of the proletariat are capable of reaching a point wherefrom to understand the whole social system, whereas those of the bourgeoisie are not. The incapability of bourgeois categories of mediation to be veridical—their systematically ideological construction—derives from the nature of the categories employed which are basically *immediacy*. Economic theory, for example, operates with an immediated reality as a given (as Marx showed in *Capital* and elsewhere) which leads to an ahistorical form of thought conceptualizing social relations presently existing as in accordance with natural laws and thus changeless. But although the proletariat is forced to start with the same intellectual tools as the bourgeoisie, it employs the theoretical category of mediation to separate itself from that class. As a result, asserts Lukács, its own production of knowledge stands on a higher scientific plane in the sense that it provides an adequate historical analysis of capitalism. The proletariat is enabled by the dialectical method to recognize the social reality underlying what is immediately given in its world, to comprehend society as a historical totality. This the bourgeoisie can never do. For the ability to go beyond the immediate implies that reality can be transformed. Although bourgeois thought—abstract rationalism—expresses the existing state of evolution of social relations, the transformation of qualitative attributes into quantifiable units, rationalization of the mode of production, etc., these are viewed as unchanging and lawlike in their fixity. The proletariat can, however, see that this rationalization of social existence results in a reification of all social forms which can only be changed by abolishing the immediate nature of those relations, a process requiring the practical abolition of the 'objectification' of the reified relations—bourgeois society itself. Thus the proletariat, the 'contradiction of history', becomes conscious of the underlying *irrationality* of bourgeois rationalism and by doing so destroys the ideological dominance of the ruling class: 'The knowledge that social facts are not objects but relations between men is intensified to the point where facts are wholly dissolved into processes—

51

in Hegel's terms, "Becoming now appears as the truth of Being".[19]

This objective requirement to go 'beyond' the 'facts', demonstrates their partial nature as falsely isolated elements of a total process. To speak of the 'facts' without reference to their social context is to Lukács to accept reification; it is because it sticks to the facts as given that bourgeois thought is unable to comprehend its own social foundation. (To what extent is non-Marxist thought necessarily empiricist, as Lukács implies? Only of course to a limited extent, and this is what provides the main source of a critique of his position. Some specifically 'bourgeois' modes of thought, as for example phenomenology, are anti-empiricist in the most extreme way in the sense of attempting to cut themselves off from *any* specific social location, in order to examine *all*.) The overcoming of reification, the achievement of real knowledge about the social world can never, however, be effected on an individual basis; only the *class* can relate to the whole of reality, for the concrete individual is unable to overcome reification and determinism, to operate a purely monistic praxis.

Hence only a class can effect change because reification is the immediate reality of every person living in capitalist society and can be overcome only by becoming conscious of the contradictions of capitalist society and aware of the immanent meaning of the contradictions for the total development of society, an awareness and consciousness only possible in a complete sense at the level of a class. The practical nature of actual proletarian consciousness (Lukács even terms it 'pragmatic') implies a change in its own objects and thus in itself if it is to achieve adequate correct consciousness.

But, as Kant pointed out, we cannot be certain that the object of our concept exists, and thus the proletariat's aspiration to a future historical totality remains *problematic*, in the sense that a dialectical theory of social change has no *real* social base and is strictly speaking ideological. Within Marxist thought such a problem has never been adequately resolved: Engels saw concepts as reflections of 'things' in a world of processes and produced a dualism between thought and reality. Marx, however, realized that the only solution was to treat thought—philosophy—as a form of reality to transform it into praxis. What is achieved by this is the necessity of seeing the present as a 'becoming' in the sense that we see the practical class-consciousness of the proletariat as a part of its historical development, as an element of its becoming. In this formulation thought and existence do not 'correspond', 'reflect' or are otherwise dualistic and opposed since their *identity* lies in the fact that they are both parts of the same real historical and dialectical process. To Lukács what this constitutes in the consciousness of the proletariat is a new possible reality arising from the dialectical contradictions of capitalism, not an idea, but praxis. Although at first a theory of praxis, it is transformed into 'a practical theory that overturns the real world'.[20]

One other essay ought to interest us from the collection. In 'The changing function of historical materialism', a lecture given by Lukács during his brief period as Minister of Culture in the Hungarian soviet, he quite explicitly articulates the theory of historical materialism as a weapon, as the intellectual armament of the proletariat.[21] It is both a science and a means of prodding the working class to activity in the class-struggle. In fact, it becomes a means of giving proletarian class-consciousness a *scientific* status. A far less subtle view of Marxism is hence delineated here, than in the earliest essays, especially in 'Reification and the consciousness of the proletariat'.

But there *are* theoretically interesting elements in this later essay, notably in Lukács's exploration of the difficulties which arise when historical materialism (it is interesting that he does not talk of *dialectical* materialism; there is in fact a duality in his work, between historical materialism on the one hand—the weapon of the proletariat and dialectical method on the other, the Marxist mode of analysis) is applied to what Hegel called 'the absolute spirit'—i.e. art, religion, philosophy. We can easily differentiate and analyse the means/modes of production of historical stages as they were reproduced in social structure: it is far less easily done with art and other symbolic artifacts, which may survive in a form not directly related to the objective conditions of society. These ideal productions may continue to have value, relevance, or even an exemplary status, leading us to believe that there is stability in the value of art and other cultural products. Lukács explains that this notion (and of course we should recognize that he is defending the production of aesthetic theory) that art may exist 'above history and society'[22] is due to the unique quality of art in its dialogue between man and nature. Interpolated, Lukács is describing art as a privileged realm of discourse between man and his material environment which is not strictly subject to the vagaries of socio-historical change, even when the form of societal development it is initially related to has disappeared. From this point of view economic laws may be seen in their true light, as truths linked to specific social structures whereas art seems to operate in a semi-autonomous way; the relation of the mode of division of labour to the art of a society differs. In precapitalist societies, for example, the influence of art on handicrafts is 'quite decisive', Lukács instancing the transition of architecture in Western Europe from the Romanesque to the Gothic style,[23] whilst in capitalist societies art becomes narrowly confined, and can exert no influence of a deterministic nature on the production of commodities since its own existence is dependent upon economic factors which separate art from the social relations of industrial production. Religion similarly becomes removed from the sphere of production in capitalist society, although it was in fact 'never able to express with such purity the relation of man to nature as was art.'[24] The tenor of this argument about art, and its seeming importance to Lukács, is a further pointer, if one was needed, to the Hegelian nature of Lukács's treatment of historical materialism. Lukács is unwilling to allow the sort of argument where art becomes—as it did to the vulgar 'scientific' Marxism which was the real orthodoxy when he was writing—merely the reflection, ideal expression or epiphenomenon of the material conditions existing in a society. The results of such an interest in saving 'art' and a non-reductionist aesthetic theory from the hands of scientific Marxism, become the source of an important contradiction in Lukács's approach to historical materialism. It will be recalled that Lukács, in defining 'orthodox Marxism' concentrated upon the dialectical method which he felt was the central and crucial characteristic of a revolutionary Marxism. Implicit in this notion was the idea that history is only knowable by using the concept of dialectical totality; but, Lukács is proposing to treat pre-capitalist society *differently* from capitalist society, and thus logically seems to be saying that the concept of dialectical totality should be differentially applied to the pre-capitalist historical stages, allowing the reader to think that he is proposing a form of relativism in order to avoid the necessity of treating art, and cultural productions in general, as determined by the existing mode of production and social relations of production, and to allow them therefore some independence of the laws of historical materialism. The rest of the essay, an extended critique of 'vulgar Marxism', need not concern us except for a revealing statement by Lukács that the difficulties he had shown to exist in the treatment by historical materialism of pre-capitalist society seem to imply a limited value for studies of a historical materialist nature, if defined in vulgar 'scientific' Marxist terms.[25]

4 Marxism III

The importance of Lukács's work in *History and Class-Consciousness* should not be seen as intrinsic to the essay collection alone. Its themes, the alienative consequences of bourgeois rationalism, the contention that the proletariat required a theoretical system suited to its transformatory role, and the argument that the connection between thought and being is no simple one, such that the former is a *representation* of the latter, but a dialectical relationship of a much more complex nature, all exerted a powerful influence on European Marxist intellectuals. In particular, the collection of young left-wing philosophers and social theorists at the *Institut für sozial Forschung* in Frankfurt-am-Main, were much influenced by the ideas of Korsch and Georg Lukács (both of whom published articles in the Institute's journal) and developed a systematic theoretical perspective in terms which owed a great deal to Lukács's Hegelianized Marxism. In France, the work of Lucien Goldmann developed many of the specifically theoretical (rather than polemical) elements of Lukács's book in a humanistic direction so as to produce a quite sophisticated sociology of literature. We shall deal with both here, as they demonstrate the systematization of an explicitly Marxist sociology of knowledge based in Lukács, and exert considerable influence today.

I The Frankfurt school: Horkheimer, Adorno, Marcuse and Habermas

Goldmann and the Frankfurt 'critical theorists' share most centrally a fundamental organizing principle, whose source, though not exclusively Lukácsian, nevertheless received its distinctive moulding at his hands. It is, in short, opposition to positivism in the realm of social theory. Elevated to the level of a theoretical programme by the Frankfurt school, this theme exercises a considerable influence on modern sociological thought, and may be considered one of the clearest (though not always acknowledged) organizing principles of a *critical* sociology of knowledge at any level. For one of the roles of sociology of knowledge—and in the Marxist view, its primary role—is a demonstration of the basis of 'scientific' statements in a configuration of socially given interests, the implication being that the separation of subject from object of knowledge is illusory, that positivism in sociology is an ideology subversive of scientific truth. In 'scientific' Marxism the reasons for this become the unscientific relation of theory to practice, and product of practice, of bourgeois thought, in the sense that the natural scientific model is not properly adhered to. By contrast, Lukács developed the idea that bourgeois social theory is ideological *because* it attempts to follow natural science methodologies: both Goldmann and the Frankfurt school take over this view that science *as such* is ideological, and produce anti-scientific sociologies of knowledge, as a consequence.

When the Institute for Social Research at Frankfurt started in 1923, its work was mostly directed to empirical and theoretical investigation of substantive aspects of capitalist and socialist societies. Max Horkheimer's accession to the directorship of the Institute in 1930, and his continued leadership of it in exile (in France and the U.S.A.) after 1933 produced a change of direction. Horkheimer and his associates—most notably T. W. Adorno and an ex-student of Heidegger, Herbert Marcuse—were interested in the development of historical materialism in a theoretically self-conscious direction. Consequently, they evolved a theoretical programme which would function in much the same way as Lukács had described proletarian class-consciousness: it would be *critical* social theory (i.e. deriving from the description of Marxism as the 'critique of political economy') opposed to 'traditional' theory.

Much in the same way as Lukács had contrasted bourgeois and proletarian thought, Horkheimer—who can lay claim to have invented the term 'critical theory' and provided its first exposition—opposed traditional and critical theory.[1] Traditional theory was contemplative, assisting in the process of social reproduction because it embedded in the work organization and division of labour by which the given social system maintains itself: as a result both science and the scientific practitioner have specific roles to play in the maintenance of existing social relations.[2]

> The apparent independence of work processes which ought to derive from their movement from the inner essence of their objects corresponds to the apparent freedom of the economic subjects in bourgeois society. They think that they act according to their individual decisions, whereas, even in their most

complex calculations, they are really only exponents of an obscure mechanism.

However, critical theory could claim to function outside of the constrictions of bourgeois society. As an 'immanent critique' of capitalist social systems it aims to undermine rather than reproduce them: by placing itself outside of the existing social organization of capitalist reproduction it aimed to bring the contradictions of bourgeois society to the level of consciousness. In that sense it operates more as an ideology—at least to 'scientific' Marxists—than as a substantive theory. In part, however, it is possible to detect some residue of the '*Geisteswissenschaften*' so beloved of Dilthey in the idea of critical theory. Importantly, Horkheimer's formulation of his programme is uncharacteristic of its time in being anti-relativistic. It has been claimed that critical theory was initially a particular political position more than anything else: I think it is far more than that, a development of the issues prominent and pre-valent in German idealist philosophy. Especially, in its opposition to the natural scientific mode of cognition—which Horkheimer saw as atemporal, relying solely on discursive logic—critical theory stressed a notion of man as the creator of historical reality, a being capable of comparing what is with what could be (echoes of Hegel's 'being and becoming').[3]

In the formation of its categories and in all phases of its procedure, critical theory quite consciously pursues an interest in a rational organization of human activity which it has set itself to elucidate and legitimize. For it is not just concerned with goals as they have been prescribed by the existing life forms, but with men and all their possibilities.

And, in the idealist tradition, truth is carefully defined and held to be 'objective' in the sense of being (metaphysically) inherent in the essence of human reality—a characteristically rationalist view. Horkheimer originally linked critical theory as a mode of cognition to a determinate structural location—the proletariat—for whom it provides knowledge in a motivating way.[4]

Those viewpoints which [critical theory] takes as the goal of human activity for historical analysis, and above all the idea of a rational social organization corresponding to the general will are immanent in human labour, without being present to individuals or in public opinion in a correct form. It is the property of a specific interest to experience and perceive these tendencies. Marx and Engels theory claims that this will happen in the proletariat. But in this society, the situation of the proletariat does not provide any guarantee or correct knowledge

either . . . 'hence' . . . the differentiation of its social structure
which is fostered from above, and the opposition between
personal and class interests which is only overcome at the best
of times, prevent this consciousness from acquiring immediate
validity.

It is in statements like these that we can see a clear connection
between the Frankfurt school and Lukács: the idea of theory being
produced to motivate working-class consciousness by intellectuals
who were not of that class, but could provide it with the means of
achieving an essentially philosophical goal—the realization of
human reason. Like all neo-Hegelianism, it tends to treat science as
something alienative because it isolates elements rather than treating
of the totality: Horkheimer describes how bourgeois economic
theory may be *transcended*, rather than replaced with a *more* scientific economic theory. Science is seen as divisive of the totality which
could be achieved in a human unreified world not subject to a purely
technical rationality: science implies technical control and is thus
contrasted with historical and social knowledge. In agreeing with
Lukács that science *was* reification, the Frankfurt theorists laid the
basis of anti-scientific social theory reducible in the main to a sort of
philosophy. Interestingly, this leads back to the old neo-Kantian–
neo-Hegelian arguments which had involved Weber, and led him to
elaborate a special method for sociology, of '*verstehen*', modelled on
Dilthey's hermeneutic methodology of the '*Geisteswissenschaften*'.
Science as a naturalistic enterprise consequently becomes the main
domain of traditional theory, and scientific Marxism an attempt to
vulgarize the important dialectical system Marx evolved; 'science'
becomes the symbol of an authority system, a structure of social
relations which negates a truly rational organization of society. Indeed the triumph of technical-manipulative-rationality is given a
substantive context by Horkheimer *et al.*: fascism. Science, from
being wrong because contemplative, becomes false because it is
employed by a repressive mode of domination, to become domination itself.

The anti-scientific epistemology developed by Horkheimer relied
to a great extent on Hegelian ideas, especially in its definition of
theory as 'self-knowledge of the object'. As Horkheimer himself put
it: critical theory 'constructs the unfolding picture of the whole, the
existential judgment contained in history'.[5] History achieves a metaphysical reality as a process in which a historical subject—man—
realizes itself. Knowledge of reality becomes a judgment, an evaluation, in terms of a goal of rational social organization. Horkheimer
and Adorno extended this 'metaphysical humanism' on to a substantive level in their analysis of fascism. According to critical theory,

technical rationality is the main cause of reification: bourgeois rationalism becomes identified with the sources of the authoritarian personality and fascism. For Horkheimer and Adorno, fascism becomes the self-destruction of the liberal Enlightenment; the goal of *'Entzauberung der Welt'* (as Weber put it) in its forms of natural science and empiricist epistemology leads directly towards a situation in which science (antithetical to 'culture') and logic become instruments of domination—fascism is thus the 'truth' lurking behind capitalist society. Thus there is a tendency for the early Frankfurt-school theorists—but not, significantly, for Marcuse (Marcuse saw critical theory as the negation of philosophy, as a transformatory *social* theory and was thus more concerned with structural aspects of capitalist society—cf. *Reason and Revolution*)—to seek the negation of the negation as the essence of revolution, to deny any positive aspect to bourgeois society. As such, the source of revolutionary transformation tends to be seen as external to the existing social system—an 'external negating subject'—which though it may be identified as the proletariat, is not defined structurally.

The similarity of the viewpoint of critical theory towards science, and the anti-objectivist phenomenological philosophy of Husserl should not go unnoticed. Both are rooted in the crises of German idealism, and both provide essentially metaphysical solutions to fundamentally epistemological problems. But the development of Frankfurt-school thought, especially in the direction of psychologism, has seen a certain convergence of these two initially disparate positions, primarily in the work of Jurgen Habermas.

After the war, Horkheimer and Adorno tended to develop their theoretical programme in an increasingly apolitical direction such that it became a critical theoretical stance, rather than the tool of a 'theoretician whose only concern is to accelerate a development which should lead to a society without exploitation'.[6] Habermas exemplifies this evolution of critical theory. He is a philosopher primarily interested in the development of sociological theory, and especially concerned with the sociology of knowledge in his aim of developing a theory of ideology. Thus he has involved himself in the work of transforming critical theory from a philosophical–political orientation into a sociological–epistemological theory. In his inaugural lecture as director of the Frankfurt Institute, Habermas showed his aims to be oriented towards the unification of *Erkenntnistheorie*—theory of the conditions of possible knowledge—and *Erkenntniskritik*—the critique of knowledge, both in structure and content—to create an eventual linkage of philosophy of history and theory of knowledge.[7] One of the main elements of his work has been the attempt to reconcile Marx and Freud (a theme beloved of Frankfurt intellectuals—cf. Fromm, Marcuse, etc.) and to develop a theory of ideology based upon the communicative relationship of psycho-analyst and psycho-analysand. Habermas has also seen fit to develop Hegelian ideas in a sociological direction to complement his view of Marxism as a critique of ideology, rather than as positive science. Taking over from Hegel's Jena lectures (1803–6) the notions of 'language', the 'tool' and 'family property' as three basic instruments of spirit, he transformed them into concepts of *communication*, *labour*, and *interaction* which would replace the concepts of productive forces and relations of production. Quite clearly, Habermas employs the Young Marx against 'scientific' Marxism, arguing that Marx was wrong in believing his work to be a natural science rather than a critique of bourgeois society. In fact, he argues, Marx's concepts of relations and forces of production are too limited to properly take account of modern society: they should be replaced with concepts more suited to analysis of the institutional framework of society, and centrally the concept of 'symbolically mediated interaction'. As a result, Habermas argues, it is possible to understand social systems initially in terms of the type of legitimizing ideology which they employ, the configuration of norms, cultural traditions and modes of symbolic communication. Science and technology function as supporters of institutional domination in capitalist society by legitimizing it as a viable social system.

In his essay, 'Knowledge and interest', the heritage of German idealism which so clearly marks his writing is systematically demonstrated. Habermas is arguing for a threefold typology of science, differentiated between natural and non-natural forms in terms of the interests which guide their characteristic modes of cognition. *In toto*, it is a continuation of the argument against positivism, against the 'reduction' of social and cultural phenomena to the level of material relationships, and it provides a polemic against the view that natural scientific theory is the paradigm of knowledge creation. Interests, Habermas argues, are what determine what shall count as knowledge, not intrinsic *autonomous* elements of cognition. In fact, cognition is inseparable from practical concern, and the attempt to impose the positivist distinction between fact and value, descriptive and normative statements, on the non-natural sciences only produces an obscuration of the interests which guide such knowledge. Husserl, giving another solution to idealism's *bête noire*, science, argued that all science did was to create a specious objectivity ignorant of the real ontology of scientific theory, its basis in the pre-scientific world of everyday life. In distinguishing advanced science from 'theory' in its original sense—an imprinting of the immutable order of the cosmos on its impersonal onlooker, which changed his relationship to the world—the separation of 'values' from theory becomes a subversion of the initial unity intended by theory. But

Husserl's critique of positive science, which focused on the conceal-
ment of scientific knowledge from practical interests, showed only
that phenomenology was incapable of producing the right relation
of theory and interest: 'What was needed was not a realliance of
knowledge with interest by an extension of the influence of theory
into practical life; on the contrary, theory through the very conceal-
ment of its true interest had acquired a pseudo-normative power of
its own.'[8]

Habermas's solution to this problem is to show how interests
underlying knowledge can be demonstrated by reference to the '*a
priori* transcendental frame' which structures the way theoretical
statements relative naively to reality. 'A specific connection between
logical rules of procedure and the interests guiding cognition can be
shown to hold for three categories of research. This is the task of a
critical theory of science which avoids the pitfalls of positivism.'[9]

Accordingly there are three types of science, representative of
three fundamental interest-orientations. The first, 'empirical analytical sciences', display a *technical* interest in cognition, the transcendental frame of reference laying down conditions for determining
the meaning of the validity of possible statements such that rules
for the construction and testing of theories are clearly prescribed. In
fact, the predictive goal of such knowledge implies that both the
logical construction of statements and test conditions reflect a
cognitive interest in keeping objectified processes under technical
control.

The second type, of 'historical interpretative sciences', are organized in terms of predominantly '*practical*' interests, 'practical'
having a special meaning for Habermas of the specific method by
which facts are elucidated: that objectivity is produced by the hermeneutic apprehension of meaning. This implies a method which
ignores the basic cognitive framework of the interpreter through
which he transmits knowledge. Consequently, 'interpretational research is guided by a concern for the maintenance and extension of
possible intersubjective understanding which is necessary for the
orientation of any symbolic interaction'.[10] It is of course arguable
whether such methodology or research really ought to be termed
scientific: its lack of a systematic means of verifying or testing hypotheses would seem to function to disqualify it from inclusion in any
but the most general notion of 'science'.

Habermas's third category of science, the 'systematic sciences of
action' or 'critically oriented sciences' which compose sociology,
economics and politics, produce nomological knowledge like the
natural sciences. But they are not in their critical forms content with
the search for laws and probabilistic statements: they also seek
to discover which theoretical statements express 'relations of

dependence' which are open to change because they are only *ideologically* stable. Based on self-reflection as their methodological frame of reference, they are influenced by an *emancipatory* interest in knowledge.

It will be clear to the perceptive reader that sciences of types one and two are basically what Horkheimer meant by traditional theory. It follows that what Habermas uses as the distinction between traditional and critical theory is not so much the notion of reproduction so central to Horkheimer's view of *science*, but rather the *type* of interest which produces knowledge. For at least the early Horkheimer and other Frankfurt writers, all bourgeois science was ultimately ideological; but for Habermas bourgeois science is not ideological simply because it is based on a technical rationality. However, the fact that it is concerned exclusively with the elucidation of mechanisms of control, and not with freedom from control, allots to it a role in the repressive domination of the institutional framework of society. Also, social science, whether rooted in bourgeois authority relationships or not, can play a role in the erection of a form of social organization in which communication free from domination, and a general and unforced consensus, could exist. For this is what makes the critical sciences *critical*, their ability to criticize prevailing institutional ideologies, interest-based scientific knowledge which functions as a constraint on non-exploitative social relations. Habermas is consequently distancing himself from the original formulations of critical theory, from scientific Marxism, especially that of the New Left (he has argued cogently that Marx's theory of class-struggle is no longer applicable to advanced capitalist societies, since technology and science have become the primary productive force. The labour theory of value is thus in urgent need of revision, since class-based distinctions no longer obtain) and from traditional Western social science's 'excessively' positivist orientation. As a conclusion to the essay, Habermas develops five theses expressing the determinate relationship between knowledge and interests. The theses contain a statement of the epistemological foundations of the theory of ideology. Habermas asserts in them that: the processes of cognition are inseparable from the creation and development of society; knowledge functions to maintain and extend human existence. Given these two general theses, Habermas extends the next three to provide a clearer understanding of the existential conditions in which interests guide knowledge. Thus, the third thesis states: 'the interests guiding cognition constitute themselves in the medium of work, language and authority', and these three media give three categories of possible knowledge; *information*, allowing increased technical control; *interpretation*, orientating action in a context of common normative traditions; *analysis*, setting consciousness free from its dependence on 'hypostatized' or reified—ideologically constructed—forces.[11] All three correspond to the transformed Hegelian concepts, and thus refer to specific institutional locations within social systems, which consequently exhibit characterizing interests— a (trivial) example being that the knowledge generated in an administrative context would be structured by an interest in the greater *control* of clerical procedures, rather than either the normative cohesion of clerical work or action by which such administration could be destroyed, or transcended.

Habermas finds it important to assert, in the fourth thesis, that 'in the power of self-reflection knowledge and interest are one' and that consequently standards of self-reflection are certain because of their basis in *language*, the only fact of which we can have certain knowledge and that which raises us above nature. This 'fact', if accepted, would mean that an emancipatory interest in knowledge does in fact aim at the accomplishment of reflection (reflexivity is important because it employs an essentially hermeneutic methodology—*assuming* that language is as straightforward as it appears), and as such provides the grounding of a true objectivity: it also takes us on to Habermas's fifth thesis: 'the unity of knowledge and interest proves itself in a dialectic which restores what has been suppressed from the historical traces of a suppressed dialogue',[12] and only in an emancipated society would communication be universally free dialogue— a 'true consensus'. Truth has thus an existentially precise location and one dependent on free and uncoerced social relations: 'To this extent the truth of statements is based on the anticipation of a life without repression',[13] and a pure theory which hides the interests guiding knowledge becomes the slave of the very interests it has concealed and is in that sense ideological: it distorts our socially given means of communication.

This over-riding concern with the mechanisms by which language, *communication*, is distorted by socially structured—even stratified— interests involves Habermas in a distinctive usage of Freudian theory, and the cognitive processes involved in the psycho-analytic relationship. Freud had been well employed by earlier Frankfurt theorists, especially Marcuse, because of his theories of sexual repression: although Freud himself had been a highly conservative man, his ontogenetic and phylogenetic hypotheses could be interpreted (as they have been by Fromm and others) to mean that modern industrial, *capitalist*, society is predicated upon an extreme psycho-sexual repression—a sort of erotic reification which is anti-humanistic in its consequences though it does allow man to achieve a high level of manipulative control over both his environment and his social organization.

Habermas employed both the meta-psychological theories of

Freud—which he uses in the Frankfurt tradition with a *critical* perspective on the notion of human cultural development as repression of human instincts—and the psycho-analytic *relationship*, to extend his notion of Marx as a *critic* of ideology which underlays his theory of ideology as 'systematically distorted communication'. Thus it is the focus on the clinical situation, from a hermeneutic viewpoint, in the dialogue between analyst and analysand which will concern us here. For Habermas views psycho-analysis as a theory of linguistic failure, a therapy by which both partners in the relationship achieve a state of self-reflection in which knowledge and interest explicitly coincide. But why should a dyadic relationship be of interest to a theory of ideology in complex social systems? The answer lies in the cultural context in which repressed dialogue comes to be repressed, and knowledge of individual emotions and feeling-states is systematically distorted. In the Freudian—or rather Frankfurt–Freudian—theory of cultural development modern society is collectively repressed; indeed such repression is one of the main conditions on which modern social organization is predicated. Consequently the 'systematically distorted communication' involved in the therapeutic dialogue between analyst and analysand includes 'the hidden pathology of collective behaviour and entire social systems'.[14] Our knowledge of ourselves may thus suffer from a distortion systematically produced by our institutions and normative systems, which extends to socially available knowledge of the actual workings of the social system in which we exist. The psycho-analytic relationship, in which what was distorted communication becomes a free dialogue, is thus the model of an emancipatory transformation of society to a level in which an unforced consensus is possible in general terms, and in which, again, knowledge and interest may coincide.

My very short and general treatment of Frankfurt critical theory and its extension into sociology of knowledge by Jurgen Habermas should be concluded by a summing-up of the influences exerted in that direction by Lukács. As I have constantly pointed out, that which is behind both Lukács and Frankfurt is as important as that which is explicit in their connections. German idealist philosophy produced a whole constellation of epistemological problems and responses to the attempts to bypass it both by Marxism and positive science. Clearly what has emerged for the sociology of knowledge from both Lukács and Frankfurt is a consequence of the conflict between all three of these mutually antagonistic positions. Both Marxism and positivist social science produced empirically based knowledge unavailable to idealism which controverted many of its tenets, yet both were unable to resolve the epistemological problems raised by idealism (largely because they were unimportant to them) and also both were unsatisfactory as theories of knowledge, Marxism because of its insistence on a determinate structural location for true knowledge, and positivism because its model of knowledge seemed to exclude the important questions about truth completely. The only solution was anti-positivist critical theory, which contained the old philosophical problems but suggested that their resolution was a *historical* problem that lay in the production of a specific sort of social transformation. In the case of Habermas, who gets nearest to some sort of empirically adequate work, the substance of this solution revolves around a more or less idealistic conception of social systems as ideological systems primarily. The *consequences* of this for Habermas's sociology of knowledge are discussed elsewhere, but suffice it to say at this point that Habermas views knowledge as something dependent for its content and structure on the interests characteristic of specific formations. Though Lukács was perhaps more concerned with promoting social revolution than is Habermas, the linkage between his work and that of Habermas resides in this conception of interests, though for Lukács they would have a more determinate social basis in the sense that capitalism as a whole systematically produces knowledge—generating interests suited to its goal of reificatory rationalization.

II Lucien Goldmann: sociology of knowledge and sociology of literature

In discussing the appropriation of Lukácsian approaches to the sociology of knowledge by writers of the Frankfurt school, I pointed out the preponderant interest in methods of distinguishing between natural, historical and social sciences. Broadly speaking, it may be argued that sociologies of knowledge serve as a polemic against the methodological imperialism of natural science paradigms, especially when conceived as vehicles of a unification of Marxism and neo-Hegelian dialectical philosophy. Lukács, in seeing the proletariat as capable of performing an empirical revolution of epistemological issues, conflated the Marxian concept of socialist revolution with the Hegelian idea of the end of history, and the self-knowledge of the object. Within this constellation of intellectual positions, a fundamental antipathy to positivist scientism was engendered. It could lead, logically, to a humanism, a view of history which centred around the idea of an *essential man*, involving a basic individualism. Lucien Goldmann's work in the sociology of literature is based in a Lukácsian sociology of knowledge and distinctively contains these elements of neo-Hegelianism, humanism, anti-positivism and historicism.

Without discussing the contributions Goldmann has made to the sociology of literature in depth, it would be difficult to show in what ways he has employed sociology of knowledge substantively. The dictates of space, however, preclude all but passing references to Goldmann's *magnum opus*—*The Hidden God*—and I am forced to concentrate on Goldmann's small book *The Human Sciences and Philosophy*, first published in 1952. This book—really an extended essay—is however particularly suited to my task of analytic exposition, since it contains in mostly assertive form the majority of predicative concepts which Goldmann employed in his empirical work.

Conceived as a polemic against trends in the development of sociological theory, both methodologically and substantively, the book contains quite a clear statement of the theoretical tools Goldmann employed in his analyses of Kant, Racine and Pascal, and later, Robbe-Grillet and other modern writers. In stating and defining his theoretical postulates, Goldmann was concerned to demonstrate that philosophical issues—though they may have been expunged from the natural sciences, ought to occupy an important role in the knowledge which the 'human sciences' produce of social and historical reality. He wished, in a sense like Lukács, to preserve a realm of philosophic discourse for Marxism because he believed that philosophy dealt with *'fundamental truths concerning the relations of men with other men and of men with the universe'* and consequently that such truths existed in the foundations and methodology of the human sciences.[15] Of course what this produces—as indeed it must—is a confusion: we can never be sure what Goldmann intends as the proper methodology for the human sciences or indeed whether they should exist separately from philosophy at all. Rather we are left to oscillate, as does Goldmann, between decidedly non-empirical philosophic generalizations about human social existence, and empirical statements about the existential conditions under which particular methodologies are produced. In fact the confusion proceeds from the concept of science which Goldmann employs. In a critique of scientism, one expects *definitions* of science and scientific knowledge: but Goldmann only provides *identifications*. Natural scientific knowledge is based on a model—that of the physico-chemical sciences—whilst 'human scientific' knowledge is variously termed a *'synthesis of justified* abstractions'—'concrete' rather than 'abstract'—or the study of men's 'actions' in terms of its 'structure', motivation and the 'changes that it undergoes', and directed towards grasping 'the essential aspects of human life'. There is simply no conception of 'human scientific' knowledge being systematically defined, or related to operational conditions.

Given these confusions, present I think in most anti-scientism directed at historical and sociological knowledge, Goldmann does present a coherent sociology of knowledge, which I will expose.

Goldmann argues that sociology, especially in its non-Marxist forms, has become a mere servant of organized capitalism, being increasingly oriented towards support and furtherance of the aims of 'technocracy'. In this process it has moved towards a resolution of 'microsociological' problems, rather than the larger issues of historical change. At one time a critical discipline, sociology—and in particular American sociology—has concerned itself with ways of explaining and mitigating the problems of adjustment to a technological, sophisticated, capitalist society and has meant that research 'has lost sight of the qualitative changes in social structures and of the historical dimensions of social facts'.[16] The reasons for this methodological interest in minutiae is not merely a function of the subservience of sociology to the interests of capitalism, but a result of the confusion over scientific values and the relationship between natural and social facts, and the subordination of social science to the methods of the physico-chemical sciences:[17]

> for some centuries now we have had one value that is changeless and is shared by all social groups, the *control of nature*. This value has permitted the construction of an important corpus of physico-chemical sciences that are at once a-historical, non-dialectical and extremely efficacious in an operational sense.

The human sciences when subjected to a similar methodological premiss, seem however to produce little in the way of 'positive' results (we are justified in asking: positive to whom?). 'Exact' science seems not to work in the context of social theory. The possibility of a highly technological society, though (e.g. with self-regulating economic mechanisms, and productive forces consigned to the hands of specialists), would allow the social sciences to function in this way and to assist in the prevention of any human interference in the ordering of such a society. Goldmann, then, is arguing that an attempt to make sociology scientific is an attempt to prevent it seeing society as a whole, as in a historical context open to change. Sociology of knowledge he conceives as a basis of criticism of such a sociology, since it is directed towards analysis of the existential bases of sociological methodologies. His view of sociology of knowledge implies that it is directed towards the creation—or preservation—of historical, philosophical and humanistic sociology and against modern forms of a historical, 'scientific' sociology.

The critique of a historical sociology is founded on a conception of sociology as a discipline indistinguishable in principle from history:[18]

> Every social fact is a historical fact and vice-versa. It follows that history and sociology *study the same phenomena* and that

67

each of them grasps some real aspect of these phenomena; but the image which each discipline gives of them will necessarily be partial and abstract . . . [it is necessary to] abandon all abstract sociology and all abstract history in order to achieve a concrete science of human reality, which can only be a *historical sociology* or a *sociological history*.

In fact, he argues there cannot be *concrete* sociological knowledge that is not historical—'concrete' meaning a 'synthesis of justified abstractions'—the justification coming presumably from a location in premisses of which Goldmann approves, but which implicitly seem to be correspondence to human needs, or wider values. Such values will be involved in the mode of analysis of Goldmann's sociology of knowledge, which will provide:[19]

An understanding of the main currents of contemporary [i.e. up to 1950] sociology, the nature of their relation to contemporary social reality, the direction of their movement at the centre of this reality, and the social frameworks which are capable of promoting, or, conversely, of reducing their positive value as instruments of knowledge.

In providing such an approach, and particularly in his equation of sociology and history, Goldmann is arguing for a crucial epistemological distinction, between empiricist rationalism on the one hand, and dialectical thought on the other. Simply, Goldmann maintains that rationalism-empiricism holds a sharp distinction between subject and object—I and We—and does not employ any more than a purely positivist history. Dialectical thought replaces the I–We dichotomy with a historical We—employing a philosophy of history and a specifically historical epistemology. It thus posits a historical consciousness, which goes beyond the I of rationalism: what this consciousness seeks are: 'transformations of the acting subject in the dialectical relation Men–World; i.e. *transformations of human society*'. Such a view produces a particular notion of the content of social-science knowledge:[20]

the object of the historical sciences [i.e. Goldmann's history-sociology] is *human actions of all times and places* in the degree to which *they have had or now have an importance for or an influence on the existence and structure of a human group and, implicitly thereby, an importance for or an influence on the existence and structure of the present or future human community*.

A definition which includes not only 'collective phenomena', but also the action and behaviour of significant historical figures—in so far as they exert an influence upon or in their work express the values and beliefs of the social group they come from or represent. Of course, this further distinguishes natural and 'human' science: physics for example is involved in the explanation of externally sensible facts, whilst sociology-history must comprehend the *meaning* of an action for actors, in two ways: in respect of a *conscious* meaning to the actors, and its *objective* meaning in their social, economic and political contexts. This dualistic model of course produces problems: what is the relation between 'individual consciousness and objective reality' (in fact, the role of ideologies) in the theoretical and methodological development of the sociology of knowledge?

This problem of 'ideologies' Goldmann presents in terms of the issue of objectivity in social sciences. Discussing the work of Lukács, Weber and Durkheim, he presents the methodological arguments as the distinguishing feature of the non-Marxist as against Marxist sociologies. There are two main aspects to Goldmann's argument here. First, he asserts the 'partial identity of the subject and object of knowledge' because of its basis in the human, historical and social contexts of scientific cognition: hence objectivity must be quite a different problem to natural as opposed to humanistic social science. Second, any separation of 'material' and 'spiritual' aspects of human reality must produce dangerous abstractions because of the 'total' nature of that reality—a neo-Hegelian conception taken straight from Lukács's critique of 'bourgeois' social science.[21] Consequently the social theorist must seek to recover the 'concrete and total reality', involving in the study of social facts the 'history of theories about these facts' and their location in a total societal and historical context.

To Goldmann the notion of objectivity employed by Weber and Durkheim was inadequate because it relied upon the individual sociologist to ensure it, and did not deal with the—postulated— identity of subject and object in humanistic social science. However, though Lukács differs from them in respect of this point, all three writers share a belief in two main points; one, science alone cannot logically establish value-judgments: two, the theorist must prevent deformation of his analyses by personal values. But recognition of these points, though necessary to science, is not sufficient for objectivity. Durkheim for example does not see any ontological difference between natural and social facts, such that a lack of objectivity in natural scientific work is merely a personal idiosyncrasy whereas basic evaluative presuppositions are *prior* to research in the human sciences, because of the divergencies between interests and values of social classes: there are not socially *shared* conceptions of the values underlying social science as there are underlying natural science.

Both Weber and Durkheim are *conservative* sociologists because of their situation as representatives of bourgeois values, argues Goldmann, and the social contexts in which the German and French middle classes were situated when they produced their work: Durkheim's 'Cartesian optimism' expresses the 'optimistic tradition of a bourgeoisie which had been disturbed but little by the development of a proletariat capable of setting over against it—its own socialist vision'.[22] On the other hand, Weber was a member of a bourgeoisie challenged by a vigorous socialist movement, containing within it the theoretically powerful tradition of Marx and Engels. To Goldmann this explains both Weber's interest in Marx's work and his methodological prevarications, his awareness of the influence of value-judgments in social-scientific work. However, Weber contended that it was possible to distinguish between values which, as it were, selected objects of study—which were ineradicable—and values which influenced the conduct of research, which could be eliminated: in that sense he was unwilling to posit any social determinism of thought. Lukács, however, in Goldmann's view, overcame the deficiencies of non-Marxist sociology because he was willing to accept fully the consequences of viewing all thought as socially determined (this is not in fact correct; Lukács wanted to reserve autonomy to aesthetic knowledge—cf. section on Lukács, pp. 53–4 above), which both Durkheim and Weber had rejected. Although this is a serious misinterpretation of particularly Durkheim's work (which is discussed elsewhere) in that it dwells too greatly on his dictum—'treat social facts as things'—ignoring *The Elementary Forms of the Religious Life* and *Primitive Classification,* Goldmann contends that this externalization of objects of study has characterized modern non-Marxist sociology. Methodology, in the narrow sense of the practice of research, has replaced theory as the goal of sociological work, in the sense of being directed to the reduction of human facts to the same level as objects of the physical sciences.

But of course the adoption of a 'social determinist' position and the consequent recognition of the socially given influences of value judgements on science poses the problem of *relativism*. Goldmann takes over Lukács's solution to this problem—the potential—or 'imputed'—consciousness of the proletariat (cf. pp. 44–6), the class which will provide itself as the negation of bourgeois society and its reification. The notion of the proletariat as potentially both subject and object of social-scientific knowledge, as in fact the realization of the Absolute Idea in Hegelian terms, Goldmann recognizes as an essentially metaphysical concept: it is valuable as an 'ideal concept' rather than as an expression of reality. Rather, the problem of relativism has to be solved in a different way, Goldmann arguing that this involves the 'synthesis' of two elements which relate in part to Lukács's sociology of knowledge.

1 Goldmann contends that 'perspectives and ideologies', in their consequences for scientific thought, are differentiated such that: 'some value-judgments permit a better understanding of reality than others'. The *method* of differentiating between the veridicality of contending sociologies is thus to test their ability to explain how other theories 'as a social and human phenomenon, reveals its infra-structure, and clarifies, by means of an immanent critical principle, its inconsistencies and its limitations'.[23]

2 The development of a theory which has the 'widest possible form and range of comprehension', which is to Goldmann, Marxism. However there are some problems for Goldmann with respect to this solution of relativism.

First, there are limitations on the knowledge available to 'ascend-ing' classes which may not hold for 'reactionary' classes. Second, there may be limitations which prevent 'possible consciousness'—the maximum knowledge of a class—from being completely true. How-ever, despite these limitations, it is possible for individuals to go beyond the level of knowledge of all the social classes existent in his time. This possibility is given by an eclecticism on the part of this hypothetical individual—he synthesizes all elements of truth pro-vided by the perspectives of the different classes and allies to this synthesis 'elements of understanding' not socially current. Hence the scientist, in some circumstances, due to his search for 'truth' as a moral value and his aim of producing the most comprehensive knowledge of reality, may enlarge 'the limits of real consciousness of a class in a given epoch': his situation as one exposed to differing theories allows him, in acknowledgedly exceptional circumstances, to produce an extension of objective truth beyond the limitations of the group of which he is a member. Crucially, then, this will involve the analysis of ideologies, the potentialities of differing class view-points for exposing the 'truth'. For a *dialectical* sociology of know-ledge, it follows, a method '*genetic*', '*material*' and *psychic*, must be employed:—'the *total* character of human activity and the indissoluble bond between the history of economic and social facts and the history of ideas'[24] must be encompassed. Goldmann's developed sociology of knowledge rests, apart from its groundings in neo-Hegelian con-cepts of totality and a concept of society derived from Marx, on a notion of social life as made up of three 'major structural elements'. The first of these—the 'specific importance of economic life'—is quite clearly Marxian in the sense that it refers predominantly to the concept of mode and forces of production. However, the other two—'the predominant historical function of social classes', and 'the notion of potential consciousness'—are quite decidedly additional to the Marxian concept of society, and relate to Goldmann's view that the recognition of the existence of true science implies concepts of true and false consciousness in social life (e.g. in the sense that there cannot be at the same time both true *and* partial consciousness) deriving from his contention that 'the category of totality is the carrier of the scientific principle in the understanding of social life'.[25] In the positive scientific analysis of Marx, the approach exemplified by his later work, the concepts of mode, forces and relations of production were the primary elements of his theoretical system, prior to all other conceptualizations and requisite to any analysis of social structure. Quite clearly, Goldmann is going far beyond this in asserting a *separate* structural element of potential consciousness. The *linkage* between Goldmann's quasi-Marxist conception of potential consciousness and orthodox scientific Marxism lies of course in his definition of social classes. Goldmann castigates non-Marxist sociology both for its 'ignorance' of social classes and its refusal to define social groups such as classes in terms primarily of position in the mode of production, and consciousness. His definition provides a bridge in the sense that it contains three elements, two structural and one structural-conceptual; classes *must* be defined, then, if they are to provide an adequate base of sociological analysis as: (1) having a determinate 'function in production'; (2) in terms of their social relations with other classes; (3) the basis of what Goldmann terms 'world-views': 'From the end of antiquity up until our own time *social classes have constituted the infrastructure of world-views.*'[26]

Now this had important consequences, both for Goldmann's conceptions of potential consciousness and for the whole of his sociology of literature. It leads to two main conclusions which involve the definition of class *in terms of* consciousness (rather than vice versa, which is the straightforward Marxist position). First, the ultimate location of the infrastructure of 'a philosophy, a literary or artistic current' is no other social group but a class and its linkages with society. Second, 'The maximum of potential consciousness of a social class *always* constitutes a psychologically coherent world-view which may be expressed on the plane of religion, philosophy, literature or art'[27] (my italics). And this is the arbiter of Goldmann's definition of ideology: ideologies are *partial*, world-views *total*. World-views consequently only exist in classes—and classes which have a continuing influence on the 'totality of the human community'— ideologies being the productions of non-class social groups and declining social classes. The circularity of this definition of class, and the non-empirical distinction ideology–world-view should be obvious to the reader. Classes are those social groups which possess 'world-views': world-views are then the expression of a class's *total* potential consciousness. Ideologies—partial knowledge of society—are produced only by social groups. Classes then cannot produce ideologies and no existent 'world-view' can be attributed to a group. The concept of *'potential consciousness'* then is central to Goldmann's sociology of knowledge: how does he present it?

Returning to the argument about differentiation between types of science, Goldmann argues for a distinction between three qualitatively different scientific methods based on an ontological distinction between 'inert', 'living' and 'conscious' existence (experimental knowledge of the 'chemistry of life' and the possibility of its creation in the laboratory of course falsifies this distinction): physicochemical, biological and human sciences, the fundamental concept in the latter being that of potential consciousness.[28] Indeed it is the 'principle instrument of scientific thinking in the human sciences'. Whilst natural science takes into account two stages of knowledge, its 'ideal norm' and the actual level of knowledge achieved, social science must take into account an 'intermediary factor': 'the *maximum of potential consciousness* of the classes which constitute the society under analysis'.[29] But of course the actual distinction of potential from real consciousness must be made, in the sense that real consciousness is the result of the actual conditions under which a class-consciousness exists: potential consciousness expresses the possibilities available to that class within its given social structure. Real consciousness is thus the 'collective consciousness' of a class at a determinate point in its history: this 'fact' (taken quite clearly from Lukács's analyses of proletarian consciousness in its actual and 'imputed' senses) is of great importance in the study of literary works since it allows the analyst to see intellectual and artistic phenomena as *'expressions* of a collective consciousness' (my italics), with the resulting contention that:[30]

> Every manifestation is the work of its individual author and expresses his ways of thinking and feeling, but these . . . are not independent entities with respect to the actions and behaviour of other men. They exist and may be understood only in terms of their intersubjective relations which give them their whole tenor and richness.

Class position in fact produces, on the basis of the totality of relations between individuals and society, what Goldmann calls a 'psychic structure' common to the members of that class.[31] But this does not mean that *all* intellectual productions represent class positions: only those which express a shared structure can be termed representational. World-views, consequently, are 'social facts' represented in coherent and adequate form by great philosophical and artistic works, whose content is determined by: 'the *maximum of potential consciousness* . . . of the social class in general'.[32] The sociology of knowledge is able to study world-views at two different levels: at the level of *real* consciousness, or in terms of their coherent expression in art, literature and philosophy—the two levels being of course complementary, though the second is much clearer: it has formed the corpus of the majority of Goldmann's work in the sociology of literature (and particularly the concept of 'tragic vision' as applicable to the writing of Pascal, Racine and Kant—in terms of its status as a bourgeois world-view). Curiously, Goldmann argues that the *number* of world-views is determinate in the sense of being smaller than the number of classes in history: a typology of world-views would thus seem to be methodologically *prior* to the identification of social classes, and leads of necessity to a fundamentally idealist sociology of knowledge which would postulate social groups as 'carriers' of specific cognitive systems.

There is certainly an unresolved tension in Goldmann's work between idealism and materialism expressed best in his attempts to formulate a sociology of knowledge. But of course it affects his substantive work as well, and that is no more clearly shown than his adoption of the concept of 'tragic vision', which he takes from the young Lukács who wrote *Die Seele und die Formen* (*The Soul and the Forms*—a treatise on literary criticism, 1911) to characterize the attitudes implicit to the French seventeenth-century *noblesse de robe* and their involvement with Jansenism. In *The Hidden God*, then, Goldmann uses the concept of tragic vision—which means in Lukács's formulation the vision of a world which God has left, and yet has to be lived in by the tragic hero with the eye of God upon him—to describe the world-view of one element of the middle class and its problems of adjustment to social and political pressures, through his analysis of the philosopher-theologian Pascal and the playwright Racine. Of course the concept of tragic vision is in a sense pre-Marxist: its rooting in Lukács derives mainly from the neo-Kantian influences upon him. But, as I have argued elsewhere, *any* sociological analysis of intellectual phenomena is brought to employ idealistic conceptions unless it declines into a dogmatic materialism. It is to the merit of Goldmann to have produced a corpus of substantive work in which the tensions between idealism and materialism produce a coherent explanation of the multiple interrelations of society and its cultural manifestations.

5 Max Scheler

I

I have argued elsewhere that one distinctive element of the sociology
of knowledge is a critical concern with the employment of a positivist philosophy as the basis of scientific cognition when applied to
the social rather than natural world. Nowhere does this concern
appear more clearly than in the work of Max Scheler. It could almost
be said that Scheler devoted his life to an anti-positivist crusade, a
war against the 'cult of science' that he saw as the characteristic
ethos of Western society and which was responsible for the conflicts
and social pathologies of modern life.[1] And although Scheler provided a critique of positivism from a diametrically opposed position
to Lukács, Mannheim, the Frankfurt theorists and Goldmann, they
still shared views of the role of science in modern capitalist society.
Scheler was an élitist who saw sociology of knowledge as an essentially political tool: it would provide the 'foundation of all cultural
politics' and constitute a method of resolving the ideological conflicts
prevalent in Weimar Germany immediately after the First World
War, by allowing the politicians involved in these conflicts to see the
limitations of their viewpoints. It would allow one-sided political
views to be overcome by a *Weltanschauunganalysis* showing their
class-determined nature. Along with Lukács, Goldmann, Horkheimer, Mannheim, etc., Scheler sees positive science as a one-sided
mode of cognition; its *rationalism* a manifestation of the modern
social atomization of the old spirits of '*Volk*' and '*Gemeinschaft*'
which had characterized pre-capitalist German (and European)
society. *Science* is seen by Scheler—in the sense of a *Weltanschauung*
—as the product of a specific class, in the same fashion as the
Marxist writers saw it: the product of a bourgeois class interested in
the creation of the means of control of both natural and social world

75

by technically rational methods (cf. my discussions of Lukács, Goldmann, Mannheim and the Frankfurt school, pp. 54–74). Part of the reason for his employment of similar conceptual elements to those of the Marxist writers lies in Scheler's recognition that Marxism provided a one-sidedly accurate analysis of the tensions fundamental to capitalist society and its awareness of the connections between social classes and the social knowledge of a society. Indeed, Scheler's theory of *'ressentiment'*—a sort of class-based resentment of social organization—was based to a certain extent on the notion of proletarian class-consciousness as a specific form of *ressentiment* against bourgeois society. In an important sense Scheler was anti-bourgeois, anti-capitalism, as well: though of course his ideal society was opposed to that of the Marxists, for he favoured an élitist, community-based society in which everyone knew his place and the right to rule was placed in the hands of those best fitted, socially, genetically and intellectually: in fact, the aristocracy.

To a very important extent, Scheler's sociology of knowledge is rooted in his phenomenological analyses. It attempted to explain 'how the deep-lying ontological and epistemological relationships among men are adapted to the cosmic order',[2] and how these relationships were adapted in terms of their social determination. In this, Scheler was effecting a compromise between a Marxian notion of consciousness as socially determined, and an idealist theory of knowledge. Rather than locate the determination of knowledge forms solely in a structural factor such as the relations of production, Scheler's theory stresses the co-determination of thought by both intellectual and material factors—what he called '*Ideal-und-Realfaktoren*'. In other words he wished to preserve the 'Eternal essences' which characterized his phenomenological position as analytic components of a sociology of knowledge, and the '*Idealfaktoren*' were elements which with *Realfaktoren* co-determined knowledge. There was an absolute realm of ideas quite separate from the real world of material objects: their unification lying in the realm of the social. The sociology of knowledge would thus trace out the points at which—and to what proportionate degree—material factors, social, economic and psychobiological, interacted with parts of the realm of absolute ideas to make them active in the social world and play a determinate historical role. Hence, no idea could have any social or historical reality unless it were associated with 'interests, instinctual drives and collective drives', but the actual meaning or content of ideas is autonomous and develops according to the separate laws of the intellectual–cultural sphere.

Scheler's *Wissenssoziologie* proceeded from his critique of Comtean positivism and embodies important elements of his theory of élites, and indeed his whole élitist preconceptions about social organization. Particularly, Scheler felt that this new discipline could assist the ruling élite to maintain social order:[3]

> Through what he called perspectival vision, Scheler hoped that the ruling élite would be able to select the truth out of every social perspective. The élite would then be able to integrate all of these truths into a social program that would win the allegiance of all citizens. *Wissenssoziologie* could thus become another form of social cement. It would enable the ruling class to hold the society together and direct it according to their superior vision.

Scheler's sociology of knowledge also proceeds from another direction as a response to Wilhelm Dilthey's '*Weltanschauungs-philosophie*' which had been so influential in German social science and philosophy from about 1890 to 1930, and which was an attempt to see the intellectual world in terms of a limited number of *Weltan-schauungen*. These *Weltanschauungen* formed the bases of all philo-sophical systems and were founded in the lived experience of the thinker, so that any philosophy or intellectual position would only be understood as an expression of one of the basic *Weltanschauungen* and that it was only *true* in so far as it was *contingently true* in rela-tion to the lived experience of its author or authors. Dilthey thus raised relativism to the level of a philosophical system which negated absolute truth. Scheler, though he accepted the concept of a limited number of *Weltanschauungen*, operated consistently (due to his Catholicism) with a concept of absolute truth which he employed to alter the very notion of '*Weltanschauung*' itself. What Dilthey had observed, he argued, were in fact artificial constructions (*Bildungs Weltanschauungen*) produced by a conscious intellectual process; these constructions varied according to the 'basic cultural men-talities' of the societies of the world, or as Scheler termed them—the 'relatively natural *Weltenschauungen*',[4] which lay behind them. These relatively natural world-views were closely related to the fundamental 'organic' basis of the culture they supported and con-sequently changed only very slowly over time. Dilthey's *Weltan-schauungen* were culturally specific and related only to the European cultural world: what was needed was a wider typology of both rela-tively natural and artificial world-views. The foundations of both of these, relativistic, world-views, Scheler said, lay in a constant and absolutely unchanging world-view *beyond* historical or social de-termination. Hence there was an absolute realm of truth behind history and society, and which Scheler believed could be appre-hended as the *essence* of human thought and knowledge by phenomenological methods. Consequently, rather than subsuming philosophical analysis of *Weltanschauungen* under science, as Weber had done,[5] Scheler argues that philosophy could posit and determine the objective cognitive value of *Weltanschauungen*, by its employment of a particular methodological and substantive mode of analysis: the sociology of knowledge. To Scheler, then, sociology of knowledge arose partly out of his confrontation with Dilthean relativism (and constituted a form of epistemology). But, as we have said before, it also is rooted in his critique of the bourgeois ethos of science and Comtean positivism. It is possible to find a third influential element, in Marxism, and it is clear that Scheler's careful discrimination between '*Realfaktoren*' and '*Idealfaktoren*' is a consequence of his reading of Marx and particularly Lukács, as well as his contacts with Marxists working in the field of the sociology of knowledge.

II

In the long theoretical introduction Scheler contributed to the collection of essays he edited, *Versuche einer Soziologie des Wissens* (Leipzig, 1924) he associated sociology of knowledge with epistemology, logic and developmental psychology.[6] In fact, Scheler wished (his) sociology of knowledge to replace both classic philosophical epistemology and Comtean and Spencerean theories of knowledge. Both were, though for different reasons, too closely attached to Western cultural developments and both tended to see science as the paradigm of knowledge, rather than as an element of it.

Comte and Spencer, and later Durkheim as well, tended to see positive science as the most advanced form of knowledge, logically superior to philosophy, metaphysics and religion which were held to constitute obsolescent modes of cognition. Comte even developed a theory of human cultural and social development on the basis of a typology of knowledge forms, with 'religious' knowledge as the most primitive form, metaphysics ('philosophy') an intermediary stage, and positive science as the third and most advanced level of human knowledge: a liberating knowledge which transcended the two lower levels of knowledge because it enabled men to 'see in order to foresee' ('voir pour prévoir'). But Comte, Scheler argued, was unaware of the fact that—though he rightly credited science with being the dominant *mode of cognition* in modern capitalist society—all he was doing was producing a manifestation of the ethos of the European middle class, an ethos concerned solely with control and domination in its drive for economic profit. Rather, Scheler said, we ought to see religion, metaphysics and positive science as three independent and equally valid modes of cognition: Comte had simply assumed that religious and metaphysical thought was directed to the same ends and had essentially the same goal as positive science, without realizing that they were fundamentally different and that the latter was based in the 'spirit of capitalism' and is merely a 'class philosophy of modern industrial enterprise, bent solely on the expansion of power' which would end with the abolition of the bourgeois class.

Scheler's elaboration of sociology of knowledge begins with a group of formal 'axioms', which lead to a theory which takes the three modes of cognition as the basic systems of human knowledge in terms of a differentiation of the motivations which underlie them. There are *three* axiomatic principles of sociology of knowledge. First:[7]

> The knowledge which each man has of being a *member of society* in general is not empirical but a priori knowledge. It genetically precedes the stages of his self and self-value consciousness: no I without a We; and genetically, the We always has a content before the I.

Consequently all our 'basic' knowledge, that received naturally as it were, is phenomenologically constituted as socially ordered knowledge. Scheler's second axiomatic principle states that the relations implied by such participation in a shared consciousness, depend on 'the essence structure of the group' and may be apprehended by ideal-types. (What Scheler means is that there is a group 'ethos' comprised of the 'drives' and past mental history of its members; we shall deal with this notion at length later.) Apprehension of this 'essence structure' is thus primarily by hermeneutic means, since what is involved in the process itself is basically a transference of *meaning*. Fundamental to this axiomatic principle is Scheler's contention that hereditary functions exist 'for the acquiring of certain types of knowledge' and that differences in societies in terms of their cultural productions are based on these inborn 'talents' rather than on social differences among classes. This leads Scheler to an important distinction between two categories 'essential' to sociology of knowledge: 'group soul' and 'group mind'. 'Group soul' is in fact the 'relatively natural *Weltanschauung*' referred to earlier (cf. p. 77 above) and was composed of the folksongs, folk-language, customs, mores and popular religions, etc. of the society. 'Group mind'—what Scheler came to call 'artificial constructions' (*Bildungs-weltanschauungen*) or 'educated' world-views—comprised the relatively sophisticated and systematized culture, the state, law, educated language, philosophy, art and science, which was built 'on top' of the group soul. Sociology of knowledge, Scheler felt, was primarily concerned with the group mind, the élite production of knowledge and would trace:[8]

the downward flow of knowledge from the top of society and determine the manner of its distribution over the various groups and strata with time as well as the ways in which this distribution is organised by society . . . [and] deals chiefly with the group mind.

In his later work,[9] Scheler was to stress the processes by which what he termed 'absolutely natural *Weltanschauungen*' were broken down into concrete cultural manifestations in history, and thus produced a fragmentation of the absolute truth and values contained within this primal *Weltanschauung*. In his distinction between 'group soul' and 'group mind', Scheler had adverted to the *sociological* distinction of the two categories: 'group soul' (relatively natural *Weltanschauungen*) was a property of a whole social system, and was thus 'impersonal': but 'group mind' was the *personal* property of the élite class and required the activity of creative individuals to produce it. The translation of a realm of absolute truth and values into concrete but relative forms Scheler called *functionalization*. The process of *functionalization* was differentiated in terms of the varying ways in which societies encountered the world, these variations affecting their 'mental structure' to the extent of eventually dominating it, in terms of both concepts and modes of cognition. There were, he argued, two aspects of functionalization.

First, although different societies apprehended reality differently, each conception of reality could be true since they were viewing the same ultimate reality from different perspectives. The conditions under which knowledge was produced thus did not affect its validity, though they did select the objects of knowledge.

Second, Scheler continued his belief in a 'supratemporal metaphysical sphere of truth in which the individual incarnations of truth participated'.[10] There was in fact, he believed, a realm of eternal ideas which imparted true validity and ultimate unity to all the functionalizations of truth in history, which were thus grounded in the eternal logos beyond history. And this brings us to the third axiomatic principle of Scheler's sociology of knowledge: it is a 'law' of epistemology, he asserted, that there is a *fixed* structure of knowledge of reality which extends to all the spheres of human knowledge and constitutes in that form a 'constant' of the human mind. Hence there are five spheres of irreducible reality, and although their content is open to historical rearrangement each is given as irreducible with human consciousness since there is an *essential* order which they represent and which in turn determines their *pre-givenness*. The 'spheres' are:

1 The absolute sphere 'of the real and valuable, of the sacred'.

2 'The sphere of a co-world, ante-world and post-world', e.g. history and society.

3 Spheres of 'the outer and inner world' which include the sphere of one's body and its environment—I believe this is a distinction which Scheler meant to refer to social-psychological knowledge.

4 Sphere of that 'meant as alive'. (Biology?)

5 Sphere of the 'corporeal inanimate world which is dead and appears as dead'. (Physics, etc.)[11]

Given these three anxioms, Scheler was able to argue that:[12]

> the sociological character of all knowledge, of all the forms of thinking, perception, cognition, is indubitable: not, of course, the content of all knowledge and still less its objective validity [which was given by the 'spheres' and their essential determination] but the *selection* of its objects according to the *ruling social interest perspective* . . . the 'forms' of the mental acts by which knowledge is won are always and *necessarily sociologically* co-conditioned i.e. by the structure of society.

As remarked earlier, systematized or sophisticated knowledge meant to Scheler a 'relatively artificial or "educated" world-view' and in his demonstration of the co-conditioning process, he developed a typology of these world-views ordered in terms of their artificiality:

Least artificial   1 Myth and legend
                    2 Natural folk-language
                    3 Religious knowledge
                    4 Mystical knowledge
                    5 Philosophic-metaphysical knowledge
                    6 Positive knowledge of mathematics, natural
                      science and *Geisteswissenschaften*
Most artificial   7 Technological knowledge.

The change of such knowledge being directly proportionate in its rate to the degree of artificiality: clearly myth and legend, being least artificial, are the closest to a 'relatively natural *Weltanschauungen*' and are thus less open to social change than technological knowledge which is the province of a small social group and open to fairly rapid change.

Though he repudiated positivism, Scheler employed an evolutionary theory of knowledge in terms of its concrete manifestations: as societies became more complex and developed their material resources they also developed differentiated knowledge systems. He talked about this process of social and cognitive evolution in terms of a theory of drives which provided the translation between '*Realfaktoren*'—material forces—and '*Idealfaktoren*'—intellectual and normative systems. There were, he believed, three main human

81

drives: the 'power of blood', the 'will-to-power' and the drive for 'economic profit'. But rather than existing at equal strength throughout history, they were historically and socially differentiated in their effects, each drive being predominant at a specific stage of growth of a civilization, which may be ordered into three characteristic 'phases' (there are interesting parallels between Scheler's drive theory of cultural growth, and Spengler's cyclic theories of civilization):

1 A phase of blood (i.e. kinship) relations forming the independent variable of events and determining the organizational form of groups, limiting the scope of what can happen for social and mental organization.

2 A phase of factors of political power which are directed towards activities concerning the efficacy of the state.

3 A phase in which the economy is causally primal, and 'economic factors' determine real events in the sense of opening and closing 'the sluice gates of the spirit'.[13]

Consequent upon these distinctions, one can see a role for Marx's analyses which applied, Scheler felt, to the modern period when the economic drive had replaced the 'will-to-power' of feudal society; it was thus a mistake of historical materialism to claim historical generality, since it was in error in assuming *one* independent variable (relations of production) to operate throughout history. There was in fact no one independent variable but three stages which determined the organic growth and decline of national cultures and whole civilizations.

The importance of Scheler's theory of 'co-determination' in sociology of knowledge thus rested on his distinction between material and mental factors: the *actualization* of ideas in a society is determined by prevailing material conditions, their selection as objects of knowledge in terms of the values and goals of the ruling group. Élites thus take up elements of the absolute world of ideas and spread them to the imitative masses: their actual acquisition of these ideas being dependent upon two factors, their 'general cultural ethos' and the drive structure—as Scheler put it, 'a doctrine of human drives is a *necessary presupposition* for sociology'.[14] In a sense then it is possible to understand Scheler's sociology of knowledge as in tension between three elements, also three ontologies: a philosophical reduction to an absolute realm of absolute truth and value; a physiological reduction to a theory of human drives; and a properly sociological analysis allotting causal adequacy to social structural elements. We shall return to the consequences of this tension later.

In a sense knowledge and the social-economic sphere are *both* determined by the drive structure of the élite. History can thus be seen as a result of two ahistorical spheres: *mind* absolute yet impotent, and *instinct* (or drive) powerful but directionless; the process of history becomes the acquisition of an ideal normative realm by a naturally amorphous world. The '*Idealfaktoren*' thus possess an almost 'cybernetic' control function: contrary to Marx, Scheler believed that material factors determine only the realization of 'spiritual'—or cognitive—potentials rather than contents or meanings:[15]

> It is always only the difference between the *real* works and the works that are potentially *possible* according to the laws of meaning, that can be explained by the history of real conditions and events in the progress of the history of mind. The *fatalité modifiable* of real history by no means determines, therefore, the positive *intellectual content* of the works of the mind, but it rather hinders, releases, retards or accelerates the actualization and realization of this intellectual content. To employ a metaphor: it opens and closes in a definite *manner* and *order* the sluice gates of the spirit.

In taking account of Marxism, Scheler was actually directing his remarks against one primary source: Lukács's *Geschichte und Klassenbewusstein* which had then only recently been published (1923). Lukács had tended to argue that proletarian thought was capable of producing truth, whilst bourgeois thought was in principle (because of its partiality) limited to false knowledge, ideology, on the basis of a conception of thought and knowledge as being solely class-determined. Scheler categorically denied such a premiss:[16]

> If there really was no instance in human thought which allowed one to transcend all class ideologies and interest perspectives, then all possible true knowledge would be an illusion, and all knowledge would only be a function of the deficiencies of the class struggle, as the economic interpretation of history argues.

Class *was* important, though, to a sociology of knowledge, since it functioned to an important degree as a selector of objects of knowledge and attitudes. Scheler even went as far as to differentiate between the cognitive and evaluative tendencies of 'lower-class' as against 'upper-class' thought, which he felt expressed why the masses were radical and the ruling élites conservative:[17]

Tendencies of lower class	*Tendencies of upper class*
1 Prospective time consciousness	1 Retrospective time consciousness
2 Emphasis on becoming	2 Emphasis on being

3 Mechanistic conception of the world	3 Theological conception of world
4 Philosophical realism	4 Philosophical idealism
5 Materialism	5 Spiritualism
6 Induction	6 Deduction
7 Pragmatism	7 Intellectualism
8 Optimism with regard to the future	8 Pessimism regarding the future (past is Good Old Days)
9 Search for contradictions	9 Search for identities/ harmonies
10 Emphasis on environment	10 Emphasis on heredity

Scheler did not, however, indicate as to exactly how these tendencies were developed, or indeed how they manifested themselves or were held by individuals: they were, he said, after all, general inclinations unconsciously held, the crucial point being that once made conscious they could be shaken off. To Scheler's position, which made a radical distinction between ideology and knowledge, and allotted a trans-cendent character to truth, Marxism was wrong in seeing ideology as an absolutely fixed limitation of the knowledge of a social group. Once prejudices could be elucidated through the use of sociology of knowledge, they could be consciously eradicated.

In developing a theory which served to unite materialist and idealist theories of knowledge, Scheler was attempting to show that know-ledge was not something that could be looked at as either a material or mental product alone, but as something which owed its origins and form to the socio-historical conditions in which it was pro-duced (which include, as previously described, psycho-physiological factors), the previous intellectual history of the group producing it and also the realm of absolute truth and values of which it was a part. The easiest way to demonstrate the construction of his model of 'co-determination' of knowledge and thought is to present the way in which he linked up drives, social structures and intellectual con-ditions for the three modes of cognition which constituted a typology of knowledge forms in human history: religion, metaphysics and positive science (see Figure 1).

Each knowledge-drive-organization system has a distinctive social origin; religious knowledge in social classes, metaphysical know-ledge in 'vocations', and positive scientific knowledge in 'estates'.[18]

Of course, the splitting up of knowledge into three irreducible realms gives to Scheler's sociology of knowledge the task of showing in what ways we can talk generally about them in terms of the ways they may exist in specific social structures. It should be quite clear to the reader that Scheler's definition of knowledge is fairly narrow:

	Drive	Goal	Personality type(s)	Social form
Religion	self-maintenance through salvation	salvation through God-contact	charismatic leader, 'holy man', ecclesiastic, 'homo religiosus'	church sect communion
Metaphysics	wonder at existence of the world and things (reality dependent on *absolute* being)	wisdom through intuition	wise-man sage	'school'
Positive Science	need to control nature and society	world picture of mathematical symbols made through experiment induction and deduction	'researcher —scholar'	'international scientific republic'

Figure 1 *The three modes of cognition*

it characterizes the thought of élite groups ('group mind') and is specifically dependent upon education; socialization for example being carefully distinguished from knowledge as the responsibility of the general cultural ethos of society ('group soul'). Consequently his sociology of knowledge is unspecific about generally available knowledge—a result of the critique of Marxian pan-ideologism implied by Scheler's *Ideal-und-Real-faktoren* distinction. Thus the modes of cognition which Scheler sets out give us only a partial sociology of knowledge confined to élite groups: we are left with an untheorized element of reality defined by the term 'relatively natural *Weltanschauungen*' which, though it is the basis of knowledge in theory, is not located as a practical determining element empirically. Of course there is no real attempt by Scheler to ground his sociology of knowledge in empirically available observation or even to suggest for example other than vague associations between particular posited drives and specific socio-historical systems. Schelerian sociology seems in fact to contribute most to Scheler's work as the 'Catholic Nietzsche' and as an apologist and ideologue for German élitist culture, and very little to sociology of knowledge. We shall return to this later, and discuss the general role of his sociology of knowledge in élite theory.

III

Our concluding remarks on Scheler will be brief. As is pointed out later in this work, Scheler's theory represents something of a dead end. Incapable in principle of contributing to a scientific study of the determinate connections between knowledge and social structure because of its essentialist theory of truth as the resident of an absolute and empirically unavailable realm of reality, it can only function within the terms of a philosophical discussion. And this is all, in fact, that Scheler claimed for it. He rejected in most senses of the term a social science which would look for laws of social organization or change believing that it was only the counterpart of positive natural science, and thus consigned either to the level of a limited mode of cognition or as a specific ideological representation of bourgeois society. As a writer very much influenced by Catholic theology and philosophy, Scheler embraced a corporalist and hierarchic view of how social life ought to be organized. Consequently, as well as stressing an absolute (and ultimately deistic) realm of truth and value, he was constrained to see knowledge *in the world* as something partial, and only a limited image of the true knowledge transcendentally possible. The overtly Catholic nature of his work was, however, ameliorated by his understanding of the value of Marxist approaches to social reality, although he characteristically sought to limit their validity to a specific historical and cultural location, counteracting the evolutionist paradigm of knowledge (which of course Marx, as much as Durkheim or Spencer, employs) by his inclusion of the irreducible (and *idealist*) spheres of religion and metaphysics alongside *materialist* positive science. Scheler is not, however, without followers. Within the Catholic sociology of religion movement his work is looked upon quite favourably and has been employed in a modified form by Werner Stark, who takes over the essentialist conception of truth and uses it as a foundation of his neo-Kantian and formalist approach to sociology of knowledge and religion. Stark is also, of course, a practising (and preaching, to judge by his books) Catholic.

We will end this section by a quotation from Scheler which sums up many of the strands of his work and expresses very clearly the metaphysical and almost theological cast of his theories:[19]

The human mind is not only differently filled in different epochs; it is differently constituted. In this respect there are many different truths. They all spring from the perception of the same ontic realm of ideas and value orderings, however. Hence behind all the apparently exclusive universes of validity there lies the one real dimension that imparts true validity and ultimate unity to all of them. Thus we give up as relative, as historically and sociologically dependent on the particular standpoints, all orderings of *goods, goals* and *norms* in human societies, as expressed by ethics, religion, law and art, etc., and retain nothing but the idea of the eternal logos, whose transcendent secrets cannot be explored, in the form of a metaphysical *history*, by any one nation, any one civilization or even all cultural epochs that have emerged so far but only by *all together*, including all future ones—by temporal and spatial co-operation of irreplaceable (because individual) unique cultural entities working together in complete mutual solidarity.

6 Max Weber

To the limited extent that we can call upon a 'Weberian' sociology of knowledge, any explanation of that sociology must deal pre-eminently with one important aspect of Weber's work; his conceptualization of 'rationality'. Weber saw socio-historical change as working inexorably towards a greater rationalization of human activity, not all at once or in the same direction, but generally moving towards a situation of greater technical-purposive control over nature, society and culture. Those of his studies which can be seen within the framework of a sociology of knowledge concern themselves primarily with this topic, and involve a consideration of religion, law, music and art. Weber treated all of these as demonstrating (at least in the West) an increasing rationalization, the reasons for which are dependent partially on criteria intrinsic to these knowledge forms, and partially on the influence of socially produced interests. Part at least of the development of religion is due to the degree to which prophets, holy men and other charismatic figures had their religious movements routinized and institutionalized in accordance with the social interests of both their adherents, and church and state. To deal with a Weberian sociology of knowledge with any real adequacy thus requires us to consider Weber's conceptualization of the types of rationality and his methodology of sociological study, as a way into seeing his sociology as a whole.

All of Weber's sociological work is consciously anti-Marxist, though at several points Weber does indicate his acceptance of some Marxian notions. There is a current general movement to see a closer association between Marx (i.e. rather than Marxism) and Weber than has hitherto been possible (cf. A. Giddens's work, especially *Capitalism and Modern Social Theory*, Cambridge, 1971), but it does seem to me to founder at a number of points, which crucially involve the theorization of the relationship between society and culture: I shall deal with this during my general discussion of Weber. It is enough to state here that the important concept of 'elective affinity' which Weber employed to provide the bridge between material interests, social formations and ideas, specifically excludes any Marxian notion of the pre-givenness of the structural variables characteristic of socio-historical periods. Though Weber was centrally involved in study of capitalism and its rational, Western development, he approached the social system of capitalism in a way somewhat different to Marx: for the crucial notion of Marxian theory—capitalism as the production of surplus value by the exploitation of the labour time of the worker —is almost completely missing from Weber's conceptualization of capitalism, which concentrates pre-eminently on the market relations and ethos of calculative rationality. Weber *does* take socio-technical substrata as requisite to a sociological analysis, but only as *one* aspect of that analysis: a complete explanation (or the nearest that can be got to one, since Weber did not believe in the possibility of complete explanation) would thus involve specification of the interdependencies of social-structural variables; interests of social groups; and ideas. All three fuse into specific configurations at certain times, but none is held to be determining of that configuration; structure sets the conditions and limits, but within that wide field ideas gain an affinity with the interests of a social group, and may thus serve to alter the structural conditions, so as to lead to a new framework of action and meaning.

II

There is one important reason why Weber's sociological theory is antithetical to a sociology of knowledge, if by that we mean a theoretical approach which contains as its basic postulate a determinate relationship between social structure and knowledge. For Weber's intellectual heritage, especially neo-Kantianism, tended to enforce a separation of knowledge and social or material elements, which derived from the initial Kantian division of phenomena and noumena, on a prioristic grounds. This was developed into an important methodological distinction in German thought (and which Marx was trying to overcome by transcending mind and matter in *practice*) that there was one set of methods for the natural sciences, open to causal explanations, and another set of methods for the 'cultural' sciences—including sociology—which were dependent on intuitional criteria, explanation being conducted hermeneutically in terms of *meaning*. It follows that what Kant called things-in-themselves (natural phenomena) were specifically separated from social phenomena in terms of the knowledge we can have of them, for a thing-in-itself is basically unknowable; it is only available to us in terms of our cognitive apparatus—the categories. But this means that the mode of understanding social phenomena—other consciousness—must involve specification of meaning-relationships, for other people are not things-in-themselves as such, but reasoning individuals like us. Kant had also held that the laws which ordered the physical world were discontinuous with regard to the human world, the natural corollary being that knowledge of human life could not be conducted in terms of causal explanation at all, since it did not conform to natural laws but was in principle *free*. Methodological individualism is the logical consequence of this, the tendency to see aggregates as solely that, rather than as wholes which possess super-individual qualities. As an epistemology, Kantianism denies significance to the empirical in so far as the determination of cognitive axiomatic frameworks is concerned, for it is based in the assumption that knowledge cannot be explained experientially. The development of post-Kantian philosophy, especially romantic idealism in the work of Fichte, Hegel and Schelling, moved away from this in allotting a historical character to knowledge: reason thus was not seen to be limited by categorial structures, but was open to a historical transformation. The consequence of this view was not however a movement towards (except in Feuerbach and Marx) an empirical study of culture, but rather the creation of vast metaphysical systems in which reason assumed the status of an 'absolute idea' (Hegel). Idealism, thus conceived, exerted a considerable influence on the development of legal, economic, historical, aesthetic and sociological thought in Germany, and led directly to the concepts of *'Geists'*, or historically unique cultural totalities, as the reference points of empirical study. Thus Marx could see capitalism as a world historical *system* of social relations precisely because he took over the idealist conception of *'Weltgeist'* (world spirit) and transformed it from a metaphysical to an empirical concept: the actions of individuals must be seen not in terms of their own stated or perceived ends, but as components of a wider system which has compulsive power over them. The forces and mode of production give rise to particular social relations of production, to which all individuals are more or less subject, and which they can themselves control only by collective action to change the ownership of the means of production. Socio-economic systems, to Marx, have a super-empirical nature, a holism which implies that social change means the transformation of the entire social system. Marxism thus becomes a critique of both Hegelian and Kantian idealism, which both received extensive reformulation towards the end of the nineteenth

90

century. Thus neo-Kantianism and Dilthean *'Geisteswissenschaften'* represent an updating of idealism to deal with historical and social phenomena, the subjects of the 'cultural sciences'. The great methodological debate in Germany, around the turn of the century, over the correct method for social/cultural science was fought out between these two positions; neo-Kantianism, in the work of Windelband, Rickert, Cohen and Natorp, argued for an *a priori*, logical distinction between social and natural science in terms of their methods. Thus natural science dealt with generally repeatable, lawlike phenomena and employed a generalizing or 'nomothetic' method, whilst cultural science analysed meaning-complexes, and the unique non-repeatable phenomena of human history using a qualitative and individualizing, or 'idiographic', method (the terms 'nomothetic' and 'idiographic' are Windelband's). Dilthey however opposed *'Naturwissenschaften'* and *'Geisteswissenschaften'* in terms of their subject matter: whilst the neo-Kantians had seen reality as indivisible except in terms of logical categories, Dilthey thought that science could be classified wholly in terms of the differentiated subject matters it dealt with. Weber rejected all three positions, Marxism, neo-Kantianism and Dilthey's historical relativism: they were all either empirically or methodologically inadequate to an understanding of science in general and social-historical science in particular. However, Weber does accept some of each of these positions: methodologically he tends to be anti-holistic:[1]

> Interpretative sociology considers the individual and his action as the basic unit, as its 'atom'—if the disputable comparison for once may be permitted. In this approach, the individual is also the upper limit and the sole carrier of meaningful conduct. . . . In general, for sociology, such concepts as 'state', 'association', 'feudalism' and the like, designate certain categories of human interaction. Hence it is the task of sociology to reduce these concepts to 'understandable' action, that is, without exception, to the actions of participating individual men.

Weber also takes up one aspect of Dilthey's approach to cultural science—the concept of *verstehen* (understanding) as the primary method of apprehending actors' meanings—since his methodological individualism led him to see social phenomena as involving relations between socially constructed meanings. Finally, he recognizes the validity of some aspects of Marx's approach to the interpenetration of social and economic variables; but he proposes analytic categories to sophisticate the analysis. In most Marxian analysis, there is no distinction between 'economic', 'economically determined' and 'economically relevant' phenomena or actions; everything is reduced to a single universal causal sequence, and it was this possibility in Marxism to which Weber was centrally opposed. Now whether Weber was right in his interpretation of Marx (he was of course unable to read any of the 'Hegelian' texts, such as the 1844 manuscripts, or the *Grundrisse*) he did see himself as going beyond the limitations of economic determinism. In this context it is as well to remember that Weber did *not* oppose causal explanation in sociology: on the contrary, he saw the erection of a properly scientific sociology as centrally concerned with the specification of causal links among social phenomena. However, causality was not for Weber something that could be reduced in sociological explanation to any one set of phenomena, such as the economic variables, but rather involved a multiplicity of causal factors. Thus, whilst Weber could recognize the importance of economic variables, and the ways in which they could limit or extend the contexts in which social action took place, he saw that social action had itself a power which could influence and change the economic variables, or could affect and be affected by other non-economic variables. It is in this sense that he distinguishes economic, political and military power, whilst Marx merely allows political power to be the expression of the control of economic forces: Weber is careful to look into the various institutional components of social systems, and even breaks down the notion of economic class into a multidimensional theory of stratification. But despite his opposition to Marx's philosophy of history and social theory, Weber has had a comparable influence on the development of the sociology of knowledge: Lukács and Mannheim, to take only two examples, owe a great deal to Weber. We are left then with a problem—why should the work of a sociologist never directly involved in the sociology of knowledge have been so influential for it, and this in the face of a specific work (*The Protestant Ethic and the Spirit of Capitalism*) which *can* be taken to oppose the Marxist analysis of religious thought as a product of material circumstances? As I have been at pains to point out throughout the present work, any sociology of knowledge properly termed is committed to postulate a determinate relationship between social structure and knowledge, allotting some causal significance necessarily to the former. Weber's idealist background led him to an approach which in some crude senses negates a sociology of knowledge—*if* we interpret him as defining religion, say, independently of its societal contexts, or law, music, etc. as only *contingently* social phenomena. Now it is not necessary to treat Weber so crudely, for his aim was always to investigate the relationship between 'ideal' and 'material' phenomena but in a way which did not make either of them the basis of the other: all social phenomena, said Weber, are produced by the mutual interaction of ideal factors—ideas, values, beliefs— and material factors, such as the mode of economic production, disposition of social groups or even climatic environment. What sociology should be doing, he thought, is to find a method by which such analyses can be carried out, and that is why he placed such a premium upon the development of causal explanations, though he did recognize the difficulties of achieving such explanations given the existing state of development of social science. In this context he allied a certain amount of pragmatism to his Kantian rationalism: knowledge, he felt, could never be total and always stops short of a complete understanding of reality, so that our ways of producing knowledge are not limited by any idea of the 'correct' way to produce knowledge. Any real science is defined not by the nature of its methods or any strict conception of its subject matter, but by the problems it deals with. His methodology, as a result of these views, contains two main elements: an attempt to produce an analysis of the effective causes of social phenomena, and a hermeneutic technique for producing analytic concepts. 'Interpretative sociology' is consequently a very apt characterization of how Weber worked: he wishes to *understand* the social context of human action in the way in which its 'meaning' (both objective and subjective) as 'social' can be generalized into types *and* laws. The means by which the understanding of meaning is generalized by reference to empirical reality is by means of 'ideal-types', abstract conceptualizations which are a mixture of actual empirical observations and *a priori* assumptions concerning social phenomena. Ideal-types are thus neither descriptions nor hypotheses, but tools to be used in the conceptual and explanatory organization of a confusing social reality—they allow us a way in to understanding the problems we wish to explain. But their status, and their role in producing explanations is problematic. In one sense the notion of an ideal-type as an abstraction from reality derives straightforwardly from what we have referred to as Weber's philosophical background, Kantianism: all scientific concepts are 'unreal' or abstract in the sense that they are selections from a concreate reality which can itself be only known incompletely.[2] The concept of ideal-type also contains the notion of understanding by intuition, involving the consideration of ideas, norms and 'value-concepts' as subjects of sociological study, and whilst Weber felt that analysis of these subjective phenomena was requisite to his work, he was at the same time opposed to the possible reduction of that work to the level of idealist theory which forced him to define ideal-types as conceptually necessary but empirically unreal. The ideal-type is in fact a way of including both individualizing and generalizing methods within one instrument; and it also by way of this function manages to produce a linkage between social-structural variables and cognitive, evaluative or simply cultural variables. Ideal-types become a way of indicating possible connections or comparisons between general social facts, ranging from entire social systems to small groups, and groups of ideas and values defined in terms of individual manifestations—the writings of Baxter or Calvin for example, as indications of the 'Protestant ethic' which can be used to open up the ways in which that ethic came to be espoused by particular social groups and thus have some influence over their social action and the organization of their social and economic relationships.

In treating Weber's types of rational social action analytically, we must have recourse to the clarified notion of ideal-type, and understand the complexity of its relationship to Weber's substantive sociological work. Weber's own definition of the ideal-type is instructive at this point:[3]

> [The ideal-type] is achieved by enhancing unilaterally one or more points of view, and by bringing together a mass of single phenomena, some extensive, some hidden, some more so, some less, some not at all, which combine with those unilaterally accentuated points of view in a uniform set of ideas. It is not a representation of the real, but it attempts to lend significant means of expression to its representation. It is meant to point the way for the formation of hypotheses. It is a structure of ideas which has the significance of a purely ideal delimiting concept, by which reality is measured for the clarification of certain significant elements in its empirical content, and with which it is compared . . . [the ideal-type] is a Utopia, and for the historian there is an increasing task to establish in each single case how near or how far apart reality and the ideal stand . . . [it will] guide research in a way which leads to a sharper comprehension [of the problem at issue]. If it leads to this result, it has fulfilled its logical purpose in manifesting its own unreality.

—and we have to be clear that the ideal-type is *not* an 'average', an 'ideal essence' behind social reality, or an ideal, in the sense of normative-evaluative, concept (though it may be used to analyse such concepts): it is ideal only in the sense of being a 'pure, *logical* type'.

Now, the types of social action which Weber distinguished are important not just for their relevance to his general sociology, but also for their possible use as types of knowledge-system, as in fact ways of linking up social action with the knowledge produced by that action and also that requisite to it. Thus, most clearly, we can say that what Weber calls '*Zweckrational*' action—technical-purposive (instrumental) action—is most appropriately employed to characterize the mode of cognition employed by scientists in their work. It also may describe (or, as an ideal-type, point to) the structure of scientific knowledge and the way in which it is related both to a determinate type of social activity, and a specific structural location in a social system. The beauty of the ideal-type formulation used in this respect lies in its employment as a conceptual tool which is completely 'adequate on the level of meaning' and which allows us to use it to examine both 'rational' and 'irrational' phenomena and, particularly in this context, knowledge.[4] Thus ideal-types are primarily useful for the analysis of collective meanings, ideas and values which can be related to social-structural conditions in general terms in a way which retains elements of both the objective and subjective meaning of the cognitive elements studied, but which in no way assume that knowledge (for actors) can be defined in purely logical terms.

The types of social action which Weber distinguishes between are:

1 *'Zweckrational'*—*'instrumentally rational'*—action; what might also be termed technically-purposive action for it refers to action that is determined by an actor's employment of means in relation to specific rational ends, such means involving the actor's expectation as to the behaviour of natural phenomena, and other social actors.

2 *'Wertrational'*—*'value-rational'*—action is intended by Weber to apply to action orientated in terms of some *absolute* end (e.g. human freedom, salvation, absolute virtue, beauty, etc.) which does not regard means as specifically connected to it, and cannot guarantee achievement of that end.

3 *'Affektuel'*—*affectual*—emotional action which is 'determined by the actor's specific effects and feelings'.

4 'Traditional' action; customary, habitual social action ingrained by tradition into an accepted—and almost automatic—mode of action.[5]

Coupled with this is Weber's concept of *social relationship*—the context within which a plurality of actors' behaviours takes account of each of the others' actions and is oriented in terms of that action—as Weber puts it: 'The social relationship thus consists entirely and exclusively in the existence of a probability that there will be a meaningful course of social action—irrespective . . . of the basis for this probability.'[6] Weber also discusses types of ways in which social action regularly occurs, in a sense a typology of micro-systems of action. Thus what Weber terms 'usage' is the ideal-type of regularized action natural to the actual existence and continuing practice of a specific group; whilst 'custom' is used if that practice has some long-standing customary basis. Against these two, Weber sets a third type, action 'determined by self-interest' which consists of repeated group *Zweckrational* action, where 'actors' conduct is instrumentally oriented toward identical expectations'.[7] These are the bases of social action considered rationally, in their interpenetrating relationships and as regular occurrences. But what makes social action repeatable, apart from either its customary or self-interested nature? What provides the limitations on action which we experience every day and thus provides the notion of a social order in terms of which action is more or less orientated? This can only be a *belief* in a legitimate order, Weber says (unless it is recourse to some purely coercive means), and to the extent that such a belief does govern action, then such an order exists, either as a '*convention*' or as a legal system in which deviation is restrained by the application of formal mechanisms of compliance. Thus a system of domination is produced in terms of the extent to which certain demands are recognized by social actors as legitimate and are complied with on that basis: without going into Weber's sociology of domination, it is clear that the empirical determination of social action, relationships and usage is structured in terms of the system of *legitimate* authority exerted by a recognized group of power holders. The basic mode of integration of a society thus centres around the creation of a belief in the legitimacy of the power relationships in that society: domination may initially appeal to material, affectual or ideal motives for its support, but its continued existence depends upon its ability to establish and cultivate an 'ideology', a belief by which its claim to legitimacy can be made socially acceptable.[8]

Thus, when we employ Weber's typology of social action as the basis of a sociology of knowledge, we are led into showing the relationship between action, knowledge and the form of domination (e.g. in terms of the type of claim to legitimacy—charismatic, traditional or rational–legal—which is made). It is not possible here to go into all the suggestions Weber's theoretical sociology makes towards a sociology of knowledge, since I have not the luxury of space or time to do so. Nor would it be appropriate in this work, which needs must provide merely an analytic overview of significant writers' work. In any case, we must now examine the ways in which Weber uses the central concept of 'rationalization' in his substantive work, and trace the connections between that and his theoretical adumbration of the meaningful rationality of social action, as it exists in the two works which most nearly approach a sociology of knowledge—*The Protestant Ethic and the Spirit of Capitalism* (*PESC*) and *The Rational and Social Foundations of Music* (*RSFM*).[9]

III

Both of the long essays I will discuss here share a common topic:

the process of *rationalization* which has characterized Western social development, as Weber calls it *'Entzauberung der Welt'* (disenchantment of the world). Now this process, which has been associated with the transformations of Western society, has produced a movement in all areas of life towards a greater emphasis on *'Zweckrational'* social action, at the expense of *'Wertrational'*, affectual and traditional action. But rationalization is in no sense a unitary phenomenon, or even a progressively unilinear development: capitalism itself is not even specifically rational, for 'adventurer' capitalism tends to be founded on traditional social action and exists throughout history. Modern types of capitalism in the West are specifically anti-traditional in the way that they seek profit rationally and systematically. Weber's study of Calvinist Protestantism does not assume it to be the source of rationalism, indeed, as he is careful to point out, his study of the Protestant ethic as a particular form of rationalism —the idea of a calling and of devotion to labour in it—emphasizes the extent to which those components are in fact 'irrational' in ultimate self-interest terms. What is significant is the extent to which certain ideas available in the ethics of Calvinist theology and in the other branches of 'Ascetic Protestantism' allowed the social groups which held those beliefs to act in a way which made them economically active to the extent of seeing acquisition of wealth in a rational and systematic way as an affirmation of their religious values. Labour in the social world becomes for the ascetic Protestant loaded with the highest positive ethical evaluation, and at the same time the principal means by which the Calvinist could alleviate his radical uncertainty concerning his salvation.

Thus the evolution of Calvinist theology is completely tied up for Weber with the process of disenchantment of the world. Protestantism replaces the loose discipline and semi-magical ritual of the traditionalistic Catholic church with a coherent and continuous discipline and a repugnance of magical elements. Whereas Lutheranism, because of its social and political location, becomes a Protestant legitimation of the *status quo*, Calvinism with its stress on a world created solely for God, whose motives are beyond human understanding, and a belief in the predestination of an elect for eternal grace, created such a radical break with both traditional religion and Lutheranism that it set its adherents a monumental task in finding a meaning in their lives and in the world. Thus what Calvinism produces is a social-psychological drive of such intensity and directness —the radical uncertainty of salvation—that it constitutes a positive element in the development of a specifically capitalist *'Geist'* (or *system* of values). Uncertainty about predestination is itself a sign of its lack; the Calvinist is thus led to hold himself out as one of the chosen in order to alleviate his feelings of great inner loneliness and thus eliminate any notion of salvation through church or sacraments (and thus provide the logical conclusion of the '*Entzauberung der Welt*'). His social activity in the world can be orientated solely for the glory of God: only intense activity in a calling (and, moreover, a gainful calling) can give certainty of grace—'God helps those who help themselves'. Thus, only the rational acquisition of wealth could create the conviction of salvation for the Calvinist. Moreover, the approach to the calling was itself of religious significance: it had to be methodical and systematic, a constant application of woeful activity towards desired and instrumental ends. In that sense economic activity, which was both gainful and could be carried out methodically, was the most obvious type of calling.

The conjunction of these elements in 'Ascetic Protestantism' Weber demonstrates most forcefully in his analysis of the principal predestinarian sects, and in the writings of Richard Baxter (Weber also refers to Spener, the Pietist, and the Quaker Barclay): they indicate very directly the way in which religious values constrain activity towards rational, calculative and profitable capitalism. Baxter stressed that the *enjoyment* of wealth, rather than its possession, was a great sin; only ceaseless activity serves God's will, and time-wasting as well as unwillingness to work is a great sin. A stress on hard labour and sexual asceticism is part of this ethical system, which also specifically demands work in a *calling*, systematic, methodical and rational—all else is worthless. There is a positive injunction also to choose the most gainful calling or callings, for both wishing to be poor and desiring charity are ethically wrong. This Puritan value-system opposed enjoyment and hedonistic consumption, reserving expenditure solely for necessary and practical things (defined by the calling). Altogether it functioned so as to encourage acquisitive activity in a continuous rational way which accumulated capital that could only be used for further investment. Coupled with this entrepreneurial function, the Ethic also legitimizes an unequal distribution of wealth in terms of signs of grace and positively supports the notion that low wages encourage the productivity of those who cannot aspire to membership of the elect: 'Now naturally the whole ascetic literature of almost all denominations is saturated with the idea that faithful labour, even at low wages, on the part of those whom life offers no other opportunities, is highly pleasing to God.'[10] It is clear, says Weber, that all of the elements he isolated within the secular—but still ascetic—spirit of capitalism of Franklin exist in an earlier religious form. An 'elective affinity' exists between the religious ethic of ascetic Protestantism and the spirit of capitalism, in the sense that the social group of Calvinists, etc., found that the ideas of their theology were consonant with the practice of a certain type of social activity: ultimately this practice, disengaged from its specifically religious location meant that the ideal of asceticism, of rational and systematic labour, conformed with the *interests* of a social stratum (the bourgeoisie) keen to advance itself economically and politically. Nowadays the rational ascetic pursuit of profit is almost wholly disengaged from religion, since it no longer requires its ethical support. Weber saw clearly that ideas only have a reality in so far as they are linked to a system of social action. The significance of Calvinist and ascetic Protestant theology thus lies in its historical role in a precise social context: and the genesis of a socio-economic system—capitalism—can be seen to lie in the development of a rationalized and disenchanted religion. Weber is not saying that capitalism as such has an 'ideal' foundation, but that it is crucial to see that the development of ideas, values and interests which are characteristic of a modern, legal-rational capitalism, were generated by the roles certain religiously orientated groups played in institutionalizing a mode of social activity which had important psychological consequences for them. Clearly, we cannot see ascetic Protestantism as simply a set of ethical principles, in the same way that we cannot see capitalism as just a 'spirit': both have precise structural locations within determinate social systems. What Weber's suggestions of a sociology of knowledge produce is an approach which stresses the role of social selection of ideas and values. We are unable to understand the rationalized structure of modern society and modern knowledge forms without a reference to the role certain systems of ideas have played in the activity of groups strategic to the processes of social change. What characterizes all or most of these groups in the West has been the tendency to 'rationalization', which has itself characterized the nature of their social activity.

In his essay on music, Weber gives an indication as to how his analysis of the social processes underlying rationalization links up cultural with social-structural changes. Western music is distinctive in terms of its possession of two important elements: its systematic rationality always in tension with melodicism, the irrationality of 'chord-alien' tones; and its exclusively characteristic polyphonality which emphasizes the study of counterpoint as essential to musical production as an autonomous art. Rationalization of music thus involves both technical and social transformations for Weber; polyphonic musical rhythm and the institutionalization of a social group of musicians/composers/instrument-makers as practitioners of a cultural specialization. Unfortunately, only the final section of the essay deals with the social, as distinct from the purely rational, foundations of music. However, Weber does give a coherent analysis of the interrelated nature of technical changes involving the sophistication of resonating bodies—an exclusively Western invention—which provides the basis for all modern string instruments. On the one hand rationalization was achieved by practical developments—the eventual production of standardized notation, and specific instruments—and on the other by changes in the social organization and societal role of music. Thus certain instruments, notably the organ, which is the basis of all keyboard instruments, have functioned in specific institutional settings. The organ has, since the rise of the monasteries, been a religious instrument (before then, its use was mainly secular, as a court instrument), and the main vehicle of musical rationalization initially: 'Where the organ penetrated in to the Monasteries it became representative of all technical musical rationalization within the church. Also important, it was used for musical instruction.'[11] The organ, by its greater association with religion—the centre of all medieval knowledge production—received a continuous development: by 1200 it was capable of three octaves; in the thirteenth century theoretical treatises were beginning to be written on it and by the fourteenth century its role in cathedrals was almost universal. Technical development accompanied its enhanced role and with the development of the windchest it was able to work harmonically such that singing by many voices (polyvocality) could be ordered in terms of it. Western polyphonality thus has a great deal to owe to the organ, and to its social and economic patronage by the church: 'In a period without any market, the Monastery organization was the only possible base on which [the organ] could prosper.'[12] This meant that the task of building an organ was handled by those who were also players of the instrument: the builders consequently having a considerable influence on musical rationalization. Importantly, the men who did this were in many cases secular organ builders: it was their practical knowledge and ability which most influenced the development of organ music and technique. However, the organ remained an ecclesiastical instrument devoted to art music in the Catholic church, specifically distinguished from the singing of laymen—it is only quite recently (since the seventeenth century) that it has accompanied the congregation. Thus, ascetic Protestantism —especially Pietists and Lutherans—tried to change the role of the organ into an accompaniment of the congregation, which turned it away from any further influence on art music, or certainly diminished that influence.

The development of a specifically orchestrated, secular music in the sixteenth century itself freed music from the guild organization of musicians and manufacturers of the feudal period which had limited technical development (whilst making it possible in some collective context) in terms of a fixed market. The establishment of musical roles in the rise of court orchestras, and the development of humanistic music theory leads to, Weber says, the attempt to rationalize instruments for orchestras. The demand of the court orchestras of the sixteenth and seventeenth centuries, both in technical and aesthetic terms, produced a set of standardized string instruments—violin, 'cello, viola—which were melodically suited to Renaissance music, and provided, once their roles were established, the foundations of both modern orchestral and chamber music.

The rise of the piano, from its more limited antecedents the clavichord and clavecin, signifies one important element in the secular rationalization of Western music, which has developed an economic base in terms of both the manufacture of pianos and the creation of a sheet-music industry: as Weber notes, the piano was (and to a certain extent still is) a feature of northern European middle-class homes. Indeed, 'pianistic culture' is essentially Nordic, Weber says, because the piano as an indoor instrument is suited to the life-style of the northern middle classes, centred on the house. In southern Europe, the piano is nowhere near as important (though it was invented in Italy) either musically or as a significant part of middle-class furniture.

IV

The way in which Weber handles the conceptualization of his theoretical and substantive sociology, leads, as I have shown, towards a non-determinate analysis of the relationship between social structure and knowledge. In any case, for Weber, society is two things —meaningful social action organized in terms of social relationships of a regularized nature, and power. Thus material factors, and especially economic organization, have a secondary role in the explanation of social change, for neither the forms of social action, the structures of social relationships, nor the system of imperative co-ordination can be deduced from economic relationships, the level of technological development, or even the social relations of production. These can be taken account of as limiting, or partially causal variables: the real elucidation of social phenomena comes from determining how the constellation of important factors links together in the actual empirical case. Ideas may themselves enter into a sociological analysis as distinct elements, which are connected with material interests of social groups at a later stage. Hence a Weberian sociology of knowledge is committed to allotting some autonomy to ideas or knowledge, in the explanation of any historical and social reality. Thus whilst it is impossible to comprehend Weber's theory of social change without reference to the structural and material conditions of rationalization, that process is itself unthinkable without the realization that the development of rational concepts and systems of thought is not the result of a reflection of material factors, nor simply the superstructural ideology of a specific socio-economic system (though elements of rationalization *are* ideological, as Weber recognized in his analyses both of science and rational-legal bureaucracy). We shall see the consequences of this in our discussion of Mannheim's sociology of knowledge.

7 Durkheim

When we approach the problem of discussing a characteristically Durkheimian sociology of knowledge, we are almost immediately faced with the realization that, as Parsons pointed out, there is a fundamental tension in Durkheim's work between determinism and voluntarism, and between positivism and idealism.[1] This in part derives from the fact that Durkheim located his sociology of knowledge in his study of religion and as a result it does not exist separate from that other enterprise. But this secondary location does have one virtue in that it makes clear Durkheim's methodology at the outset: in treating religion as a necessarily collective and thus social phenomenon he locates the sociological conditions of knowledge in similarly collective phenomena. Religion, then, is in the best positivist tradition a less developed form of scientific knowledge, and all our categories of understanding flow from it, or rather *through* it, for religion is but the symbolic representation of society and a cognitive expression of the relationship between human social organization and its natural environment. But the treatment of knowledge as coterminous with religion—or at least, the *categories* of knowledge rather than its precise content—leads directly into the methodological and epistemological difficulties to which we have referred. These derive from (1) Durkheim's methodological orientation, and (2) his consequent conceptualization of society and the 'social'. We will discuss the Durkheimian sociology of knowledge with regard to these two elements, and we will use three main works by Durkheim to illustrate our points: *The Rules of Sociological Method* (1895), *Primitive Classification* (1901–2), and *The Elementary Forms of the Religious Life*; *EFRL* (1912). However, we will not exclude some consideration of Durkheim's other major works—*The Division of Labour in Society* (1893) and *Suicide* (1897).

To an important degree Durkheim developed his sociological theory within the context of two differentiated philosophical traditions. Methodologically, Durkheim conflates positivism and organicism.[2] Now, in principle, the two are not mutually exclusive: positivism, as a reformulated empiricism, merely stresses the rule that the explanation of phenomena must be in terms of those phenomena themselves, and not resort to extra-empirical 'facts'. Organicism goes *beyond* this in constructing its conception of the world on an organic model which stresses the connection, or analogy, between society and biological organisms. Society, to organicism, thus has a life of its own over and above those of its members; it is an holistic entity. Positivism *may* be anti-holistic in the sense of leading to a radically conceived methodological individualism, as in the work of Mill. But certainly in Comte's original association of positivism and organicism the two were taken as complementary, largely because positivism was not then completely associated with a straitened conception of scientific method. Despite reasonable but not insurmountable philosophical differences between positivism and organicism, however, the political consequences of the two positions are sufficient to make their inclusion within a social theory problematic. Positivism and the methodological individualism which it connotes are both a product of liberal radicalism, and have their roots in the political philosophy of the Enlightenment: it has precise and important links with both empiricism and materialism. Organicism, on the other hand, was profoundly conservative in its basic elaboration and particularly so in the work of de Bonald and de Maistre, who stressed the superiority of society over individual as an antidote to the corrosive idea that society could be rationally constructed; society and its consequences—e.g. language—were divinely created and were basically unchangeable: 'Individual reason and experience must be justified in terms of the collective historical experience of mankind. Social structure can be modified; it cannot be created or destroyed.'[3] Organicism is thus both *holistic* and *idealist* precisely because of its political orientation. Society, rather than the individual, is the real and ultimate being. But society is conceived here not as a material or phenomenal entity first and a cultural or normative entity second: society to organicism is a primarily idealist conception in which the actual structural organization of its units is subordinate to some organizing ideal (cf. Hegel, Comte).

Durkheim resonates the consequences of both traditions in his work: early on, organicism is tempered by positivism (*The Rules of Sociological Method*; *Division of Labour in Society*); in the later work the reverse is true and organicism comes to overwhelm positivism, especially in *The Elementary Forms of the Religious Life.*

What results from these two analytically important elements is a correspondence theory of knowledge. For Durkheim, societies are organized in relation to the human needs of their members, and the social solidarity which characterizes them may be differentiated in terms of their size and complexity: at an early stage people are held together by the fact that their lives and modes of living are very similar, their solidarity is 'mechanical', a simple response to the shared conditions of social life which exists at the level of 'collective consciousness'. With a larger population, society becomes more differentiated and complex and a new source of solidarity is requisite —'mechanical' collective consciousness is now inadequate to the task of producing social integration—and the division of labour becomes the primary focus of 'organic solidarity', since advanced and complex societies most completely approximate to the conception of society as organism.[4] Hence, society is conceived as a system which seeks to perpetuate itself as a living body in which social action by groups and individuals must be seen in the context of the needs of the system. Sociology, as a positive science, deals with this aspect of society, and has a distinctive subject matter in so far as social phenomena exhibit both a super-individual and functionally coercive reality. Now knowledge (and thought of any type) does not exist apart from the social existence of men, and since society, though we can conceive of it as having an external power over men, is real only in so far as it exists in the collective consciousness, then knowledge, beliefs, ideas are simply aspects of that collective consciousness, whose basis is the form of society itself. Consequently, concepts and the categories of understanding are not given, but are created by the facts of social life; in short, the forms which thought takes are constructed as *representations* of social organization in terms of its collective nature. Society is thus a moral collectivity, and the analysis of the social conditions of knowledge must logically proceed from an understanding of the way in which society receives its first systematic conceptualization as a collective representation: religion. Reinforcing this substantive interest in religion as the most fundamental expression of social solidarity is the positivism with which Durkheim orients his methodology. Religion palpably exists as a way in which men at all levels of social development orient their lives and carve up the world into sacred and profane areas; it has a constraining effect on their action and is as a result a *social fact*. Whatever science might say about the veridicality of the claims religious thought makes about the world, its social existence is irrefutable. Nothing which actually exists can be, to a positivist, 'wrong': as a social fact it is something requiring explanation as to the reasons for its persistence and the various historically differentiated forms which it takes. Durkheim's sociology of religion cannot in consequence be seen as anything like a *critique* of religion: 'it is an essential postulate of sociology that a human institution cannot rest upon an error or a lie, without which it could not exist',[5] and thus as religion is a human institution, it is 'true' in so far as it expresses human needs and human existence.

As was pointed out above, positivism and organicism have clear political correlatives which we can translate into ontological statements about human (social) nature: positivism postulates voluntarism in the sense that it allows men the possibility of choice in the structure of their social organization since it is anti-holistic. Organicism, and idealism in general, disallows voluntarism: it is determinist in making individuals subject to the superior individual—society—and it methodologically constrains the sociologist to conceptualize his subject matter in holistic terms. It is against this potentially confusing background that we have to see Durkheim's sociology of knowledge, for it displays all the contradictions that such an eclecticism can produce.

II

The methodological basis of all Durkheim's major work is contained in *The Rules of Sociological Method*. Therein Durkheim sought to present his positivist organicism (which Parsons calls, in his *Structure of Social Action* (pp. 351 ff.), '*sociologistic* positivism') as a coherent and scientific approach to the study of society. Its themes, briefly stated, are these:

1 The data of sociology are susceptible to a naturalistic explanation: 'The first and most fundamental rule is: *Consider social facts as things.*'[6]

2 The data of sociology can be delineated in terms of their *exteriority* to the individual: they are things in the same sense that natural phenomena are things, not open to change in their basic structures. In the terms of positivism they are also exterior to the individual in the sense of being 'objective' realities, delineated from *individual* facts which are 'subjective' realities.

3 And following on from the above points is that which stresses the coercive power of social facts as one of their most distinctive qualities: 'types of conduct or thought are not only external to the individual but are, moreover, endowed with coercive power, by virtue of which they impose themselves upon him, independent of his individual will.'[7]

Constraint is therefore an intrinsic characteristic of social facts but not the chief definer of their 'social' nature; for, Durkheim says, we can distinguish between individual and social facts. Universality alone does not make social facts social: 'It is, however, the collective aspects of the beliefs, tendencies and practices of a group that characterize truly social phenomena.'[8] Social facts thus have a reality of their own. But that is not to say that 'social' means 'material' facts. On the contrary, Durkheim maintains that society is not a material entity at all, but 'psychic': 'social life is constituted wholly of collective representations',[9] and we must interpret this to mean that he saw society as a fundamentally normative system, a structure of beliefs and values which constrained men to act in certain ways with the ultimate goal (recognized or not) of reproducing the society in a more or less stable form. But whilst he conceptualizes society as an 'ideal'—a system of social relationships oriented about certain ideas and values—this does not mean to say that Durkheim reduces sociological explanation to purely psychological phenomena:[10]

> *The determining cause of a social fact should be sought among the social facts preceding it and not among the states of the individual consciousness* . . . [the conception of social fact specifically implying a functional analysis here] . . . *the function of a social fact ought always to be sought in its relation to some social end.*

Hence, though psychology can provide a stepping-off point for sociology, it cannot go any way towards explanation of collective phenomena: social facts require a sociological science to understand them.

Clearly Durkheim is led to postulate a particular sort of social entity as the subject of sociological research—the 'group mind' and its manifestations as 'collective representations'. This leads directly to an approach which treats knowledge and social structure as inextricably connected for it locates in 'the social' the source of all generally available knowledge. The 'collective habits', as Durkheim calls them, are the basis of all moral and legal rules, values, aesthetic standards, political and religious beliefs which do not exist as simply individual manifestions but instead as the *rules* behind individual things. Social facts, then, are characteristically coercive, and collective in the sense of existing *apart* from independent manifestations; the scientific method by which these facts are to be apprehended and explained is empiricist. Durkheim does not believe in a deductive science, or the requisiteness of theory prior to research, and he differentiates between science and ideology in terms of a dichotomy between starting from 'the facts' and starting from ideas about the facts. Empiricism, taking facts as givens and constructing theory inductively, is the method of science, whereas starting from ideas about society to produce deductive statements is the method of ideology. Of course, Durkheim is somewhat naïve in this: his

107

characterization of social facts itself proceeds from non-empirical assumptions about social solidarity, and the belief that society requires its order to be produced and maintained by coercive means. Though Durkheim repudiates it, sociology can only advance through analysis of its concepts prior to an appeal to the given. In social life reality is structured by our concepts as much as it exists independent of our existence: we must modify our concepts in the light of empirical evidence, but 'the facts' cannot determine our concepts in advance. Durkheim was quite correct to contrast his work with that of Comte and Spencer, which dealt with the 'ideas' behind state, family, contract, etc. as if they were some actualization of an immanent concept, rather than dealing with those institutions as social realities. Ideas might function to some extent in producing social realities—the 'things' which are distinctively social—but it is ideological to introduce them as elements of an explanation: 'They [ideas] cannot be perceived or known directly, but only through the phenomenal reality expressing them.'[11] It follows that sociology cannot advance by studying the *idea* of morality, or of economic calculation, but only by examination of the *actual* moral rules which govern conduct or the *actual* economic organization of a society. Society, social order and the coercive power of social facts are thus empirical 'givens' to Durkheim, which are not as a result open to individual or voluntary change: positivism is thus made to reinforce organicism and the idealism which is its basis. For the 'facts' which Durkheim adduces to be social are not natural or even material facts, they are untested assumptions, a meta-theory, about the constitution of social reality. However, I will not at this stage commit myself to a criticism of Durkheim's methodology: suffice it to say that this methodological confusion is at the bottom of his sociology of knowledge.

The correspondence theory of knowledge appears in the *Rules* in so far as Durkheim attempts to characterize scientific causality as a movement between the 'surface' and the 'essence' of reality; the existence of identically repeated characteristics in phenomena he takes to necessarily produce the conclusion that they are closely connected with the nature of the thing studied, which he illustrates by reference to law: 'if to a given group of acts there is attached also the peculiarity of a penal sanction, an intimate bond must exist between punishment and the intrinsic attributes of these acts.'[12] It follows that 'collective representations' are, as social facts, the 'surface' manifestations of the social 'essence': systems of values, beliefs, norms and knowledge correspond to an underlying social reality which is their ultimate foundation.

As well as positing an empiricist (yet idealist) conception of scientific knowledge, Durkheim also cut out any subjective element from the realm of sociological analysis. Quite obviously empiricism insists on the primacy of sense-perception for producing data; positivism however goes beyond this in forcing a radical (and ultimately arbitrary) distinction between objective and subjective data, so as to exclude as far as possible the latter from science: 'We lay down as a principle that social facts lend themselves more readily to objective representation in proportion as their separation from the individual facts expressing them is more complete.'[13] Now we will see that this led Durkheim into a situation where, in his study of religion, the conceptualization of 'sacred' as distinct from 'profane' could only be couched in subjectivist terms, and which pointed away from positivism towards a voluntaristic theory of action.

III

Durkheim's first systematic attempt to deal with the issues raised in *The Division of Labour in Society*, *Suicide*, and *The Rules of Sociological Method* concerning the actual relationship between society, collective representations and human cognition appears in the long essay he wrote with Marcel Mauss, *De Quelques Formes primitives de classification* (1903).[14] Durkheim and Mauss were dealing with secondary anthropological and ethnographical data about primitive systems of classification, in an attempt to demonstrate one aspect of Durkheim's thesis that society is the basis of the categories of understanding, hitherto allotted either to individual activity—empiricism —or to inbuilt capacities of reason, as in rationalism (especially Kant, Descartes). Durkheim was convinced that his sociologism could provide an explanatory basis for the understanding of the structure of human knowledge—though not its actual contents— and the data which he and Mauss survey in the essay is intended to provide the means to a 'crucial experiment' about the genesis of the capacity of classification in social organization and physical environment.

The data surveyed, collected mostly between about 1870 and 1900 (though some is considerably older), covers Australian aborigines, Zuni and Sioux Indians, and Chinese natural philosophy. As with the later book on religion, Durkheim takes the Australian aborigines to have the most primitive form of social organization and, consequently the most simple classificatory system. The North American Indians and Chinese, though their classificatory systems are more advanced, represent elaborations on this basic classificatory schema because they possess more differentiated societies which, however, are still founded in the two-moiety system which characterizes the Australians. Durkheim employed an evolutionary schema to study the development of collective representations, locating societies along a continuum from primitive to advanced, in terms of which all could be classified. Thus aboriginal society was held to be basic social organization, the simplest form of society which was the foundation stone of all more advanced social forms. One could, in Durkheim's terms, analyse such societies so as to see where collective representations began and how they were originally produced: more complex societies and collective representations were just elaborations on that basic theme, and if the most simple society could be understood, Durkheim presumed, that would provide the means to understand highly differentiated societies like our own. The assumption that primitive society provides the simplest statement of social reality is highly questionable, as is the evolutionary schema with which Durkheim operates. However, the validity of Durkheim's method is not as important as his substantive conclusions at this stage.

Classification is a particularly appropriate topic for Durkheim since it is one of the basic categories of understanding. Yet man could not of himself individually have produced it (Durkheim ignores the possibility of genetic endowment), and things do not in nature present themselves as grouped: 'Every classification implies a hierarchical order for which neither the tangible world nor our mind gives us the model.'[15] However, all religions, even the most primitive, possess cosmologies, ways of ordering the world of nature into some sort of coherent unity. This can be seen at its most simple in the totemism of Australian tribes, which divide up into two 'moieties' comprising several clans, and containing precisely defined marriage classes associated with totemic animals of the clans, for example:

Moiety I { Marriage class A / Marriage class B } Emu clan Snake clan Caterpillar clan (etc.)

Moiety II { Marriage class A′ / Marriage class B′ } Kangaroo clan Opossum clan Crow clan (etc.)

only A–A′; B–B′ marriages being allowed. In this way the natural world is classified, so that the social organization of men is reflected in a distinction of animal species. Although most tribes have a more complex social organization than this, the two-moiety system underlies them: although there are larger numbers of clans, and more complex relationships between marriage classes, this involves a greater number of species. It is clear, Durkheim and Mauss argue, that generally speaking the Australian system employs moiety as *genus* and marriage class as *species* and thus groups natural objects 'in accordance with social groups'.[16] The authors discuss a number of examples of different tribal organization and systems of totemic classification to show that the more complex the social organization, the more complex is the presentation of the classificatory system in terms of its basic elements. One point should be noted: Durkheim and Mauss are careful to point out that classification is relatively arbitrary at this stage (a contention expressly denied by Lévi-Strauss; see especially *The Savage Mind* and *Totemism*); *inside* the totemic divisions there are no clear distinctions.

Although this system is not found everywhere in Australia, it can be shown that its basic principles continue to operate, in the sense that, for example, the right to certain controls conferred by particular totems correspond to specific social groupings, making both controls and the things associated with them part of the same class of beings. The importance of such classificatory schemata does not lie alone in their social construction, for they have a reflexive importance for the social development of these primitive tribal forms. As Durkheim and Mauss show, social changes in the tribal organization may take place in terms of the classification system itself (which underlies what Durkheim and Mauss miss in their analysis: totemism is a normative system working by naturalistic analogy to produce a system of social relationships, and is in fact the society itself, not a representation of it). Thus a tribe, becoming large, may segment into groups ordered in terms of orientations to particular elements of reality: logical relations hence mirror social relations: 'clans formed within each moiety are logically related to each other. Thus in Australia it is rare for the crow to belong to one moiety other than that of thunder, clouds and water.'[17] Fragmentation of the clan system must result, it follows, in disintegration and incoherence in the system of classification, because it denotes an incomplete totemic system: 'There is thus a close link, and not an accidental relation, between the social system and this logical system (totemism).'[18] Much greater systematization of the classificatory system, including a reliance upon analogic relational categories, is evident in the Zuni and Sioux tribes of North America. The Zuni, in fact, possess a remarkably coherent system which is very highly integrated with their social organization. Every aspect of natural reality has a precise location in an analogical relational classification, based on a division of space into seven regions which encompasses the whole universe and includes specifically social functions. Now the Zuni classification scheme is at first sight quite different from the Australian, but is based on social division of the clans within the pueblo. Even though it is a classification by topological rather than social location of totemic clans, Durkheim and Mauss insist that topography only becomes the secondary basis of classification: its primary basis is

111

the two-moiety system, the same as the Australian. In Zuni mythology, in fact, such a distinction—between the 'people of winter' and the 'people of summer'—is preserved, and points to the conclusion that the Zuni produced their advanced form of social organization by sub-division of each moiety. Thus the Zuni system 'is really a development and a complication of the Australian system', and Durkheim and Mauss discuss the Omaha tribe of the Sioux as an intermediary stage between the two systems 'thus to discern how the one developed from the other'.[19] The Omaha are intermediary because they retain both a classification by clans, and a prototypical regional system. The tribe is divided into two moieties each of five clans with patrilineal descent such that totemism is in decline. When the tribe is camped, it forms a circular site within which each clan has a specific place. The two moieties are placed to right and left of the direction of the tribe's movement such that each moiety has a semicircular area, within which each of its clans has a precise position *and* specific social functions determined by what is held to be 'subordinate to them and over which their influence is thought to be extended'.[20] Both clans and things then are orientated in terms of their social functions with regard to the centre of the camp and not in terms of specific orientations topographically derived.

It is thus possible to conclude, Durkheim and Mauss say, that classification by clans and totems precedes that by orients: also the inevitable localization of clans which results from such a system (e.g. specific clans are classified in relation to specific phenomena, and neighbouring clans by the differentials in distance or phenomena between them) leads directly on to orientational systems:[21]

> The camp has only to be oriented in a fixed way and all its
> parts are immediately oriented along with everything, things and
> people, that they comprise . . . all things in nature are . . .
> thought of as standing in fixed relations to equally fixed
> regions in space.

Such orientational systems conflate tribal and cosmic space (the pueblo is the centre of the universe to the Zuni): clearly both systems are based in the reality of the social organization of the tribe, in turn both structuring and limiting its development. It is no accidental relation that the Zuni possess both a highly systematized cognitive system and a great degree of social concentration and conservatism.

The orientational system of classical China—the foundation of Taoism—also comes under the scrutiny of Durkheim. It is infinitely complex, and as well as space and natural phenomena also contains a (binomial) classification of time: each of these elements being co-ordinated to form a vast interdependent system which produces astronomical, astrological—geomantic and horoscopic—divinatory knowledge. But despite its complexity and elaboration, still the same social foundation exists as in totemism and North American orientational classification. Social solidarity in fact can be clearly seen to play an important part in the Chinese system, since divination functions to legitimate social classifications as well as natural distinctions: mythologies, therefore, which play a significant role in divination may thus be seen as systems of classification also (which is, of course, Lévi-Strauss's stepping-off point), but ones which are importantly pre-philosophical: they can provide the *base* for a philosophical and thus ultimately scientific classificatory method.

There is a continuous development visible in human cognition for the Durkheimian perspective, which is given in the social development of whole societies. Although Durkheim and Mauss exclude any real sociological analysis from their treatment of the anthropological data, contenting themselves with a baldly stated argument which does not take account of differentials in the production of knowledge by social groups (e.g. in all of the examples, an undifferentiated society is *assumed*, in the sense that social divisions do not imply for Durkheim differential ability to influence totemic desiderata, etc.; the Australian tribes, Zuni, Sioux and Chinese society are all *assumed* to be organic wholes such that 'collective representations' may be taken as expression of those wholes). They nevertheless provide the basis of a framework for treating the social bases of cognition:[22]

> It was because men were grouped and thought of themselves
> in the form of groups, that in their ideas they grouped other
> things, and in the beginning the two modes of grouping were
> merged to the point of being indistinct. Moieties were the first
> genera, clans the first species. . . .
> Thus logical hierarchy is only another aspect of social
> hierarchy, and the unity of knowledge is nothing else than the
> very unity of the collectivity, extending to the universe.

Durkheim believed that in showing classification to be a 'collective representation' he had produced a method by which the debate between empiricism and rationalism could be resolved. For classification in primitive society, though it had a religious and mythological form, exhibited many of the speculative characteristics of scientific classification, and it followed that if one of the 'categories of understanding' could be shown to have a social base then it was in principle possible to demonstrate that the others were also 'collective representations' initially, and that their systematic development was related to changes in complexity and solidarity of social structure. So, in *EFRL*, Durkheim set out to show that primitive religion is a 'collective representation' which contains within it all of the elements of cognition, and that those elements derive essentially from the social organization and solidarity of the primitive society. Also, primitive religion—most near to being an uncomplicated and direct reflection of society—contained within it *all* the elements of 'even the most advanced' religions. The corollary to this is clear, even though Durkheim mysteriously ignores it: whatever the functional specialization of 'advanced religion', the fact that it is the basis of cognition should mean that it still has precise connections with developments in our modes of cognition. Yet, unless we are prepared to treat science or philosophy as identifiably religious, that clearly is not the case. Religion has almost no relationship with modern philosophy, and no connection whatever with science, and consequently modern production of knowledge must exist apart from the 'collective representations' of society, which religion continues to produce, as Durkheim argues. In consequence we must see the Durkheimian sociology of knowledge as being highly limited: it cannot in principle take account of 'modern' knowledge, or even knowledge produced in relatively low-level civilizations, because of its reliance upon a conception of knowledge as a *reflection* of social organization. It is, thus, a sociology of 'primitive knowledge', or rather a sociology of various forms of undifferentiated knowledge; science, specifically, is beyond its grasp.

The reasons for this failure lie at two levels. First, Durkheim's positivism constrains him to a correspondence theory of knowledge oriented to a particular type of corresponding relationship—society: religion, which excludes the possibility of a more sophisticated sociology of knowledge relating knowledge-producing groups to the type or function of the knowledge they produce and its social consequences. Second, his organicism or extreme sociologism leads to a treatment of societies as organic wholes founded on a shared and *equally available* normative system: the division of labour, for example, is not a potentially divisive mechanism at all, but merely an advanced method of ensuring social solidarity within a complex organic whole (my point being that it can have *both* consequences, rather than one alone). Thus the primacy of social control—social facts as exterior, coercive agents—in Durkheim's sociology produces a focus upon 'collective representations' as normative systems which ignore differences in the amount of control available to various groups in the society, and thus make knowledge-forms a straightforward representation of a continuous and relatively unified social reality. *Empirically*, Durkheim does allow for differential access to the means of controlling collective representations, and the possibility of a breakdown of social control in his concept of 'anomie' (cf. *Suicide*), but *theoretically* the stress on social solidarity which derives from organicism produces a restrictive concept of collective representations, which cannot handle their empirical differentiation in advanced social systems.

I shall bear these two points in mind in my subsequent discussion of Durkheim's 'Sociology of (undifferentiated) knowledge', based on the *EFRL*.

IV

The whole of Durkheim's 'crucial experiment'[23] about the relationship of society to religion, and thereby to the categories of understanding, rests on the validity of his theory of social development. For, if Australian totemic societies really do constitute the essence of the fundamental form of human social organization and do represent the first stage of social development, such that more advanced societies may be said to be elaboration on that basic theme, then Durkheim has proved an indubitable relationship between society, religion, and cognition. If such a positivist evolutionism is, however, without empirical foundation, then the status of the *EFRL* dwindles, for Durkheim has forfeited his claim to the empirical generality of his conclusions. Alternatively we may argue that what *are* important are his conceptual distinctions and implications, for in fact the majority of his empirical case has been falsified by the advance of anthropological knowledge. It is in the conceptual and theoretical field that Durkheim's last major work is of importance, but this does not unfortunately extend to the sociology of knowledge: I shall clarify this.

As I have remarked, the occasion for Durkheim's study of religion was its palpability as a social institution, its status as a 'social fact'. The continuing existence of religion in social life could not be possible unless it were some sort of 'reflection of reality' and not an illusion as had been asserted by the naturalistic positivists. In many respects the *EFRL* is an attack upon naturalistic positivism which Durkheim saw as leading to two main types of theory of religion, 'animism' and 'naturism'. Both saw religions as illusions, pre-scientific explanations of natural or psychological phenomena to which Durkheim opposed his own explanation by invoking his category of the 'social'. There was a reality, a positive empirically apprehendable type of phenomena reflected in religions which was neither natural nor psychological but uniquely and identifiably *social*. That is, Durkheim was presenting a functional argument: religion is important because of its consequences for social solidarity. Indeed, the functional argument is the basis of his justification for an evolutionary schema of religion.[24]

At the foundation of all systems of beliefs and of all cults
there ought necessarily to be a certain number of fundamental
representations or conceptions and of ritual attitudes which,
in spite of the diversity of forms which they have taken, have
the same objective significance and fulfil the same functions
elsewhere;

and primitive societies' religions show these basic elements more
clearly as they are reduced almost to essentials.

There are then, two main aims in the *EFRL*. First, a theory of
religion in the sense of a theory of the social conditions and social
origin of religious belief and activity. Second, a theory of the social
conditions of knowledge which, though it derives from the first aim,
exists separately from it for Durkheim. The structure of knowledge
and the problem of how it is possible in a universal form—the problem which rationalism and empiricism have debated—is solved empirically for Durkheim by an appeal to the 'social facts'. His theory
of religion provides the context for a sociology of knowledge because it led him to conceptualize religion as pre-philosophical and
pre-scientific knowledge (similarly to Spencer and Comte), and as
having a crucial part to play in the establishment of the categories
of understanding—time, space, class, number, cause, substance,
personality, etc., those 'most universal properties of things' by which
all other things are located. Religion provides the 'framework' of
the mind; 'when primitive religious beliefs are systematically
analysed, the principal categories are naturally found. They are
born in religion and of religion; they are a product of religious
thought.'[25] And since religion is 'eminently social', a 'collective
representation', then it follows that the categories also are socially
formed, and that the endless debate between 'apriorism' (rationalism)
and 'empiricism' can have a scientifically validatable conclusion.
This conclusion links up the truths in both positions, but makes each
dependent upon the other:[26]

So between these two sorts of representations [individual
empirical knowledge and socially formed categories] there is all
the difference which exists between the individual and the
social, and one can no more derive the second from the first
than he can deduce society from the individual, the whole from
the part, the complex from the simple. Society is a reality
sui generis . . . [and] the representations which express it have
wholly different contents from purely individual ones.

It is important to remember that Durkheim does not restrict himself to the cognitive aspects of knowledge, but stresses the importance
of institutionalized moral controls which both derive from and

orient the categories so that they become the means by which individuals internalize the moral authority of society. One can thus speak of a 'moral necessity' which underlies the categories, for they perform a social control function as well as being agents for the transmission of knowledge. In the meaningful sense of the term, the categories provide a cosmology, a way for men to relate to and know the social universe in which they live: they provide the means by which the social continuity is maintained, and it follows that their development must depend upon the possibility of social changes within a society such as to affect the whole system of collective representations. In fact, Durkheim says, our whole conception of knowledge is something subject to historical development: what is known, its form and content, is continually altering and both objectivity and truth are dependent upon the collectivity, the society or social group: human reason is the legitimate subject of study for a *historical-social* science, since it is both genetic and collective.

Durkheim's method of analysis is to show, firstly, that totemism is *the* 'elementary' religious form, and then to subject it to a systematic analysis which focuses on the conceptual distinctions it makes between 'sacred' and 'profane' things and places, and 'belief' and 'ritual', in order to demonstrate his hypotheses about religion and about cognition. What such a religion produces are collective representational systems which have specific social action meanings for their participants: they produce concepts which have a more than individual importance, concepts which have a collective and thus universal meaning to social actors. Religions are not systems of ideas alone, whose rites are merely contingent upon beliefs, but rather only in so far as ideas have consequences for action does religion exist for the believer, and it is the religious organization itself which as a consequence is most significant:[27]

> The cult is not simply a system of signs by which the faith is outwardly translated; it is a collection of the means by which this is created and recreated periodically (e.g. by the 'collective effervescence' which it produces). Whether it consists in material acts or mental operations it is always this which is efficacious.

The 'reality' which believers believe in may not exist transcendentally, but it does exist socially. For what is at the source of religious reality is *social* reality, but it is presented in an 'ideological' and distorted form because of the need of a society to maintain a continuous conception of itself. 'Idealization' provides this function because it posits an atemporal continuity: society can thus be represented religiously in part truly, for the 'ideal' can represent the 'idea' of society as a moral system rather than just a physical aggregate or geographical location. Religion thus becomes an 'eternal' aspect of

humanity: society needs to uphold and reaffirm collective sentiments and collective ideas which 'make its unity and personality'
such that there is a continual need for a 'living cult'. Apart from
these control functions, religion is cognitively similar to science,
wanting to translate natural human and social phenomena into an
intelligible language: 'the attempt is made by both [science and
religion] to connect things with each other, to establish internal
relations between them, to classify them and to systematize them.'[28]
What distinguishes the two is the critical component of science, yet
this is something developed from religion in the sense that it
relates to the creation of *concepts*. Concepts are linked directly to
language: they change as it changes, which is very slowly; they are
impersonal and capable of being universalized and this is what gives
them their character as mechanisms of human communication.
Both language and the concepts it contains are produced by society,
by human social organization, and: 'The ideas which correspond to
the diverse elements of language are thus collective representations.'[29]
Science is a historical development of the collective representations
and its validity rests on both technical criteria (e.g. experimental
control) and the general ideology of its practitioners: scientific concepts are valid, Durkheim says, because there is a *faith* in science
which is not dissimilar to religious faith.[30] Science then remains a
'collective representation', with its structure and methodology dependent on the social context in which it exists and therefore becomes a systematized and refined 'religion' in its own right. And
here we are presented with a paradox; the critical component of
scientific knowledge, which allows it to develop independent of the
society in which it exists in the sense that extra-scientific criteria are
specifically excluded from its mode of internal development, cannot
be explained by Durkheim. The reason for this, which motivates
Durkheim to ignore the problem of relating his sociology of knowledge to modern knowledge forms, is that the recognition of a critical
component makes science voluntaristic rather than socially determined in the structure of its activity. It is indeed true that science
requires a type of 'faith'; but this faith is as wholly conditional upon
empirical criteria as religion is not. Thus, the representations which
science produces are open to change irrespective of social considerations. And whilst Durkheim is correct to note that science can
operate like a religion, he cannot convert that description into an
explanation of science as such; all he has told us is that belief in
reason can provide a functional alternative to belief in a God or
gods, and that the two objects of belief are related through having a
similar social basis. Clearly then, Durkheim is not concerned with
the important question of how society actually produces both
knowledge and a structure of knowledge, and how social changes

affect that production (and vice versa) at higher than the primitive level, although he does suggest rather vaguely that all societies go through periods of 'creative effervescence' during which 'new' concepts are formed: the French Revolution is to him one such occasion. For demonstrating that cognitive categories are 'social' is not the same as showing how—or why—their relationship to reality produces data, capta, sense impressions or even concepts that we term knowledge. That is, recognizing Durkheim's basic hypothesis to be true—that the source of general concepts can only be society (as both a physical and normative system)—does not tell us a great deal: that thinking conceptually is coeval with being socially human goes nowhere towards clarifying determinate relationships between society and the structure and content of knowledge. Durkheim's sociology of knowledge then remains in a limbo: whilst it is theoretically suggestive, it does not tell us enough to produce a coherent approach in itself. The value of Durkheim's work then lies precisely in his demonstration of the real connections between social organization and moral community, and the construction of axiomatic categories within *primitive* societies: as I have shown, the extension of his sociology of knowledge to more differentiated societies is extremely problematic.

8 Karl Mannheim and the production of a 'relationist' sociology of knowledge

I

At one time Mannheim's name was synonymous in the English-speaking world with sociology of knowledge, and he can be said to have provided one albeit derivative paradigmatic formulation of the field. Both Weber and Lukács share in the genesis of the Mannheimian approach, and it can fairly be said that Mannheim presents one of the logical extensions of the complementary elements of both Marxian and Weberian social theory. In doing so however he gave himself a number of problems; his sociology of knowledge has pretensions towards being a science ('cultural' rather than 'natural') yet its methods are primarily philosophical. Thus whilst Mannheim is concerned to produce a sociological epistemology as a critique of the formalism and abstract nature of philosophic theories of knowledge, his methods of doing so are philosophical. The technical language of concepts which he employs remains non-empirical; references to the 'social' are always couched in categorical terms, for whilst Mannheim understands with Weber the significance of sophisticated conceptualization in sociological study he is, unlike Weber, incapable of making conceptualization empirically justifiable and we are left unsure as to what a Mannheimian sociology of knowledge actually is. In part this problem of cognitive location is itself amenable to an empirical study as a case for the sociology of knowledge; Mannheim's times, especially in Germany, were characterized by a cultural anomie having its strongest effect in politics. As with Scheler, Mannheim sought means of ameliorating the destructive ideological politics of Weimar Germany in a mode of thought which could indicate the assumptions and truth-contents

120

of political ideologies, its means of doing so involving demonstration of the social foundations of the ideas involved. But Mannheim located the truth-content of ideas wholly in their societal contexts, rather than in some transcendental or universalist conception of truth. Like Dilthey, he saw cultural formations as socially and historically specific; sociology of knowledge is to him the inquiry into the social conditions under which certain '*Weltanschauungen*' appear. Unlike Dilthey, who accepted completely the relativism of his approach, Mannheim recognized the nihilism implicit in a relativist sociology of knowledge and sought to avoid it first by devoting a special and limited role to scientific knowledge, and second by arguing that although all non-scientific knowledge is socially relative it is possible for a 'free-floating intelligentsia' to produce a knowledge of social life which has general validity. Naturally his own world must be seen in terms of this theory of a '*freischewebende Intelligenz*', for what he called the 'relationism' of his theoretical viewpoint is wholly tied up with it.[1]

Mannheim saw a relatively classless European intellectual élite as providing the source of a 'dynamic mediation' between both left and right political blocs: the terms under which such a mediation could be achieved, the erection of a 'science of politics', were to be accomplished by Mannheim's relationist sociology of knowledge. It is important to note that Mannheim does set a specific limitation on the sociology of knowledge which gravely impairs the possibilities of its achieving scientific status; it is to deal wholly with *ideologies* (e.g. including both conservative *ideology* and radical *Utopia*) for it is to be the means of a resolution of ideological conflict. The focus of Mannheim's work is then ideology, and sociology of knowledge is the means by which ideologies are investigated. The definition of non-scientific knowledge is that it is socially limited by its contextual location (apart of course from that available to the intellectual élite) to being simply a representation of the interests and values of the group which holds it; it is true for them only, and there is no way in which its general validity can be judged, since no general social context exists.

As far as intellectual debts are concerned Mannheim is thoroughly Weberian, in the sense that his conceptualization of society is in terms of a structure of meaningful social actions of individual actors. He employs the concept of ideal-type as a methodological tool and also discusses rationality and traditionalism as polar antitheses in ways very similar to Weber. The neo-Kantian heritage is also significant in unifying Weber and Mannheim—both took the central notion of reality as ultimately an unknowable entity, something about which man could only have an imperfect knowledge—for it leads both to see social reality as a meaningful structure, rather than as a natural, or simply material entity. Mannheim's work was also influenced in this direction by his period as a student of Edmund Husserl; as we shall see Mannheim's methodological distinction between 'objective', 'expressive' and 'documentary' meanings, is based on a phenomenological distinction between ways by which an intentional object (in this precise case, '*Weltanschauungen*') is presented to consciousness.[2] The phenomenology of Max Scheler, which was of course directed specifically towards a sociology of knowledge, had some influence also on Mannheim, although he does take issue with the metaphysical consequences of Schelerian sociology. This concentration on ideal factors led Mannheim to conceive of his sociology as concerned primarily with ideological systems; in consequence even his suggested resolution of European political problems relies on the assumption that political synthesis requires above all the creation of a total world-view composed of Fascism, Communism, liberalism and conservatism.[3]

Let me now turn to substantive discussion of Mannheim's writing on the sociology of knowledge.

II

In his first writings on the sociology of knowledge (cf. the long essay, 'The problem of a sociology of knowledge', written in 1925, and the earlier essay, 'On the interpretation of Weltanschauung' of 1923, referred to as 'PSK', and 'OIW' respectively) Mannheim saw himself as contributing to the history of ideas, and in that sense employed metaphysical concepts to study the 'problem-constellation' presented by the cultural sciences, which in his view had tended to abandon epistemology in favour of the sociology of knowledge. The conditions necessary to a sociology of knowledge thus become the auspices of Mannheim's initial approach to the sociology of knowledge and he presents his theoretical starting points in terms of a statement of the factors necessary to a sociological understanding of thought. But his consideration of the problems involved is not scientific but philosophical, for the essay is mainly devoted to an understanding of the principal 'philosophic–systematic' standpoints which develop a sociology of knowledge, and an elaboration of his own 'dynamic standpoint'.[4] He is concerned above all with the 'broad ultimate principles' on which philosophically divergent groups base their approaches to the 'problem'; and the larger part of the essay is given over to a critique of Scheler's contribution to the *Versuche einer Soziologie de Wissens*, which had given a phenomenological and metaphysical outline of the sociology of knowledge (cf. p. 78 above). Mannheim felt that the debate in Germany between historicism and phenomenology had been a decisive event in the formation of a special field of problems open to a *Wissenssoziologie* approach.

In his initial approaches to a sociology of knowledge Mannheim was at pains to link up the cultural relativism implicit in the Dilthean distinction of natural and social science. The apprehension of *Weltanschauungen* posed what appeared to be important problems: if one was to produce a cultural sociology of any significance it would have to grasp the basis of the connection between world-view and social reality with some scientific adequacy. Mannheim's argument is phenomenological: it is wrong in principle to treat *Weltanschauungen* as theoretical constructions which are wholly rational in their construction and meaning. To understand how a world-view is created and given societal meaning involves us in comprehending it as a 'pre-scientific totality', it follows that to transform pre-scientific categories of experience into logical elements is a reification and distortion of cultural reality.

Mannheim's 'cultural sociology' is predicated, then, upon a phenomenological methodology which tries to go beyond cultural objectifications—works of art, philosophical treatises, theological utterances, etc.—to comprehend the totality of *Weltanschauungen*: understanding is to be achieved by transcending all immanent meanings of such objectifications, only using them as *vehicles* by which the totality is made available and given to us through them. Cultural sociology, and consequently the sociology of knowledge, is to be a Husserlian endeavour which attempts to interpret connections between social-historical contexts and cultural productions by reconstituting the totality of meaning which a given world-view embodies in terms of an analysis of the intentional acts by which *Weltanschauungen* are presented to consciousness. With his distinctions between 'objective', 'expressive' and 'documentary' types of meaning, Mannheim pointed towards the use of phenomenological analysis as the way in which a hyper-relativist sociology could be constructed. Ethnomethodology in this respect owes more to Mannheim than it does to Schutz, for as Garfinkel himself acknowledges, his sociology has as its methodological centrepiece the 'documentary method of interpretation' postulated by Mannheim.[5] The way out of any approach which sees society as essentially meaningless—which is both Mannheim's starting point and the ethnomethodologist's finishing point—is to erect a situationally specific concept of meaning: it is the meanings actors themselves put upon the social interactions they engage in, which are important. It is not enough for Mannheim to accept an 'objective'—i.e. behaviourist—account of social action, for when we are studying social relationships we are involved with interpretations of meaning, and positivism is inadequate for that: hence 'expressive' and 'documentary' meanings have to be sought since their elucidation indicates the actual patterning of understandings upon which a world-view relies. These meanings are not particularized but point beyond themselves to a *totality* of meaning, and thus to the *Weltanschauung* itself.

A focus upon meaning involves any sociology in the search for hermeneutic methodologies, ways of *apprehending* meaning. Historicism comes directly to mind in this context, and Mannheim appropriately developed a historicist sociology of knowledge.[6] In 'OIW' he had developed the notion that *Weltanschauungen*, as total systems of meaning, were to be seen as historically specific entities with precise socio-temporal locations, using the concepts of 'documentary meaning' to refer to the reception of a cultural production in such a context and thus to provide a means of characterizing *Weltanschauungen* in terms of the ways in which they are formed socially at particular historical periods. The invocation of documentary meaning in a historicist context thus gives an (phenomenologically considered) 'objective' status to Mannheim's sociological methodology and functions in much the same way as Weber's *verstehen* method. That is to say it is wholly interpretive in its typological forms, for Mannheim claims that concepts such as the 'spirit' of capitalism can be constructed by its use. In fact, of course, 'historicism' itself is constituted as a *Weltanschauung* in this method, which points to the complete relativism of Mannheim's approach. In 'PSK' Mannheim portrays himself as constructing a phenomenologically based 'dynamic' sociology of knowledge (as a contrast to Scheler's 'static' sociology of knowledge)—the 'dynamism' coming from his interpretation of the nature of historicist explanation. Now it is at this point that Mannheim's method of documentary interpretation is specifically linked up with historicism—for its veridicality as an interpretative method depends upon:

> its location within the historical stream from which the interpreter attempts to reconstruct the spirit of a past epoch, i.e. the Hellenic and Shakespearian 'spirits' have been received and understood differently by different generations. But this is not to say that such knowledge is worthlessly relative, but rather that we should try to grasp the meaning and structure of historical understanding in its specificity . . . rather than reject it merely because it is not in conformity with the positivist truth criteria sanctioned by natural science.
>
> ('OIW')

The clear corollary of this is that to understand the spirit of an age we must employ our own: the *Weltanschauung* of an epoch depends

124

as much on the *Weltanschauung* of the epoch studying it as anything else. Our knowledge of history thus becomes—if it is to be 'meaningful'—completely relative.

Mannheim's conception of the development of sociology of knowledge, which he elaborated in 'PSK', has a precise connection with his own approach to the subject. He saw four main phases of the intellectual developments giving rise to the emergence of a distinctive approach to thought in terms of its social basis, which may be summarized as producing a situation in which thought and knowledge were seen as *relative* and as subject to *criticism*. An 'oppositional science' which postulated a relativized, socially based, sphere of knowledge was formed by successively rising classes (bourgeoisie and proletariat) who employed the concept of ideology as a central part of their critical approach.[7] When generalized, this oppositional science could be held to apply to the totality of systems of ideas and the underlying social reality. Since all social groups seek to develop a complete view of the world, the subject matter of a sociology of knowledge includes the ways in which they perceive their common reality: knowledge is atomized or relativized into the intellectual productions and specific cosmologies of social groups within a society. The process of knowledge *production* is thus historically and socially interpenetrated, and although Mannheim recognizes that there is a reality not embodied wholly in any single conception, each systematic standpoint (i.e. of social groups) will give a different interpretation of that reality. In principle there cannot be *any* complete knowledge of the social world. Once concepts appear, they are taken account of by social groups in terms of their interests and values to the extent that even scientific knowledge embodies philosophical–systematic preconceptions.

There are four major 'pre-existent systematic positions' on which a sociology of knowledge may be founded: *'positivism'*, *'formal apriorism'* (i.e. neo-Kantianism), *'material apriorism'*, by which Mannheim means Schelerian phenomenology, and *'historicism'*. There are fundamental drawbacks in each of these, especially in regard to their epistemological and ontological assumptions. Positivism—though it has produced two sociologies of knowledge, Marxist and Durkheimian—is false because it disallows 'meaning' as an element of explanation and 'its methods are entirely inadequate especially in treating intellectual-spiritual-artistic reality'.[8] Neo-Kantianism remains philosophical wishing to comprehend thought in a wholly immanent fashion: it is 'wrong' for it holds a non-relativist conception of truth and bases its theory of cognition on the paradigm of scientific-mathematical knowledge. Schelerian phenomenology is unacceptable because of its dualism, the Catholic opposition of eternal and temporal reality (cf. my remarks on

125

pp. 86–7) and its absolutism in respect of history which gives it a 'static' nature. Historicism thus becomes the corner-stone of a 'dynamic' sociology of knowledge, which treats truth and knowledge as existentially variable: 'the central problem of a sociology of knowledge will be that of the existentially conditioned genesis of the various standpoints which encompass the patterns of thought available to any given epoch.'[9]

Mannheim wished to make his sociology of knowledge separate from any Marxist conception of the nature of the relationship between material interests and intellectual attitudes. In this he was quite clearly Weberian in approach, perceiving that to ascribe the limitations on knowledge production solely to material motivations of interest was insufficient. It was insufficient not simply because it gave a major role to only one element of motivation, but also because it referred the locus of that 'interest' to simply one type of social aggregate—an economic class. 'We cannot relate an intellectual standpoint directly to a social class; what we can do is find out the correlation between the "style of thought" underlying a given standpoint and the "intellectual motivation" of a certain social group.'[10]

Social groups are 'committed' to certain 'world postulates', (commitment may involve the function of material interests) which constitute the arena of the history of knowledge. Such 'world postulates' are expressive of a commitment to past, future or present social orders. Having disposed of the concept of class as requisite to the adequate characterization of the sociology of knowledge's subject matter, Mannheim associates 'style of thought' with social *strata*, such that it is possible to distinguish social from *intellectual* strata (a Weberian stratificatory notion) in terms of their definition on the basis of more differentiated criteria. 'We mean by "intellectual stratum" a group of people belonging to a certain social unit and sharing a certain "world postulate" . . . who at a given time are "committed" to a certain style of economic activity and of theoretical thought.'[11]

To link up strata and world postulates involves a mode of analysis which is both philosophical and sociological: identification of world postulates—at the level of 'meaning'—followed by finding the social groups, 'intellectual strata', linked to them and the social strata corresponding in turn to them.

The actual process of change in thought, which involves the fusion of pre-existing ideologies and ideas with new ideas to produce new styles of thought with changed meanings of existing concepts, a change in the *function* of thought, is of two types: 'immanent' and 'sociological'. *Immanent* changes in the function of thought involves a change in the location of concepts within a system of ideas, whilst

126

sociological changes involve a change in the meaning of a concept when it is taken up by a group living in a different social environment. The sociology of knowledge, then, is defined by Mannheim as: 'a discipline which explores the functional dependence of each intellectual standpoint on the differentiated social group reality standing behind it, and which sets itself the task of retracing the evolution of the various standpoints'.[12]

III

With *Ideology and Utopia* (1929) the development of Mannheim's relativist sociology of knowledge reaches its peak. It does so for two main reasons. First, Mannheim is involving himself in what he had previously identified as the subject matter of sociology of knowledge: the issue of ideology and the problems of its conceptualization. Second, and in an important sense this is linked to the first point, he is motivated by a practical concern, a desire to alleviate the ideological politics which he saw as contributing to the impotence of Weimar republicanism. Thus his sociology of knowledge, which situates political claims within the nature of the commitments and functions of the social groups making them, is to be the main tool of a free-floating intelligentsia which could provide a dynamic mediation of the crisis of German and European politics and a framework under which left and right could be reconciled. The intellectual strata can, on the basis of their own social consciousness, construct a total view of the whole social process from which to build a political synthesis. Part of the source of this practical concern was Mannheim's realization that the relativism espoused in his earlier work was an unsuitable basis for the sociology of knowledge and he sought to change the emphasis of his approach towards a less extreme relativism; his notion of 'relationism' was born as a result. Also, Mannheim was led to see that relativism was opposed to any theoretical elaboration of the sociology of knowledge: in the essay he wrote for Vierkandt's *Encyclopaedia of Sociology* (1931) he noted that only such a discipline could 'hope to overcome the vague, ill-considered, and sterile form of relativism with regard to scientific knowledge which is increasingly prevalent today.'[13]

Thus whilst he did not completely reject relativism, Mannheim's emphasis in *Ideology and Utopia* on a 'relationist' sociology of knowledge signifies a movement away from the sort of Dilthean, and phenomenological '*Weltanschauung*–analysis' position which he took in his early work. This movement away from the philosophical viewpoint of historicism to the quasi-scientific viewpoint of sociology of knowledge forced Mannheim towards a more systematic conceptualization of the empirical field of the new discipline.

With this movement his work comes more into line with the Marxian approach to sociology of knowledge and specifically to the Hegelian Marxism of writers like Lukács and Korsch. But he was, as before, unwilling to accept the Marxian conceptualization of knowledge as completely class based, if that is to mean an opposition of only bourgeois and proletarian classes in modern society. For that view meant that a complete historical relativism would be the only way of treating knowledge, which he found unacceptable. The notion of relationism thus allowed the majority of knowledge to be class based because it was formed by the perspectival vision of the group which produced it. There was however the possibility that a residuum of knowledge could be gained that had a general validity because it was composed of all viewpoints, produced by a group of individuals who were relatively free of all class based limitations of knowledge. This stratum of intellectuals could function as an independent entity because its members had received an education allowing them to go beyond the world-views of the social groups from which they came. (It is interesting that Mannheim tends to ignore the possibility that élite education might itself produce a particularist world-view, which, despite the heterogeneous social composition of the intelligentsia, would make it as situationally specific as all other world-views.) Relationism merely becomes a reformulated relativism, for it simply reduces relativism to the level of an assertion that *some* knowledge is dependent on the 'subjective standpoint and the social situation of the knower', whilst itself asserting that *all* 'historical' knowledge (e.g. excluding natural scientific laws) is 'relational knowledge, and can only be formulated with reference to the position of the observer'.[14]

Methodologically then, Mannheim's relationism is quite unsatisfactory as a sociology of knowledge, for it gives us no grounds on which to suppose that the discipline itself is capable of providing any more than a representation of the values and interests of the group which works on it. And this, I think, is a direct consequence of the subject matter which Mannheim selects to be its objects of study: ideologies and Utopias. In his preliminary distinction between ideology and Utopia Mannheim had made an important division which allows us to conceptualize systems of *values* in terms of their functions for specific types of social grouping. (Mannheim talks about *ideas*, but his description of these systems argues that they are normative prescriptions rather than empirical descriptions: within his relationism of course there is no actual means of distinguishing between them. Thus there are in principle no non-ideological or Utopian ideas, which is clearly either nonsense or a devaluation of these concepts—i.e. *all* social science, logic, etc., becomes ideological or Utopian.)

'Ideologies' thus refer to systems of ideas which give a positive evaluation to either the existing social order and the interests of groups within it, or some past social order. 'Utopias' are the constructions of groups excluded from a full actualization of their interests, which propose a future social order oriented about those interests. Both of these conceptualizations of 'total' ideologies reflect Mannheim's analytic insight into the nature of the concept of ideology itself—an insight both reflexive and historical, for it deals with the development of the idea of ideology from a particularistic to a holistic viewpoint. Initially, 'ideology' had been a term which described the conceptions of individuals or specific intellectual viewpoints as mendacious distortions which depended on the individuals concerned. However, the development of a 'total' conception of ideology, dependent on a philosophy of consciousness which saw thought as structured into a unity of coherent elements which was produced by the Enlightenment and later historicized by Hegelian philosophy, ultimately led to a position in which 'ideology' was a description of the whole thought of a particular social group. Coupled with the notion that consciousness and knowledge was itself in process of continuous historical transformation, the total conception came to imply that all knowledge is socially founded and is true or false wholly in those terms. In modern terms, the discussion of the concept of ideology revolves around the issue of 'false-consciousness': truth and falsity become empirical rather than philosophical issues, and ultimately *all* thought is seen as ideological in the sense of being formed in accordance with the views, interests and values of particular social groups. Thus an originally Marxist conception of ideology—fusing 'particular' and 'total' forms of ideology, such that all non-proletarian thought is mendacious—comes to exist within the Mannheimian view of sociology as a completely relative conceptualization: all is 'ideology'. Absolute truth thus cannot exist outside of the socio-historical situation of the knowing subject; all that is possible is an evaluative, 'relational' sociology of knowledge. For the attempt to disengage sociology of knowledge from an evaluative position—and there Mannheim is primarily attacking positivism—is itself a form of absolutism assuming that a non-evaluative position is epistemologically and ontologically capable of construction.[15] This is a 'metaphysical' assumption which cannot be demonstrated: as far as Mannheim is concerned it is refuted by the relationist viewpoint which he held, and this primarily in terms of his social action theory which makes a clear distinction between the lawlike regularities of natural scientific knowledge and the individually constructed *meanings* of social knowledge. Sociology of knowledge deals (for Mannheim) with the latter exclusively, and thus is committed to the making of evaluative decisions about the areas and structures of that which it studies: its subject matter is not given to it in terms of some phenomenally contingent area of reality. This leads him to a position similar to, but not identical with, Frankfurt critical theory; a dynamic, evaluative sociology, which examines contexts under which traditional concepts and forces do not allow adjustment to 'new' situations, preventing the transformation of man, means we can evaluate the theoretical ideas which give rise to such a situation as wrong, distorting and ideological. 'A theory then is wrong if in a given practical situation it uses concepts and categories which, if taken seriously, would prevent man from adjusting himself at that historical stage.'[16]

Mannheim's definition of ideology thus becomes a conception of knowledge as *distorted* so that it: 'fails to take account of the new realities applying to a situation, and when it attempts to conceal them by thinking of them in categories which are inappropriate'.[17] It is a conception *evaluative* because it presupposes both the reality of certain ideas and structures of consciousness, and *dynamic* because these presuppositions are subject to historical change. The judgement of knowledge as ideological or Utopian rests wholly upon the relationship of that knowledge to the prevailing *conception* of reality, or minimally the various conceptions of reality which social groups have in any society. Consequently the possibility of a scientific base for sociology of knowledge, if by that we mean a regularized and demonstrable relationship of concepts and statements to empirical phenomena, has disappeared wholly for Mannheim. He relies in fact upon a purely formalistic conception in which sociology of knowledge is a 'cultural science', scientific in so far as it deals with a characteristic subject matter—knowledge of a component of intellectual culture—by some systematic and *interpretative* method, the whole while realizing that definition of concepts, etc., depends upon the social position and point of view of the sociologist. All is relational to its social context.

But there is a let-out for Mannheim from this hyper-relativism. In making the thought of the intellectual wholly dependent on his social-class position, Mannheim had linked the structure and veridicality of knowledge to its social base. But if the social basis of the intelligentsia could be shown to be non-particularist without constraining subordination to any class position, then it would in principle, he felt, be able to construct a general and total conception of socio-historical reality. Thus the intellectual productions of the intelligentsia would function so as to integrate or synthesize the five central ideological world-views of the modern period (these are: (1) 'bureaucratic-conservative' (2) 'conservative historicism' (3) 'bourgeois-liberal intellectualism' (4) 'socialist-communist conceptions' (5) 'fascism'[18]), and produce a real 'science of politics' capable of inaugurating a non-ideological European political system. It could function as a class *above* all of the ideological disputes for it would be a synthesis of the 'true' elements of each. The sociology of knowledge can play a practical role in this synthesis because it can demonstrate the extent to which 'political knowledge' is tied up with modes of social existence, and show that various political evaluations are based in the interests and ideals of specific social groups. Now these evaluations may well, as previously discussed, be 'ideological' in Mannheim's sense of the term. But they may also be 'Utopian', in the sense that they refer to a future state of affairs and work to 'burst the bounds' of existing socio-political reality in order to achieve it. Where ideologies seek to place a limitation on social change, Utopias work to achieve a transformation of the structure of society. This possibly instructive way of classifying ideas in terms of the intended social functions they will have, is deformed by Mannheim in accordance with his relativism, for the distinction between ideology and Utopia is made dependent upon the viewpoints and interests of the social groups which hold coherent viewpoints characterizable in those terms. Of course this relativization of concepts is dictated by the 'dynamic' nature of Mannheim's method, and his use of the terms ideology and Utopia makes no practical distinction between the possibilities of actual realization of any ideological or Utopian social organization: all that is possible, he says, is some sort of calculation of the relative ideological or Utopian nature of the ideas in terms of the group and its context. Now whilst it is necessary to see Utopian and ideological ideas in terms of the possibilities of their empirical actualization, Mannheim makes the calculation of possibility completely reliant upon values rather than material conditions, for without a coherent theory of social organization he has no non-relative means of working out the ways in which any posited social system is realizable. In that sense the concepts 'ideology' and 'Utopia' have no more than a contingent meaning. However, the central issue of Mannheim's analysis of Utopias is defined in terms of a set of non-relative categories—the 'ideal-types' of 'orgiastic chiliasm', 'liberal-humanitarianism', 'conservative idea', and the 'socialist–communist Utopia'. Each of these ideal-type 'Utopian mentalities' exists at specific historical periods linked to the interests and aspirations of specific social classes, and each develops against the ideologies and social formations of the period within which it functioned. Thus there is a linkage between all four which develops as each appears. The liberal-humanitarian 'Idea' thus functions as a replacement of the anarchism of chiliasm: the conservative idea exists in romantic thought as a counter-Utopia against liberalism and rationalism, and the socialist–communist Utopia rejects all three as a prelude to its attempts at a complete socio-political transformation. Utopia is in fact for Mannheim one of the most important causes of social change: each of these ideal-types thus may be taken to describe a particular impetus towards new social groupings, a new theory of social organization which forms the context under which rising social classes try to achieve change. The Utopia is then the organizing idea of social change, which has no reality beyond it: such an idealist theory of history which sees it in terms of *Weltanschauungen* with special social functions—ideologies and Utopias—in reality contributes little to an empirical understanding of the relationship between knowledge and social organization. For Mannheim remains at the speculative level of social philosophy: if we are to take his élite theory of knowledge production literally, then Mannheim himself may be presumed to be a part of the 'free-floating intelligentsia' whose role is to examine and analyse or reflect upon ideologies and Utopias articulated in the political disputes of modern Europe. His role is to provide, via the sociology of knowledge, a more inclusive ideology; a philosophical–political position capable of integrating disparate and divisive political ideologies. Thus whilst we may commend Mannheim's attempt to make his sociology of knowledge of practical significance, one element of a 'science of politics', we must at the same time recognize that it constitutes a *reduction* of sociology to the level of either politics or philosophy, or both. Like his contemporaries, Scheler, Lukács and Grünewald, Mannheim is located within a distinctively philosophical mode of approaching the connections between knowledge and society. In concentrating on the production of ideas by intellectuals, Mannheim limited his sociology of knowledge to élite knowledge: it excludes science almost completely and takes little or no account of the transmission and reproduction of knowledge on a mass scale. Education only comes into the analysis in terms of the free-floating intelligentsia, who receive a knowledge which allows them to move beyond their stratum-bound conception of social reality: the general processes of education in modern society, as they provide both a form and content to some 'mass' knowledge, are not considered. Neither is the general commonsense knowledge of reality, available to members of a society through their socialization and general social interactions; although Mannheim implicitly includes such knowledge under the five ideological groupings he provides no evidence that we can in fact apply these to any more than limited, politically conscious, social strata.

In fact the sociology of knowledge forms one, albeit early, part of Mannheim's general interpretative sociology, or social philosophy. In that sense Mannheim is a false heir to Weber: the systematic empirical reference of Weber's sociological work is completely missing from that of Mannheim. Although he takes over the interpretative and typological methods of Weber, his conflation of them with a historicist conception of society as a culturally relative system of *meanings*, means that the ultimate consequence of his work is a turning against science in the study of social life. Where Weber saw '*verstehen*' and the ideal-types as tools of a general science of history and society which could include more naturalistic methods as well, Mannheim turns against any objectivism or naturalism. He describes the search for a 'general sociology' as merely the aim of producing more effective methods of social control: the goal of such a science would be to use its predictive 'power' as a means of social adjustment to a particular institutional order. The search for a general scientific method in sociology thus constitutes an ideology which substitutes the generation of lawlike statements for the discovery of meaning-complexes of action. This search for general factors and types of universal validity at one level of sociological analysis was paralleled by a movement towards reductionism—the positing of 'drives' as eternal forms in the structure of human impulses (he means Scheler in particular here) at another. Mannheim felt that his sociology of knowledge could show the fallacies in both of these positions, for they were grounded in the presuppositions of 'traditional epistemology' (which means the neo-Kantian, and Kantian epistemological positions which make the validity of knowledge separate from the individuals holding it), which had employed natural science as the exemplification of cognitive structure, and the model of valid knowledge. In terms of his basic thesis, social knowledge is qualitative where physical knowledge is quantitative and thus the traditional position is wrong in trying to make natural science the paradigm of social knowledge. They are discontinuous forms of cognition and their conflation is itself an ideology.[19] The traditional position produced by Kant, in asking how natural scientific knowledge was possible, had produced the realization that the validity of such knowledge was not dependent upon the existential situation of the thinker but on the way in which it was presented, its logical structure and demonstrability. However, the 'validity' of social-qualitative knowledge, its 'truth', is open to both historical and social change: its appearance as a form of knowledge alongside but different from scientific knowledge forces, contends Mannheim, the realization that the concepts of 'knowledge' and 'truth' are relative to the situation in which they exist. 'There exists a fundamental although not readily apparent nexus between epistemology, the dominant forms of knowing, and the general social-intellectual situation of a time.'[20]

It is in principle possible for the sociology of knowledge to demonstrate the inter-relationships of epistemologies and their social foundations. In that sense the whole of Mannheim's work on the sociology of knowledge is directed towards making it into a 'super-epistemology', which can analyse and evaluate the existential and epistemological conditions of all epistemologies.

IV

The sociology of knowledge, as I have remarked, forms a part of Mannheim's general sociology. Like the rest of his work it is concerned with the role of élites in social change. For Mannheim, élites control everything: it is they who decide what knowledge shall consist of, how it shall be produced and by what methods it can be assessed. They also set the general framework of all 'ideological' and 'Utopian' disputation within the realm of politics, by means of the attachment of the members of an intellectual élite to other social strata as representatives, in the world of ideas, of their interests. Thus for Mannheim there are two types of élite, what we might call 'social' élites, and 'intellectual' élites. In modern society, the 'intellectual' élite, hitherto a representative of the 'social' élite of a social stratum, can function as a separate social group with a potentially unrestricted vision of the social world, precisely because its members are disengaged from the limitations imposed upon them by functioning as the expression of the interests of a particular social group. They are supposed, by virtue of their privileged position, to consider and evaluate every conception of reality produced by particular social strata and synthesize them into a total conception of the world. Mannheim's sociology of knowledge has thus a dual purpose: whilst it can operate, intellectually, as a method of research by virtue of its nature as a 'super-epistemology', it can also function as a practical tool of political action. Able to show the existential bases of ideas, it can demonstrate their partiality in terms of the social world. But its limitations as a theory reside in the nature of its formulation: its eventually philosophical relativism and reliance upon an élite theory of social organization limit it to a particular conception of knowledge as an *intellectual* edifice which excludes all technical, scientific or commonsense knowledge in order to see cognition as something ordered in respect of philosophical presuppositions. The resultant lack of any empirical relevance in Mannheim's sociology of knowledge has meant that, as an approach, it has not been influential in the construction of any *scientific* sociology of knowledge. I. L. Horowitz's description of Mannheim's conception of the free-floating intellectual is also an apt description of his sociology of knowledge itself: 'Mannheim's intellectual is a man who steadily rinses his brain with ideas, but never knows enough to wash his hands with soap.'[21]

9 Phenomenological-sociological approaches to the sociology of knowledge

The primary focus of phenomenologically based sociology has been, following Schutz and Husserl, an emphasis on the commonsense construction of everyday reality, rather than the analysis of specifically intellectual consciousnesses as entities separate from mundane everyday knowledge. Consequently a phenomenologically based sociology of knowledge explicitly rejects the implicit dichotomy in classical approaches between generalized social knowledge and the knowledge of an élite social group. It sees a precise connection between the social relationships of individuals and the meanings those relationships have to the extent that the nature of those relationships and the structure of their intersubjective meaning defines the structure and content of all knowledge. Our perceptions of reality are formed by the activity of social interaction, but not in some abstracted sense in which reality is external to the individual: interaction is the mechanism by which reality itself is *constructed* by social actors. Though I am not concerned with the work of either Husserl or Schutz, who set respectively both the methodological and sociological foundations of a phenomenological sociology of knowledge, my discussion of this approach necessarily involves some introductory remarks on their contributions.

I

Husserlian phenomenology in its distinction between 'natural' and 'eidetic' knowledge had produced a conception of knowledge as rooted wholly in the *'Lebenswelt'* ('lifeworld') in which individuals relate to each other and share intersubjective meanings. Science was thus only possible because of its rooting in everyday reality, and the practical interests of men: the attempt to make science into knowledge with a formal objectivity is in those terms an illusory abstraction which separates science from its actual basis in the consciousness of all men. Schutz's development of the anti-objectivism of Husserl's attack on science, directed to the realm of social reality, progressed in terms of a fusion of this approach with the Weberian methodology of *verstehen*. It followed that social science could not be considered naturalistically since it involved the study of meaning-structures, the ways in which social relationships were constructed in terms of their givenness as intentional objects. Schutz had attempted an elimination of any positivism from sociology, ultimately to make the study of social interaction—for there is no phenomenological concept of society or social system—the province of philosophy, one part of a general phenomenology of human existence. Any analysis of social structures must be in terms wholly dependent on interpretative criteria, involving understanding of the meanings which social relationships have for those who engage in them. This is not to say that there cannot be any objectivity in social science, but rather that it is to mean a detachment of scientific problems from the biographical situation of the scientist to the level of the autonomous science itself. What results is a theoretical system of typifications, a social world of 'puppets' with typical goals, motives and values which conform to the requirements of logical consistency and 'adequacy' at the level of meaning.[1] Social reality is to be seen as a meaning-construct rather than any natural reality: it exists only in so far as it has a meaning for its participants. Thus both Husserlian and Schutzian approaches suggest a complete exclusion of epistemological issues from the realms of philosophy and social theory, since they locate theoretical and logical concepts *a priori* in the *Lebenswelt*. All knowledge is thus a construction produced in human interaction, and the structure that it systematically has is produced in accordance with that fundamental social reality. It follows that attempts to make knowledge into something separate from social reality are misplaced and distortive: in particular the erection of the study of society into a falsely natural–scientific edifice destroys any possibility of understanding the true meaning of social reality as something constructed by the consciousnesses of individual actors and made meaningful by their intersubjectivity.

Social science is wrong not only in its ontological assumptions, but also in its methodological assumptions. For if social reality is constructed by men's consciousnesses, then its nature can only be studied reflexively, by acts of pure reflection (the 'phenomenological reduction'): any attempt to apply natural scientific methods of objective research or experimentation to the study of social reality are in these terms fundamentally erroneous. Translated into a phenomenological sociology (and we are ignoring ethnomethodology at this point) the method of phenomenological analysis becomes transformed by Schutz into hermeneutics—the interpretational method of *verstehen*. Clearly then, methodology is in fact—since it poses significant epistemological problems—a crucial concern of a phenomenologically oriented sociology of knowledge. Also it is in one important sense impossible to discuss sociology of knowledge as separate from sociology itself as an element of phenomenological research. For our knowledge of social and natural reality is in fact identical with that reality: as our knowledge changes so also changes the reality that it constitutes.

II

Peter Berger and Thomas Luckmann, in their writing on the sociology of knowledge, start from the primary viewpoint of Schutzian phenomenology.[2] But they are eclectic in the sense that they strive to include Durkheim, Weber and Marx as well in their formulations concerning the structural determinants of knowledge, and knowledge as a determinant of social structure. Also, they employ the language and concepts of social behaviourism in its symbolic–interactionist form, mapping it on to their structural theory in terms of the ways in which knowledge is internalized in the individual via the socialization process. There is thus a hierarchical theory of the social bases of knowledge: Schutzian phenomenology provides the philosophical framework and the methodology by which the anthropology and dialectical perspective of Marx, the concepts of social reality employed by Durkheim and the notion of social reality as a system of subjective meanings produced by Weber, all cohere into a single theory of the social construction of reality, reinforced by a social psychological theory of the internalization of social reality which is based in Schutz and G. H. Mead. It is from this multiple viewpoint that Berger and Luckmann seek to redefine the sociology of knowledge: it is to be 'the analysis of the social construction of reality' and 'must concern itself with everything that passes for "knowledge" in society'.[3]

Berger and Luckmann divide their major work (*The Social Construction of Reality*) into two parts, two separate though 'dialectically interlinked' analyses of society as both 'objective' and 'subjective' reality. Starting from the presuppositions of phenomenological sociology, that the intersubjectivity of face-to-face relationships is the basis or unit of social reality, and that this intersubjectivity is both mediated and generalized for us by our principal sign system, language, the authors discuss the central analytic elements

137

of their social theory. What are important in any social world are the processes of *Institutionalization, Legitimation* and *Internalization* of intersubjectively constructed social reality. These are the *chief* components, then, of any society, above the purely biological or physiological constitution of human reality. Each of these analytical-empirical categories is founded on the Marxian anthropology which sees (*vide* the Paris manuscripts) man as a species who produces his own human nature in a social environment. Thus *The Social Construction of Reality* relies upon an organismic environment made available as part of that reality and as a set of limiting conditions on the nature of that reality. Social order thus may be seen as minimally involved with human self-production in the sense that the instability of the human organism (especially in its extended childhood) requires the creation of a stable environment. Institutionalization, legitimation and internalization of social reality consequently involve the realities of a constructed social order. Central to this 'problem of social order' is the conceptualization of knowledge as something wholly social, and the concepts of 'recipe knowledge' and 'social stock of knowledge' are the means by which Berger and Luckmann accomplish this. These concepts function as the hooks on which the social world is hung: 'recipe' knowledge constitutes the categorized and communicable knowledge members of a society must have for their practical competence in routine performances. It is thus knowledge linked to everyday life, what all members must know to exist routinely in their social environment. As such, recipe knowledge forms a central element of the social stock of knowledge, which constitutes the whole corpus of available knowledge. It represents an integrated whole available to all members of the intersubjectively constructed social reality:[4]

> I live in the common-sense world of everyday life equipped
> with specific bodies of knowledge. What is more, I know that
> others share at least part of this knowledge and they know that
> I know this. My interaction with others in everyday life is,
> therefore, constantly affected by our common participation in
> the available social stock of knowledge.

Thus the social stock of knowledge constitutes a structure of sets of recipe knowledge ordered in accordance with the social roles society members have to perform, and gives to members a differentiation of reality by degrees of familiarity; 'It provides complex and detailed information concerning those sectors of everyday life with which I must frequently deal [and] provides much more general and imprecise information on remoter sectors.'[5]

The way it provides information is by making available 'typificatory schemes' of both social and natural knowledge whose validity is 'taken for granted' and only called into question when 'what everybody knows' turns out to provide problems. For the individual such consensually valid typifications are made available in terms of his biographical interests, or his knowledge of others' interests— Berger and Luckmann mysteriously call them *'relevance structures'* —or even the interests of the social stock of knowledge itself (which is culturally defined). Thus part of the social stock of knowledge is its social distribution—from purely pragmatic to esoteric, and from commonsensical to expert—and knowledge of the way it is distributed is 'an important element of that same stock of knowledge'. Having reached a significant point, at which they ought to discuss how the social stock of knowledge is actually distributed and why new interests function in the selection of areas of knowledge, and how the validity of knowledge is both achieved and systematized so that there is, say, scientifically valid knowledge, Berger and Luckmann leave to discuss institutionalization, legitimation and internalization. They do not discuss the actual mechanisms by which the social stock of knowledge is created in terms of either some cultural totality or in accordance with the interests of social groups. We are merely presented with the idea of a socially distributed stock of knowledge which it takes no great intellect to realize will consist of both everyday and technically complex knowledge, and left without the means of inquiring into the actual structure of that knowledge and its relationship to the social structure of the society of which it forms a part.

In locating the societal development of knowledge within a conceptual framework directed towards the idea of society as a way of producing social order, Berger and Luckmann are put in the position of saying that social reality is constructed by actors in order to limit their possible activity. Knowledge, if it functions as a part of this essentially repressive reality—and Berger and Luckmann are committed to argue that it *is* that reality—is a mechanism of constraint on human consciousness. This essentially Durkheimian viewpoint on the nature of social reality cuts right across the Marxian 'anthropology' which the authors claim to be using. For to posit that man is free to reproduce his social and natural conditions in limitless fashion, and then to limit that reproduction in terms of a system of external and internal constraints—institutionalization, legitimation and socialization—presents a contradiction that can only fatuously be called 'dialectical'. In truth, there is very little of a Marxian approach contained within the book.

In taking social order for granted, Berger and Lockmann necessarily limit themselves to a discussion of how social order is constructed and maintained. Thus *institutionalization,* the 'reciprocal typification of habitualized actions by types of actors', is the primary mechanism of social control. Although initially the behaviours that are habitualized are subject to modification, once they get transmitted to a new generation they assume an 'objectivity' which allows them to function as Durkheimian social facts—as both external and coercive to the individual. The reproduction of any social reality requires then that certain actor-relevant behaviours are objectified into institutions which have some externality to individuals, and which can be internalized as the natural way of doing things by the socialization of a new generation. The mechanism of transmission requires, Berger and Luckmann argue, a *legitimation* of the institutional world. This takes the form, they say, of explanation and justification of the institutions at the levels of meaning. The fact that institutions do empirically cohere without some internal logic means that an understanding of their integration involves some comprehension of the knowledge that its members have of it. Analysis of such knowledge is a prerequisite of any analysis of the institutional order. Of course this assumes that a consensus obtains on basic values and beliefs without question: agreement is taken as given on the institutional order for knowledge of it to be taken as the focus of study. Knowledge of social reality, the recipe knowledge of norms of institutionalized behaviour, thus comes to be coextensive with social reality. What is taken for granted as knowledge in a society is identical with the knowledge itself, providing the framework on which future knowledge is to be ordered. Knowledge of social order, we must assume, functions as the legitimation of social order. Now of course the way in which this knowledge is made available—language—is important as Berger and Luckmann recognize. But why a particular institutionalization occurs, or how it is maintained by the semantic knowledge of normative behaviour available to social actors, is not explained. Language *does* function as a receptacle of tradition, and necessarily so if important information about social reality is to be transmitted. But having said that one has merely begged all the questions about how and why language functions in that way in both a general theoretical context, and in some actual social situation. Thus the understanding of the 'sedimentation' into language of traditional action, whether it be by some symbolic acts or educative processes, is not achieved by merely stating that it occurs. We require a more adequate demonstration of these assertions if they are to be accepted as valid.

Similar reservations have to be noted in respect of Berger and Luckmann's discussion of roles; institutions are for them internalized by roles. By acting in a role the individual is involved in a social world: the internalization of role performance allows this world to become subjectively real to the role player. But not all roles have the same institutional importance: some strategic roles may symbolize and represent the entire institutional order of a society, as for example that of monarch. (Berger and Luckmann do not mention that such 'total' roles are so because they involve the exercise of a large amount of power or prestige, beyond a recognition that they are 'most often' located in political or religious institutions.) Roles in this sense define knowledge, implying a social distribution of knowledge and a dichotimization of knowledge into general and role specific types. Whilst they note that this in turn implies systems of social organization involving role differentiation the authors do not discuss the relationship between social structure and knowledge structure any further.

Institutionalization and role differentiation of knowledge have to be seen in a 'historical' context, we are told. They depend upon the 'degree of division of labour' (as if that were something different) and the availability of an economic surplus, so that not all activity need be concentrated on subsistence.

Integration into the institutional order is the property of legitimation, whose first aim is to make the individual's life in the social world objectively meaningful. The institutional order becomes something which the individual can make sense of and operate within: legitimation thus creates an 'overarching universe of meaning', a 'symbolic universe' within which the institutional order is located so as to place everyday life in the most general frame of reference possible. If anything can be called the central theme of Berger and Luckmann's work it is their concept of the 'symbolic universe', for it is the locus of their whole argument about the binding up of social order and knowledge. Legitimation involves the precedence of knowledge over values, within this theory. In other sociological traditions, legitimation has been either purely evaluative, normative, interest-based or at most based on *distorted* knowledge (Durkheim, Weber, Marx). For Berger and Luckmann it is *cognitive*, rooted in an explanation of how things are what they are; legitimation only becomes normative when it moves from institutional knowledge to institutional prescription. There are, analytically, four different levels of legitimation; each is cognitive-evaluative in the sense described above. They move from the simplest pretheoretical level—'incipient legitimation'—to the most abstract and general: 'bodies of theoretical tradition that integrate different provinces of meaning and encompass the institutional order in a symbolic totality. ... The sphere of pragmatic application is transcended once and for all. Legitimation now takes place by means of symbolic totalities that cannot be experienced in everyday life at all.'[6] This is what Berger and Luckmann call the 'symbolic universe' level of legitimation. It is a concept very similar to that of '*Weltanschauung*', a culturally integrating totality which encompasses

141

all aspects of life within it. It integrates all institutions and institutional roles, which become participants 'in a universe that transcends *and* includes the institutional order'.[7]

The symbolic universe allows the individual to locate his own mortality within a secure context and the society to see itself within a historical continuity: it also defines what shall be considered as 'social', including a ranking of sociability from high to low, and a ranking of other non-social phenomena in terms of it (which may mean that some men, e.g. slaves, become 'animals' rather than 'human beings'). The nature of symbolic universes does not apparently allow them to be, however secure their social base, self-constituting: they require 'conceptual machineries of universe maintenance' to function when the symbolic universe has a legitimation problem. These super-legitimating things are in the main total cognitive systems which evolve historically from mythology through systematic advances in theoretical content to theology, philosophy and now science. Such levels of legitimating theories correspond also to the Weberian process of 'disenchantment' of the world: mythology represents the most naïve level of conceptual machinery, science the most systematized and rational. The conceptual machinery of universe maintenance is of course socially organized itself: it is in that sense possible to relate the persistence of certain symbolic universes to the power of the social-structural base of the groups holding them. Clearly this leads us into a pseudo-Marxian theory of ideology or 'legitimating theories' as Berger and Luckmann call them, not wishing to designate the conceptual machineries, or even symbolic universes themselves, as 'ideologies'. We are told that *all* symbolic universes and legitimations are human products and that this means that we can only analyse them in relation to their concrete social contexts.

Thus, part of the Berger and Luckmann analysis involves study of the personnel of groups who actually produce 'legitimating theories', presumably relating their activities to the interests or 'relevance structures' of the social groups they represent. Thus whatever is 'ideological' depends ultimately upon its relationship to the nature of the society in which it is produced: of course this suggests that Berger and Luckmann, despite their avowed individualism, are being led into quite holistic concepts. The whole idea of a symbolic universe as some sort of totality representing the cultural totality of a social system leads them on to a conception of ideology which totally disregards the idea of social reality as 'constructed' by its members.

Thus, what matters is who 'inhabits' the symbolic universe: Christianity is not 'ideological' in medieval Europe because everyone inhabits its universe, from serf to monarch. In post-Industrial

Revolution Europe, however, Christianity *is* an ideology when used by the middle class against the working class, which could not be included within that universe: 'The distinctiveness of ideology is ... that the *same* overall universe is interpreted in different ways, depending upon concrete vested interests within the society in question.'[8] Such an interest-based theory of ideology is not in principle different from that of Marx, or some aspects of Weber's conception of belief systems. Thus the statement that 'the history of legitimating theories is always part of the history of the society as a whole',[9] is almost identical with Marx's conception of ideologies as expressions of the real divisions of social reality; a consequence of the historical situation in which men live.

III

The essentially derivative approach Berger and Luckmann take towards the sociology of knowledge is continued in their analysis of the internalization of social reality. Covering 'primary' and 'secondary' socialization in detail as mechanisms for converting the objective reality of the everyday world into a subjective reality for the individual, they employ G. H. Mead's symbolic interactionism to provide the framework of their analysis. The construction of reality in the child, first described by Mead in terms of the taking of concepts of 'significant other' and 'generalized other' by the child's internalization of the roles of significant and generalized others, is taken over to provide an anchorage for the analysis of the construction of subjective reality. The equation of subjective and objective reality is accomplished developmentally in the evolution of role playing: primary socialization develops the concept of the 'self' in relation to others through the parental relationship of affective significance, providing the first definition of reality for the child transmitted in the development of language. As the facility of language progresses the child learns to take the role of generalized other, through the playing of games, and other activities. Once the role of generalized other is internally conceptualized, primary socialization is at an end. Now secondary socialization takes over to inaugurate the process of internalizing institutional roles. Just what roles will be internalized depends upon the division of labour, but the process of secondary socialization always involves the acquisition of some role-specific 'vocabularies'. Role acquisition is thus a primarily cognitive rather than normative activity for our authors: what is involved in the process is the gradual development of a set of linguistically precise conceptualizations of the roles of generalized others. Role knowledge is thus composed of typifications of social activities: it conforms in fact to the Schutzian conception of what sociology should do, which is to construct a world of typical actors and typical intersubjective meanings. Such a 'puppet world' facilitates our understanding of the intersubjectively real social world.[10] The actual distribution of tasks between primary and secondary socialization may be varied historically or in accordance with the actual social distribution of knowledge, but it essentially conforms to the situation presented above. The function of this analysis within the whole theory is as a sort of 'micro-sociology' of knowledge, but it is in itself dependent upon a macro-sociological understanding of the structural aspects of socialization—institutionalization and legitimation. There is a 'dialectical' relationship between these micro- and macro-sociological components, Berger and Luckmann say, which produces the totality of socially constructed reality. We should remember that 'dialectical' here means related, or relational; the proposition that the construction of social reality cannot be understood by either analysis of socialization, or of social structure alone, but involves a study of how the one affects the other (see Figure 2).

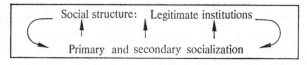

Figure 2 Constructed social reality

IV

The generalized conception that knowledge is prior to values in respect of social order, which characterizes both the Berger–Luckmann approach and the viewpoint of ethnomethodology, makes social actors into primarily cognition-centred individuals.

This knowledge is of interest to the extent to which it is socially organized, and for the ethnomethodologists this involves analysis of the 'hidden' methods by which such a knowledge is stably produced. The approach of Berger and Luckmann, though it has been called ethnomethodological, is not. It shares the intellectual heritage of Schutzian phenomenology in regard of the postulation of reality as socially constructed. But whereas the ethnomethodologists concentrate on the production and transmission of taken for granted rules about social activity, a normative order of social knowledge, Berger–Luckmann concentrate on the institutionalization of a socially constructed reality and its creation, in terms of both a role theory and a theory of socialization. For the ethnomethodologists the normative order is prior to the cognitive structure, even though it may appear that such is not the case: logical roles, they argue, depend upon a framework of normative roles which are taken for granted but not systematically recognized.[11] Berger and Luckmann begin from the assumption that knowledge is constitutive of social reality and produces a normative order of social control as a consequence of its institutionalization, legitimation and internalization.

Without unnecessarily prolonging analysis of the Berger–Luckmann approach it is worthwhile mentioning here that it is both pedestrian and derivative. In fact, its theoretically integrationist method is one of the main reasons for its limitations as a theory. For the integration of disparate sociological positions appears only to be possible at a pre-sociological level. Virtually all of the empirical insights of Weber, Marx and Durkheim, and to a lesser extent Mead, are submerged in a large speculative excursion into the superficially assimilable elements of their work. And this I think brings us to the main drawback of their work. As a sociology of knowledge their theory is quite clearly non-empirical: it belongs in the realm of social philosophy rather than social theory. For it excludes all those elements which make the distinctive theories of Weber, Marx, Durkheim and Mead *scientific*: their recourse to a set of empirical demonstrations of the main theses of these theories. The germ of this failure lies I think with the authors' insistence on the employment of phenomenology as a justification for theoretical eclecticism, for it leads them into the mistaken assumption that they can provide an integration of the sociological theories of Marx, Weber and Durkheim by treating them as equally demonstrable and available *descriptions* of social reality. The fundamental differences and tensions between these theories are simply ignored or minimized in an almost wholly gratuitous integration, and the error is compounded by the simple-minded addition of the social psychology of G. H. Mead.

However critical it is possible to be about the details of Berger and Luckmann's study, their central aim is at least laudable: the erection of a sociology of knowledge which both treats of *all* knowledge, rather than merely intellectual knowledge, and tries to build links with sociological theory proper. It is a shame that neither element of this aim is actually accomplished, but that is a function of the approach taken. For, as I have pointed out, such an integrationist methodology is acceptable at a pre-sociological level as one aspect of the construction of a general orientation to a subject-field: when it claims to provide an over-arching theory itself, the contradictions implicit in its eclectic construction emasculate it and prevent the carrying out of any coherently scientific analysis. It may be possible, as I think Berger and Luckmann have thought, to reconstruct sociology along more philosophical and hermeneutic lines, and a way into that may be achieved via the sociology of knowledge, always a pretty speculative area. However, I neither believe in the possibility of a philosophically constructed sociology nor find Berger and Luckmann's attempts to reformulate sociology of knowledge along 'phenomenological' lines particularly appealing. In the last analysis, the test of a science is its ability to provide testable 'explanations' in some systematic and theoretically precise manner. Berger and Luckmann's work seems to get excluded from the rubric 'science' by just such considerations.

10   Conclusions

The central aim of this study has been to indicate the main view-points which have been developed in the sociology of knowledge, and to analyse how exactly each has contributed to the central questions about the determinate relationship between thought and society, or, more precisely, between knowledge and social structure. I think what I have held in mind since the inception of the main theme of the study is the consideration of how in fact a sociology of knowledge is *possible*, and on what grounds it could be said to contribute both a science and a sociological specialization. For it must be recognized that such a 'discipline' could in fact be anti-sociological, in the sense that it might demonstrate that the foundations of sociology itself were in some sense 'ideological', and non-scientific. However, the possibilities of such a critical position—Gouldner[1] and Friedrichs[2] notwithstanding—actually producing a discernible change in sociological theorizing in the direction of a more 'reflexive' sociology, seem remote. At the level of sociology as a separate discipline itself, the chances seem even more remote. The simple recognition that either a type of cognitive activity—say the production of sociological theory—or the attempt to delimit the subject matter of a specific intellectual field—sociology—have in themselves a reflection of the interests of the social group engaged in them, is not an argument for their immediate abandonment as cognitive-intellectual activities. It merely makes us aware of the need for a scientific test of the concepts and theories that we employ: interests and values may play a highly significant role in the choice of issues for scientific study, but they must and can be separated out from the actual methods of investigation and explanation, as Weber recognized. Unless the aim of the sociology of knowledge is to undermine the bases of *all* knowledge, including science, then it ought to be involved in the study of the extent to which the processes of knowledge production, validation, distribution and change are interpenetrated by social phenomena, and work towards a precise determination of the effects of that interpenetration. To seek a radical devaluation of knowledge in terms of the existential conditions of its production, as for example 'bourgeois ideology', as a basic proposition of a sociology of knowledge prevents any coherent analysis of the relationship knowledge-society, and reduces it to the level of a political slogan. Similarly, to isolate the discipline from any evaluation of the importance of political, economic, etc., elements in the processes of cognition and to ignore the historical contexts of those processes diminishes its significance. For, though we cannot see any sense in which the sociology of knowledge can provide the *basis* of sociological theory, its relevance to theory is singularly important. Any general sociological theory worthy of the name must take important account of the ways in which knowledge, both mundane and intellectual, commonsense and technical, exoteric and esoteric, gets produced, distributed and forms a basis of social action. It may indeed be tautologous to state that a society, or any social system, requires a system of socially available knowledge: it is a problem requiring explanation just exactly how that knowledge relates to the maintenance and change of that social system. The sociology of knowledge consequently deals, at least initially, with the theoretical specification of how knowledge and society interpenetrate. Beyond that, it is involved with some determinate connection—either lawlike or probabilistic—between social structure and content of knowledge. It must show how knowledge comes to be differentiated so that what we 'know' about everyday life gets to be distinguished from more formal knowledge systems. The processes of knowledge differentiation, involving analysis of the acquisition of specific cognitive skills via socialization and education, are made the subject of a sociology of knowledge inquiring into the precise ways in which the structure of a social system provides a means of organizing the framework of available knowledge, of producing new knowledge and distributing both old and new knowledge, and a legitimate justification of the distinction between (crudely) 'mundane' and 'intellectual' knowledge. At least one of the primary criteria of the adequacy of any sociology of knowledge must be its sophistication in handling conceptualization of knowledge-differentiation, for this is quite clearly the most problematic element in its constitution as a scientific discipline.

The focus on the social bases of knowledge-differentiation intentionally replaces one of the traditional props of a speculative, politically orientated sociology of knowledge: the reduction of validation to the level of an evaluative presupposition based in the social position, usually in class-terms, of the thinker. Thus the

148

'normative-structural' conception of the sociology of knowledge, characterized most clearly by the various schools of Marxism, seeks to make the validity of thought contingent upon the structural location of its producers or distributors. The social and historical context of thought presents to the Marxist sociologist of knowledge the means by which he will classify it as either ideological or scientific, the latter label being assigned only to natural science and to social science which has as its goal the emancipation of the proletariat. All thought which is 'partial' in the sense of either not taking adequate account of capitalist social relations, or because it represents the interests of any class but the proletariat, thus is seen as distorting, non-scientific and ideological, invalid because its standpoint is not the 'correct' one. The assumption that all knowledge is socially based, in the sense that its validity can be judged in terms of purely social factors, provides Marxism with the central validation of its own content. For that thought which claims generality in accordance with the laws of historical development because of its identity with the working-class struggle achieves a general validity in the uses to which it is put. Marxism provides a pseudo-scientific justification for the radicalization of epistemology in that it disallows the possibility of general standards of validity: scientific knowledge, the most clearly valid, consequently appears as a general knowledge freed from the repressive conditions of capitalist production. The extension of the concept of 'science' to cover political (i.e. *normative*) knowledge by Marxism clearly makes the issue of knowledge testing into something itself political. Only that knowledge based on the presuppositions of an impending working-class revolt can be valid, and thus scientific. But the social relativization of knowledge accomplished by the Marxists has its own contradictions: it cannot adequately account for change in autonomous structured frameworks of knowledge (such as theoretical physics) and more importantly, it may lead to a position in which science itself is seen as ideological. As has been seen with Lukács, the Frankfurt school, and Goldmann, science comes to be portrayed as part and parcel of the reificatory processes of modern society, and a distortion of reality in itself. Within the Marxist paradigm the problem of adequate analysis and conceptualization of the processes of knowledge-differentiation get hypostatized into a valid-invalid, scientific-ideological dichotomization based on the economic stratification of society, and not on the stratification of knowledge itself. The issue of validation thus becomes central in a simple-minded way for any Marxist sociology of knowledge. I think what has to be recognized by any sophisticated approach to the field is that this just will not do: the whole topic of knowledge validation is too complex an issue to be assigned to a purely extra-theoretical resolution at a political level. Validation in short is a difficult problem. It is tied up with the knowledge-differentiation processes, and, it must be recognized, cannot be adequately understood at a purely sociological level. Putting validation out of court as the central issue of sociology of knowledge is thus the preliminary to a more sophisticated approach to the subject. It does not mean that how validation is effected in a knowledge field becomes inexplicable in terms of social phenomena, but it does mean that no longer will sociology of knowledge be afflicted with the role of arbiter in a political dispute between theories of society.

It must also be made clear that this study cannot propose any method of integration of the theories presented, for two main reasons. First, it is in principle not possible to effect a theoretical integration of viewpoints which logically exclude each other: that would simply be a fruitless task. Each of the major theoretical positions I have analysed operates with a particular conception of the determinacy of the relationship of knowledge and society extending even, as we have shown, to the level of the veridicality of knowledge claims. In those terms each theory is exclusive: it positively prevents integration. Second, the idea of integration seems to me anti-scientific, in the sense that it might assume consensus on non-scientific grounds to be possible and even fruitful. As I hope to have shown, reduction of sociology of knowledge to a philosophical level merely emasculates it, whilst reduction to a political level perverts it. The scientific adequacy of the subject must rest on its ability to describe and explain demonstrable relationships without changing the terms of analysis to allow either pure speculation or evaluative criteria to predominate. Clearly, either philosophical or political ideas may set the framework of a problem, but they cannot set the structure or objectivity of its resolution: that must be left to a system of autonomous technical criteria at least minimally capable of being both scientific *and* sociological. The way ahead for the sociology of knowledge lies not in its attempts at theoretical integration, but in its attempts at systematization of methodology. Within, for example, the sociology of science, advances are being made which bring our knowledge of science and the processes of its development on to a new and less contentious plane. It is not a vain hope that such advances will modify the emphasis of more inclusive theories in the sociology of *all* knowledge.

To conclude, then, I do not feel that any further analysis of the sociologies of knowledge examined in this study would be either useful or necessary at this point. The chapters each stand alone as analytic excursions into their subject matter, and provide a convenient classification and distinction of the various approaches which can be taken to the field. Having indicated my own reservations about the subject, there is nothing left but to add that advance in our understanding of the relationship knowledge–society can best be achieved by the attempt to make more scientific, and less speculative or political, our sociologies of knowledge.

Notes

Introduction

1 Cf. T. S. Kuhn's *The Structure of Scientific Revolutions*, Chicago, 1962, in which the concepts of 'pre-paradigm' and 'paradigm' are discussed in relation to their ability to characterize the development of scientific thought.
2 Cf. D. W. Hamlyn, *The Theory of Knowledge*, London, 1971, pp. 3–22.
3 Leszek Kolakowski, *Positivist Philosophy*, London, 1972, pp. 9–19.
4 See, on the whole issue of the problematic concept 'ideology', George Lichtheim's illuminating essay, 'The concept of ideology', *History and Theory*, vol. 4, no. 2 (1965).

1 Philosophy and the roots of social science: the Enlightenment

1 Peter Gay, *The Enlightenment: An Interpretation*, vol. 1, London, 1966, p. 3.
2 Ibid.
3 Cf. Gay's discussion of the 'recovery of nerve', in Gay, op. cit., vol. 2, London, 1970, pp. 3–55.
4 Herbert Marcuse, *Reason and Revolution*, London, 1954.
5 Robert Nisbet, in his influential book *The Sociological Tradition*, London, 1967, positively devalues the Enlightenment and its developments in favour of the characteristically conservative, romantic and organicist ideas of the early nineteenth century without realizing that the two sets of ideas (and values) are dialectically interlinked, the later ideas as responses to what their authors saw as the social effects of the earlier.
6 *Scienza Nuova di Giambattista Vico*, Naples, 1725. My observations and analysis are taken from the translation by Max Bergin and Thomas Fisch, New York, 1961.
7 H. P. Rickman's fascinating essay comparing Vico's methodological pretensions with those of Dilthey makes this very point, and indeed suggests even further that modern interest in Vico is itself connected

153

with Dilthey's systematization of the idea of '*verstehen*' into a coherent philosophy, where in Vico's *Scienza Nuova* it had been merely a suggestion; 'Vico and Dilthey's methodology of the human studies', in G. Tagliacozzo and H. V. White (eds), *Giambattista Vico: An International Symposium*, Baltimore, 1969, pp. 447–56.

8 Bergin and Fisch, op. cit., par. 347.

9 Alain Pons, 'Vico and French thought', in Tagliacozzo and White, op. cit., pp. 165–86.

10 Eugene Kamenka, 'Vico and Marxism' in Tagliacozzo and White, op. cit., pp. 137–43.

11 Karl Marx, *Capital*, London, 1930, book 1, part IV, chapter 13, n. 89.

12 Werner Stark, *Montesquieu: Pioneer of the Sociology of Knowledge*, London, 1960. Stark's whole book is devoted to the dubious task of proving Montesquieu to be a romantic (rather than a rationalist) who quite accepted the role of the priesthood in *ancien régime* France. By doing so he quite ignores the rationalist base of *De l'Esprit des lois* and the conscious irony of Montesquieu's treatment of the role of religion in the forming of political constitutions, not to mention his theory of religious belief as being ecologically determined.

13 R. Aron, *Main Currents in Sociological Thought*, London, 1968.

14 Montesquieu, *De l'Esprit des lois*, quoted by Stark, op. cit., p. 58.

15 William C. Lehmann's *The Sociology of Adam Ferguson*. Chicago, 1930, draws out the substance of Montesquieu's influence on the Scottish social thinkers.

16 Cf. *A Treatise of Human Nature*, Oxford, 1888.

17 The exception is, of course, Kant. As the most philosophically advanced of the *Aufklärer*, Kant's influence extends far beyond his own time, and we will examine the role of his work in the context of our discussion of Weber and Lukács, and the influence of neo-Kantian idealism upon them.

2 Marxism I: Hegel and Marx

1 David McLellan, *The Young Hegelians and Karl Marx*, London, 1969, pp. 1–3.

2 Ibid., p. 7.

3 Ibid., p. 8.

4 Ibid., p. 19.

5 Ibid., p. 20.

6 David McLellan, *The Thought of Karl Marx: an Introduction*, London, 1971, p. 15.

7 Economic and Philosophical manuscripts (1844), in L. D. Easton and K. H. Guddat (trs.), *Writings of the Young Marx on Philosophy and Society*, New York, 1967, p. 284.

8 There are two English renderings of some parts of the texts of the *Grundrisse*, E. J. Hobsbawm's *Pre-Capitalist Economic Formations*, London, 1964; and David McLellan's *Marx's Grundrisse*, London, 1971. Both have substantial and interesting introductions. The stan-

dard German edition is: K. Marx, *Grundrisse der Kritik der politischen Oekonomie*, Berlin, 1953. Eventually the work will appear as part of the standard edition of Marx's complete works now in preparation.

9 McLellan, *The Thought of Karl Marx*, p. 110.
10 Marx, Economic and Philosophical manuscripts, in Easton and Guddat (trs.), op. cit., p. 287.
11 Ibid., p. 289.
12 Ibid., p. 290.
13 Ibid., p. 290.
14 Ibid., p. 294.
15 Ibid., p. 298.
16 Ibid., p. 299.
17 Ibid., p. 299.
18 Ibid., pp. 311–13.
19 Cf. Norbert Elias's recent work on the sociology of knowledge, which finds Marx to have produced the first, and a now outdated, paradigmatic formulation of the interconnectedness of ideas and society. *Sociology*, vols. 2–3, 1971.
20 Cf. H. Marcuse, *Reason and Revolution*, pp. 267–73, for discussion of the influence of this aspect of Feuerbach's materialism on Marx.
21 Marx and Engels, *Selected Works,* vol. II, London and Moscow, 1962, pp. 403–4.
22 Marx and Engels, *The German Ideology*, Moscow and London, 1964, p. 31.
23 Ibid., p. 31.
24 Ibid., p. 32.
25 Ibid., p. 36.
26 Ibid., p. 37.
27 Ibid., p. 38.
28 Ibid., p. 41.
29 Ibid.
30 A problematic term in this context: undoubtedly Marx means theory abstracted from any *practice*—cf. Jürgen Habermas, *Knowledge and Human Interest*, London, 1972, chapters 2 and 3.
31 Marx and Engels, *The German Ideology*, p. 51.
32 Ibid., p. 60.
33 Ibid.
34 Ibid., p. 75.
35 Ibid.
36 K. Marx, *Contribution to the Critique of Political Economy*, London, 1971, p. 206.
37 K. Marx, *Capital*, London, 1957 (trs. Eden and Cedar Paul from the fourth German edition), pp. 43–58.
38 Ibid., p. 45.
39 Ibid., p. 46.
40 Ibid., p. 47.
41 Ibid., p. 50.

3 Marxism II: Lukács

1 G. Lukács, Preface to the new edition (1967) of *History and Class-Consciousness* (trs. R. Livingstone, London), 1971, p. ix.
2 Cf. George Lichtheim's discussion of Lukács's early intellectual development in his excellent *Lukács*, London, 1970, pp. 13–21.
3 Lukács, op. cit., p. 1.
4 Ibid., p. 2.
5 Ibid., p. 9.
6 Ibid., p. 10.
7 Ibid., p. 22.
8 'What is orthodox Marxism?', ibid., p. 24.
9 Ibid., p. 51.
10 Engels to J. Bloch, 21–2 September 1890; in Marx and Engels, *Selected Works,* vol. II, London and Moscow, 1962, pp. 488–90.
11 Lukács, op. cit., p. 57.
12 Ibid., p. 59.
13 Marc Bloch, *Feudal Society*, vol. II, London, 1965.
14 Lukács, op. cit., p. 63.
15 Ibid., p. 70.
16 'Reification and the consciousness of the proletariat', ibid., p. 145.
17 Ibid., p. 148.
18 Ibid., p. 149.
19 Ibid., p. 181.
20 Ibid., p. 204.
21 Ibid., pp. 223–55.
22 Ibid., p. 233.
23 This argument seems quite fallacious and misleading, since there were important social and technological developments implicit in the development of this new style, which quite cut across any purely artistic influences.
24 Ibid., p. 236.
25 Ibid., p. 239.

4 Marxism III

1 Max Horkheimer, *Traditionelle und kritische Theorie*, Zeitschrift für Sozialforschung, Heft 2, 1937 (reprinted in Horkheimer's collection of his 1930s essays, *Kritische Theorie I–II*, Frankfurt, 1968). My discussion of Horkheimer and the Frankfurt school owes a great deal to two articles by Goran Therborn in *New Left Review*, vols. 63 and 68, 1970 and 1971. All translations of Horkheimer quoted are by Therborn.
2 Horkheimer, *Kritische Theorie*, II, p. 146.
3 Ibid., p. 193.
4 Ibid., p. 162.
5 Ibid., p. 187.
6 Ibid., p. 170.
7 The essay 'Knowledge and interest' in D. Emmet and A. MacIntyre

(eds), *Sociological Theory and Philosophical Analysis*, London, 1970, pp. 36–53, is based on the inaugural lecture.

8 Ibid., p. 42.
9 Ibid., pp. 43–4.
10 Ibid., pp. 49–50.
11 Ibid., p. 50.
12 Ibid., p. 51.
13 Ibid., pp. 50–1.
14 J. Habermas, 'Towards a theory of communicative competence' in H. P. Dreizel (ed.), *Recent Sociology No. 2*, London, 1971, pp. 117–18.
15 Lucien Goldmann, *The Human Sciences and Philosophy*, London, 1969, p. 21.
16 Ibid., p. 15.
17 Ibid., p. 16.
18 Ibid., p. 23.
19 Ibid., pp. 18–19.
20 Ibid., p. 29.
21 Ibid., p. 35.
22 Ibid., p. 41.
23 Ibid., p. 53.
24 Ibid., p. 62.
25 Ibid., p. 85.
26 Ibid., p. 102.
27 Ibid., pp. 102–3.
28 Ibid., p. 112.
29 Ibid., p. 118.
30 Ibid., p. 128.
31 Ibid., p. 127.
32 Ibid., p. 129.

5 Max Scheler

1 John Staude's excellent biography of Scheler (*Max Scheler: an Intellectual Portrait*, New York, 1967) brings this out very clearly, and explicates Scheler's nationalism, conservatism and anti-socialism very clearly in terms of his choice and exposition of intellectual issues.
2 Max Scheler, *The Nature of Sympathy*, London, 1954, p. 215.
3 Staude, op. cit., pp. 200–1.
4 Max Scheler, 'The sociology of knowledge: formal problems' in J. E. Curtis and J. W. Petras (eds), *The Sociology of Knowledge: A Reader*, London, 1970, p. 175
5 *From Max Weber: Essays in Sociology*, trs. H. H. Gerth and C. Wright Mills, London, 1948, pp. 145 ff.
6 'The sociology of knowledge', p. 170.
7 Ibid., pp. 170–1.
8 Ibid., p. 173.
9 Max Scheler, *Die Wissensformen und die Gesellschaft*, Leipzig, 1926; Berne, 1960.

10 Staude, op. cit., p. 159.
11 'The sociology of knowledge', p. 173.
12 Ibid., p. 175.
13 *Die Wissensformen und die Gesellschaft*, pp. 44-5.
14 Ibid., p. 18.
15 Ibid., p. 40.
16 Ibid., p. 171.
17 Ibid.
18 'The sociology of knowledge', p. 183.
19 *Die Wissensformen und die Gesellschaft*, p. 26.

6 Max Weber

1 Max Weber, *Gessammelte Aufsaetze zur Wissenschaftslehre*, Tubingen, 1922, p. 415. Quoted by H. H. Gerth and C. Wright Mills in *From Max Weber*, London, 1948, p. 55.
2 T. Parsons, *The Structure of Social Action*, New York, 1949, pp. 602-3.
3 Adapted from the translated passage from Weber, op. cit., pp. 190-203, in O. Stammer (ed.), *Max Weber and Sociology Today*, Oxford, 1971, pp. 209-10 (see as well the discussion of the ideal-type in Anthony Giddens, *Capitalism and Modern Social Theory*, Cambridge, 1971, pp. 141-4).
4 Max Weber, *Economy and Society*, New York, 1968, pp. 20-1.
5 Ibid., pp. 24-6.
6 Ibid., pp. 26-7.
7 Ibid., p. 29.
8 Ibid., p. 212.
9 Max Weber, *The Protestant Ethic and the Spirit of Capitalism*, London, 1930; Max Weber, *The Rational and Social Foundations of Music*, trs. D. Martindale *et al.*, Carbondale, Ill., 1958.
10 *PESC*, p. 178.
11 *RSFM*, p. 112.
12 Ibid., p. 114.

7 Durkheim

1 T. Parsons, *The Structure of Social Action*, New York, 1949, pp. 409-450 ff.
2 Don Martindale, *The Nature and Types of Sociological Theory*, London, 1961, pp. 53 ff., 86-92.
3 Ibid., p. 62.
4 Emile Durkheim, *The Division of Labour in Society* (trs. George Simpson), New York, 1933, pp. 111-99.
5 Emile Durkheim, *The Elementary Forms of the Religious Life*, London, 1915, p. 1.

6 Emile Durkheim, *The Rules of Sociological Method*, New York, 1938, p. 14.
7 Ibid., p. 2.
8 Ibid., p. 7.
9 Ibid. (preface to the second edition), p. xli.
10 Ibid., pp. 110–11.
11 Ibid., p. 27.
12 Ibid., p. 43.
13 Ibid., p. 44.
14 Translated by Rodney Needham as *Primitive Classification*, London, 1963.
15 Ibid., p. 8.
16 Ibid., p. 18.
17 Ibid., p. 32.
18 Ibid., p. 41.
19 Ibid., p. 55.
20 Ibid., p. 57
21 Ibid., p. 65.
22 Ibid., pp. 83–4.
23 This is Parsons's term for Durkheim's project in the *EFRL*: *Structure of Social Action*, p. 409.
24 *EFRL*, p. 5.
25 Ibid., p. 9.
26 Ibid., p. 16.
27 Ibid., p. 417.
28 Ibid., p. 429.
29 Ibid., p. 434.
30 Ibid., p. 439.

8 Karl Mannheim and the production of a 'relationist' sociology of knowledge

1 Cf. John Heeren, 'Karl Mannheim and the intellectual élite', *British Journal of Sociology*, vol. 22, no. 1, 1971, pp. 1–15.
2 Karl Mannheim, 'On the interpretations of *Weltanschauung*' in *Essays on the Sociology of Knowledge*, London, 1952, pp. 43–63; esp. 43–4 ('OIW').
3 Karl Mannheim, *Ideology and Utopia*, London, 1960, pp. 104, 130–46, (*IU*).
4 Karl Mannheim, 'The problem of a sociology of knowledge', in *Essays on the Sociology of Knowledge*, p. 179 ('PSK').
5 Harold Garfinkel, *Studies in Ethnomethodology*, New Jersey, 1967, pp. 77–9.
6 Karl Mannheim, 'Historicism', in *Essays on the Sociology of Knowledge*, pp. 84–133 (H).
7 'PSK', pp. 137–45.
8 'PSK', p. 151.
9 'PSK', p. 180.
10 'PSK', p. 184.

11 'PSK', p. 186.
12 'PSK', p. 190.
13 *Essays on the Sociology of Knowledge*, p. 237; reprinted in *IU*, pp. 237–280 (*SOK*).
14 *IU*, p. 70.
15 *IU*, pp. 71–6.
16 *IU*, p. 85.
17 *IU*, p. 86.
18 *IU*, pp. 104–30.
19 *SOK*, pp. 261–75.
20 *SOK*, p. 262.
21 I. L. Horowitz, *Philosophy, Science and the Sociology of Knowledge*, Springfield, Ill., 1961, p. 76.

9 Phenomenological-sociological approaches to the sociology of knowledge

1 Alfred Schutz, 'Concept and theory formation in the social sciences' in Alfred Schutz, *Collected Papers I: The Problem of Social Reality*, The Hague, 1967, pp. 63–5.
2 Peter L. Berger and Thomas Luckmann, 'Sociology of religion and sociology of knowledge', *Sociology and Social Research*, vol. 47 (1963), pp. 417–27; *The Social Construction of Reality*, London, 1967 (*SCR*). See also Peter Berger and Stanley Pullberg, 'Reification and the sociological critique of consciousness', *History and Theory*, vol. 4, no. 2 (1965), pp. 196–211.
3 *SCR*, pp. 15, 26.
4 *SCR*, p. 56.
5 *SCR*, p. 57.
6 *SCR*, p. 113.
7 *SCR*, p. 114.
8 *SCR*, p. 141.
9 *SCR*, p. 144.
10 Schutz, op. cit., p. 66.
11 See, for example, Harold Garfinkel, 'Aspects of the problem of common-sense knowledge of social structures', *Transactions of the Fourth World Congress of Sociology*, 1959, pp. 51–66. Also, more recently, Alan F. Blum, 'The corpus of knowledge as a normative order' in J. C. McKinney and E. A. Tiryskian (eds), *Theoretical Sociology*, New York, 1970, pp. 235–69.

10 Conclusions

1 Alvin W. Gouldner, *The Coming Crisis of Western Sociology*, London, 1971.
2 Robert Friedrichs, *The Sociology of Sociology*, New York, 1971.

Index

161

International Library of Sociology

Edited by
John Rex
University of Warwick

Founded by
Karl Mannheim

as The International Library of Sociology
and Social Reconstruction

This Catalogue also contains other Social Science
series published by Routledge

Routledge & Kegan Paul　London and Boston

68-74 Carter Lane London EC4V 5EL
9 Park Street Boston Mass 02108

Contents

● *Books so marked are available in paperback*
All books are in Metric Demy 8vo format (216 × 138mm approx.)

GENERAL SOCIOLOGY

Belshaw, Cyril. The Conditions of Social Performance. *An Exploratory Theory. 144 pp.*

Brown, Robert. Explanation in Social Science. *208 pp.*

●   Rules and Laws in Sociology.

Cain, Maureen E. Society and the Policeman's Role. *About 300 pp.*

Gibson, Quentin. The Logic of Social Enquiry. *240 pp.*

Gurvitch, Georges. Sociology of Law. *Preface by Roscoe Pound. 264 pp.*

Homans, George C. Sentiments and Activities: *Essays in Social Science. 336 pp.*

Johnson, Harry M. Sociology: *a Systematic Introduction. Foreword by Robert K. Merton. 710 pp.*

Mannheim, Karl. Essays on Sociology and Social Psychology. *Edited by Paul Keckskemeti. With Editorial Note by Adolph Lowe. 344 pp.*
Systematic Sociology. *An Introduction to the Study of Society. Edited by J. S. Erös and Professor W. A. C. Stewart. 220 pp.*

Martindale, Don. The Nature and Types of Sociological Theory. *292 pp.*

● **Maus, Heinz.** A Short History of Sociology. *234 pp.*

Mey, Harald. Field-Theory. *A Study of its Application in the Social Sciences. 352 pp.*

Myrdal, Gunnar. Value in Social Theory: *A Collection of Essays on Methodology. Edited by Paul Streeten. 332 pp.*

Ogburn, William F., and **Nimkoff, Meyer F.** A Handbook of Sociology. *Preface by Karl Mannheim. 656 pp. 46 figures. 35 tables.*

Parsons, Talcott, and **Smelser, Neil J.** Economy and Society: *A Study in the Integration of Economic and Social Theory. 362 pp.*

● **Rex, John.** Key Problems of Sociological Theory. *220 pp.*

Urry, John. Reference Groups and the Theory of Revolution.

FOREIGN CLASSICS OF SOCIOLOGY

● **Durkheim, Emile.** Suicide. *A Study in Sociology. Edited and with an Introduction by George Simpson. 404 pp.*
Professional Ethics and Civic Morals. *Translated by Cornelia Brookfield. 288 pp.*

● **Gerth, H. H.,** and **Mills, C. Wright.** From Max Weber: *Essays in Sociology. 502 pp.*

Tönnies, Ferdinand. Community and Association. *(Gemeinschaft und Gesellschaft.) Translated and Supplemented by Charles P. Loomis. Foreword by Pitirim A. Sorokin. 334 pp.*

SOCIAL STRUCTURE

Andreski, Stanislav. Military Organization and Society. *Foreword by Professor A. R. Radcliffe-Brown. 226 pp. 1 folder.*

Coontz, Sydney H. Population Theories and the Economic Interpretation. *202 pp.*

Coser, Lewis. The Functions of Social Conflict. *204 pp.*

Dickie-Clark, H. F. Marginal Situation: *A Sociological Study of a Coloured Group. 240 pp. 11 tables.*

Glass, D. V. (Ed.). Social Mobility in Britain. *Contributions by J. Berent, T. Bottomore, R. C. Chambers, J. Floud, D. V. Glass, J. R. Hall, H. T. Himmelweit, R. K. Kelsall, F. M. Martin, C. A. Moser, R. Mukherjee, and W. Ziegel. 420 pp.*

Glaser, Barney, and **Strauss, Anselm L.** Status Passage. *A Formal Theory. 208 pp.*

Jones, Garth N. Planned Organizational Change: *An Exploratory Study Using an Empirical Approach. 268 pp.*

Kelsall, R. K. Higher Civil Servants in Britain: *From 1870 to the Present Day. 268 pp. 31 tables.*

König, René. The Community. *232 pp. Illustrated.*

● **Lawton, Denis.** Social Class, Language and Education. *192 pp.*

McLeish, John. The Theory of Social Change: *Four Views Considered. 128 pp.*

Marsh, David C. The Changing Social Structure of England and Wales, 1871-1961. *288 pp.*

Mouzelis, Nicos. Organization and Bureaucracy. *An Analysis of Modern Theories. 240 pp.*

Mulkay, M. J. Functionalism, Exchange and Theoretical Strategy. *272 pp.*

Ossowski, Stanislaw. Class Structure in the Social Consciousness. *210 pp.*

SOCIOLOGY AND POLITICS

Hertz, Frederick. Nationality in History and Politics: *A Psychology and Sociology of National Sentiment and Nationalism. 432 pp.*

Kornhauser, William. The Politics of Mass Society. *272 pp. 20 tables.*

Laidler, Harry W. History of Socialism. *Social-Economic Movements: An Historical and Comparative Survey of Socialism, Communism, Co-operation, Utopianism; and other Systems of Reform and Reconstruction. 992 pp.*

Mannheim, Karl. Freedom, Power and Democratic Planning. *Edited by Hans Gerth and Ernest K. Bramstedt. 424 pp.*

Mansur, Fatma. Process of Independence. *Foreword by A. H. Hanson. 208 pp.*

Martin, David A. Pacificism: *an Historical and Sociological Study. 262 pp.*

Myrdal, Gunnar. The Political Element in the Development of Economic Theory. *Translated from the German by Paul Streeten. 282 pp.*

Wootton, Graham. Workers, Unions and the State. *188 pp.*

FOREIGN AFFAIRS: THEIR SOCIAL, POLITICAL AND ECONOMIC FOUNDATIONS

Mayer, J. P. Political Thought in France from the Revolution to the Fifth Republic. *164 pp.*

CRIMINOLOGY

Ancel, Marc. Social Defence: *A Modern Approach to Criminal Problems. Foreword by Leon Radzinowicz. 240 pp.*

Cloward, Richard A., and **Ohlin, Lloyd E.** Delinquency and Opportunity: *A Theory of Delinquent Gangs. 248 pp.*

Downes, David M. The Delinquent Solution. *A Study in Subcultural Theory. 296 pp.*

Dunlop, A. B., and **McCabe, S.** Young Men in Detention Centres. *192 pp.*

Friedlander, Kate. The Psycho-Analytical Approach to Juvenile Delinquency: *Theory, Case Studies, Treatment. 320 pp.*

Glueck, Sheldon, and **Eleanor.** Family Environment and Delinquency. *With the statistical assistance of Rose W. Kneznek. 340 pp.*

Lopez-Rey, Manuel. Crime. *An Analytical Appraisal. 288 pp.*

Mannheim, Hermann. Comparative Criminology: *a Text Book. Two volumes. 442 pp. and 380 pp.*

Morris, Terence. The Criminal Area: *A Study in Social Ecology. Foreword by Hermann Mannheim. 232 pp. 25 tables. 4 maps.*

● **Taylor, Ian, Walton, Paul,** and **Young, Jock.** The New Criminology. *For a Social Theory of Deviance.*

SOCIAL PSYCHOLOGY

Bagley, Christopher. The Social Psychology of the Epileptic Child. *320 pp.*

Barbu, Zevedei. Problems of Historical Psychology. *248 pp.*

Blackburn, Julian. Psychology and the Social Pattern. *184 pp.*

● **Brittan, Arthur.** Meanings and Situations. *224 pp.*

● **Fleming, C. M.** Adolescence: Its Social Psychology. *With an Introduction to recent findings from the fields of Anthropology, Physiology, Medicine, Psychometrics and Sociometry. 288 pp.*

● The Social Psychology of Education: *An Introduction and Guide to Its Study. 136 pp.*

Homans, George C. The Human Group. *Foreword by Bernard DeVoto. Introduction by Robert K. Merton. 526 pp.*

Social Behaviour: *its Elementary Forms. 416 pp.*

Klein, Josephine. The Study of Groups. *226 pp. 31 figures. 5 tables.*

Linton, Ralph. The Cultural Background of Personality. *132 pp.*

Mayo, Elton. The Social Problems of an Industrial Civilization. *With an appendix on the Political Problem. 180 pp.*

Ottaway, A. K. C. Learning Through Group Experience. *176 pp.*

Ridder, J. C. de. The Personality of the Urban African in South Africa. *A Thematic Apperception Test Study. 196 pp. 12 plates.*

● **Rose, Arnold M.** (Ed.). Human Behaviour and Social Processes: *an Interactionist Approach. Contributions by Arnold M. Rose, Ralph H. Turner, Anselm Strauss, Everett C. Hughes, E. Franklin Frazier, Howard S. Becker, et al. 696 pp.*

Smelser, Neil J. Theory of Collective Behaviour. *448 pp.*
Stephenson, Geoffrey M. The Development of Conscience. *128 pp.*
Young, Kimball. Handbook of Social Psychology. *658 pp. 16 figures. 10 tables.*

SOCIOLOGY OF THE FAMILY

Banks, J. A. Prosperity and Parenthood: *A Study of Family Planning among The Victorian Middle Classes. 262 pp.*
Bell, Colin R. Middle Class Families: *Social and Geographical Mobility. 224 pp.*
Burton, Lindy. Vulnerable Children. *272 pp.*
Gavron, Hannah. The Captive Wife: *Conflicts of Household Mothers. 190 pp.*
George, Victor, and **Wilding, Paul.** Motherless Families. *220 pp.*
Klein, Josephine. Samples from English Cultures.
  1. Three Preliminary Studies and Aspects of Adult Life in England. *447 pp.*
  2. Child-Rearing Practices and Index. *247 pp.*
Klein, Viola. Britain's Married Women Workers. *180 pp.*
  The Feminine Character. *History of an Ideology. 244 pp.*
McWhinnie, Alexina M. Adopted Children. *How They Grow Up. 304 pp.*
Myrdal, Alva, and **Klein, Viola.** Women's Two Roles: *Home and Work. 238 pp. 27 tables.*
Parsons, Talcott, and **Bales, Robert F.** Family: Socialization and Interaction Process. *In collaboration with James Olds, Morris Zelditch and Philip E. Slater. 456 pp. 50 figures and tables.*

SOCIAL SERVICES

Bastide, Roger. The Sociology of Mental Disorder. *Translated from the French by Jean McNeil. 260 pp.*
Carlebach, Julius. Caring For Children in Trouble. *266 pp.*
Forder, R. A. (Ed.). Penelope Hall's Social Services of England and Wales. *352 pp.*
George, Victor. Foster Care. *Theory and Practice. 234 pp.*
  Social Security: *Beveridge and After. 258 pp.*
● **Goetschius, George W.** Working with Community Groups. *256 pp.*
Goetschius, George W., and **Tash, Joan.** Working with Unattached Youth. *416 pp.*
Hall, M. P., and **Howes, I. V.** The Church in Social Work. *A Study of Moral Welfare Work undertaken by the Church of England. 320 pp.*
Heywood, Jean S. Children in Care: *the Development of the Service for the Deprived Child. 264 pp.*
Hoenig, J., and **Hamilton, Marian W.** The De-Segration of the Mentally Ill. *284 pp.*
Jones, Kathleen. Mental Health and Social Policy, 1845-1959. *264 pp.*

King, Roy D., Raynes, Norma V., and **Tizard, Jack.** Patterns of Residential Care. *356 pp.*

Leigh, John. Young People and Leisure. *256 pp.*

Morris, Mary. Voluntary Work and the Welfare State. *300 pp.*

Morris, Pauline. Put Away: *A Sociological Study of Institutions for the Mentally Retarded. 364 pp.*

Nokes, P. L. The Professional Task in Welfare Practice. *152 pp.*

Timms, Noel. Psychiatric Social Work in Great Britain (1939-1962). *280 pp.*
● Social Casework: *Principles and Practice. 256 pp.*

Young, A. F., and **Ashton, E. T.** British Social Work in the Nineteenth Century. *288 pp.*

Young, A. F. Social Services in British Industry. *272 pp.*

SOCIOLOGY OF EDUCATION

Banks, Olive. Parity and Prestige in English Secondary Education: a Study in Educational Sociology. *272 pp.*

Bentwich, Joseph. Education in Israel. *224 pp. 8 pp. plates.*

● **Blyth, W. A. L.** English Primary Education. *A Sociological Description.*
1. Schools. *232 pp.*
2. Background. *168 pp.*

Collier, K. G. The Social Purposes of Education: *Personal and Social Values in Education. 268 pp.*

Dale, R. R., and **Griffith, S.** Down Stream: *Failure in the Grammar School. 108 pp.*

Dore, R. P. Education in Tokugawa Japan. *356 pp. 9 pp. plates*

Evans, K. M. Sociometry and Education. *158 pp.*

Foster, P. J. Education and Social Change in Ghana. *336 pp. 3 maps.*

Fraser, W. R. Education and Society in Modern France. *150 pp.*

Grace, Gerald R. Role Conflict and the Teacher. *About 200 pp.*

Hans, Nicholas. New Trends in Education in the Eighteenth Century. *278 pp. 19 tables.*
● Comparative Education: *A Study of Educational Factors and Traditions. 360 pp.*

Hargreaves, David. Interpersonal Relations and Education. *432 pp.*
● Social Relations in a Secondary School. *240 pp.*

Holmes, Brian. Problems in Education. *A Comparative Approach. 336 pp.*

King, Ronald. Values and Involvement in a Grammar School. *164 pp.*
School Organization and Pupil Involvement. *A Study of Secondary Schools.*

● **Mannheim, Karl,** and **Stewart, W. A. C.** An Introduction to the Sociology of Education. *206 pp.*

Morris, Raymond N. The Sixth Form and College Entrance. *231 pp.*

● **Musgrove, F.** Youth and the Social Order. *176 pp.*

● **Ottaway, A. K. C.** Education and Society: An Introduction to the Sociology of Education. *With an Introduction by W. O. Lester Smith. 212 pp.*

Peers, Robert. Adult Education: *A Comparative Study. 398 pp.*

Pritchard, D. G. Education and the Handicapped: *1760 to 1960. 258 pp.*
Richardson, Helen. Adolescent Girls in Approved Schools. *308 pp.*
Stratta, Erica. The Education of Borstal Boys. *A Study of their Educational Experiences prior to, and during Borstal Training. 256 pp.*

SOCIOLOGY OF CULTURE

Eppel, E. M., and **M.** Adolescents and Morality: *A Study of some Moral Values and Dilemmas of Working Adolescents in the Context of a changing Climate of Opinion. Foreword by W. J. H. Sprott. 268 pp. 39 tables.*
● **Fromm, Erich.** The Fear of Freedom. *286 pp.*
  The Sane Society. *400 pp.*
Mannheim, Karl. Essays on the Sociology of Culture. *Edited by Ernst Mannheim in co-operation with Paul Kecskemeti. Editorial Note by Adolph Lowe. 280 pp.*
Weber, Alfred. Farewell to European History: *or The Conquest of Nihilism Translated from the German by R. F. C. Hull. 224 pp.*

SOCIOLOGY OF RELIGION

Argyle, Michael. Religious Behaviour. *224 pp. 8 figures. 41 tables.*
Nelson, G. K. Spiritualism and Society. *313 pp.*
Stark, Werner. The Sociology of Religion. *A Study of Christendom.*
  Volume I. *Established Religion. 248 pp.*
  Volume II. *Sectarian Religion. 368 pp.*
  Volume III. *The Universal Church. 464 pp.*
  Volume IV. *Types of Religious Man. 352 pp.*
  Volume V. *Types of Religious Culture. 464 pp.*
Watt, W. Montgomery. Islam and the Integration of Society. *320 pp.*

SOCIOLOGY OF ART AND LITERATURE

Jarvie, Ian C. Towards a Sociology of the Cinema. *A Comparative Essay on the Structure and Functioning of a Major Entertainment Industry. 405 pp.*
Rust, Frances S. Dance in Society. *An Analysis of the Relationships between the Social Dance and Society in England from the Middle Ages to the Present Day. 256 pp. 8 pp. of plates.*
Schücking, L. L. The Sociology of Literary Taste. *112 pp.*

SOCIOLOGY OF KNOWLEDGE

Mannheim, Karl. Essays on the Sociology of Knowledge. *Edited by Paul Kecskemeti. Editorial Note by Adolph Lowe. 353 pp.*
Remmling, Gunter W. (Ed.). Towards the Sociology of Knowledge. *Origins and Development of a Sociological Thought Style.*
Stark, Werner. The Sociology of Knowledge: *An Essay in Aid of a Deeper Understanding of the History of Ideas. 384 pp.*

URBAN SOCIOLOGY

Ashworth, William. The Genesis of Modern British Town Planning: *A Study in Economic and Social History of the Nineteenth and Twentieth Centuries. 288 pp.*
Cullingworth, J. B. Housing Needs and Planning Policy: *A Restatement of the Problems of Housing Need and 'Overspill' in England and Wales. 232 pp. 44 tables. 8 maps.*
Dickinson, Robert E. City and Region: *A Geographical Interpretation. 608 pp. 125 figures.*
  The West European City: *A Geographical Interpretation. 600 pp. 129 maps. 29 plates.*
● The City Region in Western Europe. *320 pp. Maps.*
Humphreys, Alexander J. New Dubliners: *Urbanization and the Irish Family. Foreword by George C. Homans. 304 pp.*
Jackson, Brian. Working Class Community: *Some General Notions raised by a Series of Studies in Northern England. 192 pp.*
Jennings, Hilda. Societies in the Making: *a Study of Development and Re-development within a County Borough. Foreword by D. A. Clark. 286 pp.*
● **Mann, P. H.** An Approach to Urban Sociology. *240 pp.*
Morris, R. N., and **Mogey, J.** The Sociology of Housing. *Studies at Berinsfield. 232 pp. 4 pp. plates.*
Rosser, C., and **Harris, C.** The Family and Social Change. *A Study of Family and Kinship in a South Wales Town. 352 pp. 8 maps.*

RURAL SOCIOLOGY

Chambers, R. J. H. Settlement Schemes in Tropical Africa: *A Selective Study. 268 pp.*
Haswell, M. R. The Economics of Development in Village India. *120 pp.*
Littlejohn, James. Westrigg: *the Sociology of a Cheviot Parish. 172 pp. 5 figures.*
Mayer, Adrian C. Peasants in the Pacific. *A Study of Fiji Indian Rural Society. 248 pp. 20 plates.*
Williams, W. M. The Sociology of an English Village: *Gosforth. 272 pp. 12 figures. 13 tables.*

SOCIOLOGY OF INDUSTRY AND DISTRIBUTION

Anderson, Nels. Work and Leisure. *280 pp.*

● **Blau, Peter M.,** and **Scott, W. Richard.** Formal Organizations: *a Comparative approach. Introduction and Additional Bibliography by J. H. Smith. 326 pp.*

Eldridge, J. E. T. Industrial Disputes. *Essays in the Sociology of Industrial Relations. 288 pp.*

Hetzler, Stanley. Applied Measures for Promoting Technological Growth. *352 pp.*

Technological Growth and Social Change. *Achieving Modernization. 269 pp.*

Hollowell, Peter G. The Lorry Driver. *272 pp.*

Jefferys, Margot, *with the assistance of Winifred Moss.* Mobility in the Labour Market: *Employment Changes in Battersea and Dagenham. Preface by Barbara Wootton. 186 pp. 51 tables.*

Millerson, Geoffrey. The Qualifying Associations: *a Study in Professionalization. 320 pp.*

Smelser, Neil J. Social Change in the Industrial Revolution: *An Application of Theory to the Lancashire Cotton Industry, 1770-1840. 468 pp. 12 figures. 14 tables.*

Williams, Gertrude. Recruitment to Skilled Trades. *240 pp.*

Young, A. F. Industrial Injuries Insurance: *an Examination of British Policy. 192 pp.*

DOCUMENTARY

Schlesinger, Rudolf (Ed.). Changing Attitudes in Soviet Russia.
2. The Nationalities Problem and Soviet Administration. *Selected Readings on the Development of Soviet Nationalities Policies. Introduced by the editor. Translated by W. W. Gottlieb. 324 pp.*

ANTHROPOLOGY

Ammar, Hamed. Growing up in an Egyptian Village: *Silwa, Province of Aswan. 336 pp.*

Brandel-Syrier, Mia. Reeftown Elite. *A Study of Social Mobility in a Modern African Community on the Reef. 376 pp.*

Crook, David, and **Isabel.** Revolution in a Chinese Village: *Ten Mile Inn. 230 pp. 8 plates. 1 map.*

Dickie-Clark, H. F. The Marginal Situation. *A Sociological Study of a Coloured Group. 236 pp.*

Dube, S. C. Indian Village. *Foreword by Morris Edward Opler. 276 pp. 4 plates.*

India's Changing Villages: *Human Factors in Community Development. 260 pp. 8 plates. 1 map.*

Firth, Raymond. Malay Fishermen. *Their Peasant Economy. 420 pp. 17 pp. plates.*

Gulliver, P. H. Social Control in an African Society: a Study of the Arusha, Agricultural Masai of Northern Tanganyika. *320 pp. 8 plates. 10 figures.*

Ishwaran, K. Shivapur. *A South Indian Village. 216 pp.*
Tradition and Economy in Village India: *An Interactionist Approach. Foreword by Conrad Arensburg. 176 pp.*

Jarvie, Ian C. The Revolution in Anthropology. *268 pp.*

Jarvic, Ian C., and **Agassi, Joseph.** Hong Kong. *A Society in Transition. 396 pp. Illustrated with plates and maps.*

Little, Kenneth L. Mende of Sierra Leone. *308 pp. and folder.*
Negroes in Britain. *With a New Introduction and Contemporary Study by Leonard Bloom. 320 pp.*

Lowie, Robert H. Social Organization. *494 pp.*

Mayer, Adrian C. Caste and Kinship in Central India: *A Village and its Region. 328 pp. 16 plates. 15 figures. 16 tables.*

Smith, Raymond T. The Negro Family in British Guiana: *Family Structure and Social Status in the Villages. With a Foreword by Meyer Fortes. 314 pp. 8 plates. 1 figure. 4 maps.*

SOCIOLOGY AND PHILOSOPHY

Barnsley, John H. The Social Reality of Ethics. *A Comparative Analysis of Moral Codes. 448 pp.*

Diesing, Paul. Patterns of Discovery in the Social Sciences. *362 pp.*

Douglas, Jack D. (Ed.). Understanding Everyday Life. *Toward the Reconstruction of Sociological Knowledge. Contributions by Alan F. Blum. Aaron W. Cicourel, Norman K. Denzin, Jack D. Douglas, John Heeren, Peter McHugh, Peter K. Manning, Melvin Power, Matthew Speier, Roy Turner, D. Lawrence Wieder, Thomas P. Wilson and Don H. Zimmerman. 370 pp.*

Jarvie, Ian C. Concepts and Society. *216 pp.*

Roche, Maurice. Phenomenology, Language and the Social Sciences. *About 400 pp.*

Sahay, Arun. Sociological Analysis.

Sklair, Leslie. The Sociology of Progress. *320 pp.*

International Library of Anthropology
General Editor Adam Kuper

Brown, Paula. The Chimbu. *A Study of Change in the New Guinea Highlands.*
Van Den Berghe, Pierre L. Power and Privilege at an African University.

International Library
of Social Policy
General Editor Kathleen Jones

Holman, Robert. Trading in Children. *A Study of Private Fostering.*
Jones, Kathleen. History of the Mental Health Services. *428 pp.*
Thomas, J. E. The English Prison Officer since 1850: *A Study in Conflict.*
258 pp.

Primary Socialization, Language
and Education
General Editor Basil Bernstein

Bernstein, Basil. Class, Codes and Control. *2 volumes.*
  1. *Theoretical Studies Towards a Sociology of Language. 254 pp.*
  2. *Applied Studies Towards a Sociology of Language. About 400 pp.*
Brandis, Walter, and **Henderson, Dorothy.** Social Class, Language and
  Communication. *288 pp.*
Cook-Gumperz, Jenny. Social Control and Socialization. *A Study of Class
  Differences in the Language of Maternal Control.*
Gahagan, D. M., and **G. A.** Talk Reform. *Exploration in Language for Infant
  School Children. 160 pp.*
Robinson, W. P., and **Rackstraw, Susan, D. A.** A Question of Answers.
  2 volumes. 192 pp. and 180 pp.
Turner, Geoffrey, J., and **Mohan, Bernard, A.** A Linguistic Description and
  Computer Programme for Children's Speech. *208 pp.*

Reports of the Institute of Community Studies

Cartwright, Ann. Human Relations and Hospital Care. *272 pp.*
  Parents and Family Planning Services. *306 pp.*
  Patients and their Doctors. *A Study of General Practice. 304 pp.*
● **Jackson, Brian.** Streaming: *an Education System in Miniature. 168 pp.*
Jackson, Brian, and **Marsden, Dennis.** Education and the Working Class:
  *Some General Themes raised by a Study of 88 Working-class Children
  in a Northern Industrial City. 268 pp. 2 folders.*
Marris, Peter. The Experience of Higher Education. *232 pp. 27 tables.*
Marris, Peter, and **Rein, Martin.** Dilemmas of Social Reform. *Poverty and
  Community Action in the United States. 256 pp.*
Marris, Peter, and **Somerset, Anthony.** African Businessmen. *A Study of
  Entrepreneurship and Development in Kenya. 256 pp.*
Mills, Richard. Young Outsiders: *a Study in Alternative Communities.*

Runciman, W. G. Relative Deprivation and Social Justice. *A Study of Attitudes to Social Inequality in Twentieth Century England. 352 pp.*

Townsend, Peter. The Family Life of Old People: *An Inquiry in East London. Foreword by J. H. Sheldon. 300 pp. 3 figures. 63 tables.*

Willmott, Peter. Adolescent Boys in East London. *230 pp.*

The Evolution of a Community: *a study of Dagenham after forty years. 168 pp. 2 maps.*

Willmott, Peter, and **Young, Michael.** Family and Class in a London Suburb. *202 pp. 47 tables.*

Young, Michael. Innovation and Research in Education. *192 pp.*

● **Young, Michael,** and **McGeeney, Patrick.** Learning Begins at Home. *A Study of a Junior School and its Parents. 128 pp.*

Young, Michael, and **Willmott, Peter.** Family and Kinship in East London. *Foreword by Richard M. Titmuss. 252 pp. 39 tables.*

The Symmetrical Family.

Reports of the Institute for Social Studies in Medical Care

Cartwright, Ann, Hockey, Lisbeth, and **Anderson, John L.** Life Before Death.

Dunnell, Karen, and **Cartwright, Ann.** Medicine Takers, Prescribers and Hoarders. *190 pp.*

Medicine, Illness and Society
General Editor W. M. Williams

Robinson, David. The Process of Becoming Ill.

Stacey, Margaret. *et al.* Hospitals, Children and Their Families. *The Report of a Pilot Study. 202 pp.*

Monographs in Social Theory
General Editor Arthur Brittan

Bauman, Zygmunt. Culture as Praxis.

Dixon, Keith. Sociological Theory. *Pretence and Possibility.*

Smith, Anthony D. The Concept of Social Change. *A Critique of the Functionalist Theory of Social Change.*

Routledge Social Science Journals

The British Journal of Sociology. *Edited by Terence P. Morris. Vol. 1, No. 1, March 1950 and Quarterly. Roy. 8vo. Back numbers available. An international journal with articles on all aspects of sociology.*

Economy and Society. *Vol. 1, No. 1. February 1972 and Quarterly. Metric Roy. 8vo. A journal for all social scientists covering sociology, philosophy, anthropology, economics and history. Back numbers available.*

Year Book of Social Policy in Britain, The. *Edited by Kathleen Jones. 1971. Published Annually.*

Printed in Great Britain by Lewis Reprints Limited
Brown Knight & Truscott Group, London and Tonbridge

1373